POUNDING ON
BIBLE-THUMPERS

POUNDING ON BIBLE-THUMPERS:

DO YOU BELIEVE EVERYTHING YOU READ IN THE BIBLE?

C. Boyd Pfeiffer

Algora Publishing
New York

Library of Congress Cataloging-in-Publication Data —

Names: Pfeiffer, C. Boyd, author.
Title: Pounding on bible-thumpers : Do you believe everything you read in the bible?
/ C. Boyd Pfeiffer.
Description: New York: Algora Publishing, 2017.
Identifiers: LCCN 2017040914 (print) | LCCN 2017041585 (ebook) | ISBN
    9781628943177 (pdf) | ISBN 9781628943153 (soft cover: alk. paper) | ISBN
    9781628943160 (hard cover: alk. paper)
Subjects: LCSH: Christianity and atheism. | Christianity—Controversial
    literature. | Skepticism. | Bible—Evidences, authority, etc.
Classification: LCC BR128.A8 (ebook) | LCC BR128.A8 P49 2017 (print) | DDC
    230—dc23
LC record available at https://lccn.loc.gov/2017040914

Printed in the United States

To all those questioners, fence-straddlers, believers, non-believers, Bible-readers, Bible-believers, Bible-thumpers, the Baptized, un-Baptized, Synagogue-faithful, Pope-admirers, and others who might question the value of religion. To those who are concerned and questioning about creeds, rites, rituals, confessions and other dogma of the Christian Church and who, in their own skeptical way and in their anguish over religion and salvation, have helped me to ponder, think about, formulate and write these essays which consider the errors, evils, and falseness of the fables of the Bible and of Christianity.

Also by C. Boyd Pfeiffer

No Proof At All – A Cure For Christianity

And many books on outdoor photography,and fishing

Table of Contents

PREFACE

We live in a world of skepticism, as we should. We live in a world of evidence, facts, truths, proofs, of "knowing" rather than "surmising, guessing, believing, imagining," or other nonsensical ways of living that don't and won't work in our world. The prescription pills we all take, the cars we drive, the planes we board for business and vacation, the bridges we cross, the shoes and clothing we wear, the medical and surgical procedures that keep us healthy, the foods we eat, the beds in which we sleep, the building materials used to construct our homes and skyscrapers, the TVs we watch, the boats on which we travel, the electricity on which we rely, the cameras we use, and everything else has been constructed by repeated testing, experimentation, and perfecting. We live safely, comfortably, and with the confidence that it all works and continues to work for its intended use.

We don't find this confidence at all — anywhere — in the things of superstition such as astrology, flat earth theories, tarot cards, crystal balls, tea leaf readings, voo doo, ju ju, dreams, numbers, lotteries. There is no evidence — as in none — that there is any validity in any superstitions regarding Friday the 13th, opening an umbrella indoors, walking under a ladder, breaking a mirror, spilled salt, knocking on wood, black cats, etc.

When these superstitions and superstitious theories are tested, which they seldom are, the ideas within them are proven to be fanciful myths and tall tales. Were they to be tested in any logical or realistic way, they would quickly be revealed as the dust and sham that they are.

While I am hardly a student of all the world's religions, many studies have indeed shown that they, too, are built on empty promises, created from myths, developed from archaic dogmas, doctrines and rituals that may have made some sort of poetic sense in the age before widespread literacy and science. Today, they are nothing but a

---

fantastical and varyingly ridiculous repeat of humanity's many hopes and constant fears. Religions are a way of keeping the bogeyman in the closet or from coming out from under the bed.

One of the big themes of religion, including the various forms of Christianity, is prayer. Pray for the dead. Why? Pray for the young. Why? Pray for the ill. Why? Pray for the soldiers in battle. Why? Pray for the student taking an important exam. Why? What is going to happen in life is going to happen, with or without our wishes, wishes which religionists call prayers.

You can prove that prayer does not work and will not work. Check the Internet for the statistical prayer study of Francis Galton in England in 1872. This studied the life spans of various groups of the English, including the royals, clergy, lawyers, doctors, gentry, aristocracy, naval officers, army officers, artists and those in the trades. The statistical study covered the life spans from 1758 to 1843, and it showed that of all the groups, the royals had the shortest life span. This was despite the fact that the entire English population was told by their clergy each Sunday to pray for the royal family. If prayer worked, along with the best possible medical care for the royals, shouldn't that have given them an edge — a Godly edge — in life span over the others lacking this prayer of supplication?

There is no evidence that living "right" or being a good Christian of any denomination or of any other religion or practicing any rites, rituals or going to church weekly will make a person any better than an avowed atheist who cares about his fellow man and lives accordingly. There is no evidence that in a hurricane, tornado, tsunami, earthquake, flood, monsoon, forest fire, volcano, riot or war that only the bad, evil and non-believers will die and only the good church-going Christians will live. No evidence at all!

My skepticism started in a Protestant Sunday school. My thoughts of the Bible stories being told were that they were only fairy tales and hocus pocus. I was a skeptic at the age of 8 or 9. I would like to say that I was an atheist, but I would not have known that word at that age. I was and am a skeptic. I am today still a skeptic and a vehement atheist, and proud of it. I mean to use critical thinking in everything and toss out the hocus pocus and made-up magic that comes my way. I continue this life journey, discarding the falsities of creationism, the pixie dust of religion, most of the Bible, the made-up histories of myth and magic, the impossibilities of religious beliefs, the fiction of believing in fables, the worship of impossible and invisible gods.

This book is a collection of short — very short — essays on religion, Christianity, the Old Testament and the New Testament, religious rites and rituals, the necessity of wasting a perfectly good day of the week on an impossible God. They are all short, with no absolute answers, but with the idea that by thinking about the content of these essays and the possibilities suggested, you too will come to the conclusion that I reached when thinking and writing these essays.

I try to be a good person, to be fair to others, to live life well, to be good to people and spread the worth of living an honest life in the real world — and aiming to shun the superstitions of the past. While we all live in the 21st century, many people are still trapped and hobbled in a 1st century of false beliefs, myths and fables of religion.

Step up to the 21st century and continue your journey with me in leaning and studying. Read books on both sides of this tricky theological fence. Read and study the works by Christopher Hitchens - *God Is Not Great*, Richard Dawkins — *The God Delusion*, Sam Harris — *The End of Faith* and *Letter To A Christian Nation*, Daniel Dennett's many books and even my earlier book on the subject, *No Proof At All — A Cure For Christianity*.

Communicate with others of all faiths and beliefs. Join local organizations dealing with this subject, subscribe to magazines such as *Skeptical Inquirer* and *Free Inquiry*.

For those who want to continue to believe in the Bible, this "word of God," I have two words, seven letters for you — PROVE IT!

Boyd Pfeiffer

Religious Skepticism: What It Is And What It Isn't

One of the definitions of "skeptic" is: "A person who doubts religious doctrines, especially Christianity." While some look at this thought process as blasphemy, hearsay, or sacrilegious, it really is only looking at other aspects of the philosophies, theories and history of religion in hopes of further proving or disproving any or all parts of it. Note the use of the word "doubt." The definition does not say "reject."

There should be no problem with that definition, since healthy skepticism is the only way to come as close to the truth as possible with religion or any other subject. It is the way to search for truth.

Skepticism is how we treat science and history. The Christian religion has a history of 2,000 years back to the time of Jesus, and back another few thousand years if we include its foundations in Judaism and the Old Testament.

History scholars welcome all the archaeological evidence that they can find. From any time period, old books, scrolls, written tablets, personal journals, diaries, receipts, business records, catalogs, newspapers, magazines, business dealings, agricultural notes, almanacs, tools, appliances, house wares, and everything else can contribute to our understanding of an era, a geographic site, a people, a region, a religion, a culture and other aspects of life, be it from 2000 BCE or from a given neighborhood today.

Garbage heaps along with the huts, homes and hovels of hoarding and pack rat peoples are ideal sources for information. Historians and archaeologists publish their findings in reputable journals, whereupon colleagues publish pro or con papers on the conclusions of each report.

Scientists do the same thing, and all scientific journals publish studies that have worked from a hypothesis through a theory to a conclusion with that conclusion then proven or disproven in time by the repetitive, duplicate work of other scientists or additional findings to prove or disprove the original premise.

The same should be no different for religion of any kind. To rely only on the Bible for Judaism and Christianity is to deprive society of other information as to the truth or falsehood of biblical writings. Other historical references and records of the time, along with similar non-biblical records of the history of the various Christian religions since the death of Jesus, are absolutely necessary for the truth — or as close as we can come — to be realized about Christianity, Judaism and Islam.

Honest questioning and doubting, along with comparing the Bible with all possible valid information, is not blasphemy, hearsay, or sacrilegious. Those who claim so have only themselves to blame for continuing to wallow in the backwaters of ignorance as to all of the beliefs of religion, religious dogma, and religious periods involved. The truth will set you free — but only if you consider it skeptically!.

God, The Bible And Circular Arguments

Skeptic: "How do you know that there is a God or that your God is the only God?"

Religionist: "Because it is right there in the Bible. The Bible tells us that there is a God — our God and the only God — who can do all things."

Skeptic: "Who wrote the Bible to tell us this?"

Religionist: "Silly! God wrote the Bible of course! You should know that!"

Skeptic: "How do you know that all of these wondrous things, these miracles, these early Judaic and later Christian histories in the Bible are really true?"

Religionist: "Because it's in the Bible. The Bible is a historic document that tells us the truth about God, about the Israelites, about early Judaic and Christian religions."

Skeptic: "Who wrote about all these things that you believe?"

Religionist: "God wrote the Bible, or dictated to a man, or several men, all of this so that we could know the truth of the Bible and of God."

It is that type of continual circular argument that frustrates skeptics, antagonizes agnostics and annoys atheists. This circular reasoning makes the text — the Bible — this so-called inerrant Word of God — seem to be infallible. The bottom line, as even most fundamentalists will admit, is that mankind wrote the Bible, the inerrant Word of God. According to them, it could have been dictated by God to a scribe, monk, priest, etc., or perhaps over time a series of many scribes, monks or priests.

Of course, they also could have completely made this up, copied it (as much evidence suggests) from earlier pagan myths, religions, Mithraism, etc. They could also have created it as a follower of this grandiose Judaic/Christian scheme so as to gain power and prestige over fellow tribesmen and to shift them from their earlier and similar pagan religions to this new one that guaranteed tithes (an easy income and sinecure) to the religious leaders.

The irony is that most of the earlier religions — which the Christians like to place under the general category of heathen, godless, pagan religions — had rites, doctrines, dogma and man-made rituals that were then supplanted by almost identical rites and rituals of the Christians. Christians tried to characterize these religions such as Mithraism as wicked, ungodly and patently wrong while at the same time plagiarizing the pagan customs.

This shift from paganism in its many facets to Christianity may be the biggest sales job, con artistry and bait-and-switch game in history. Now that is something to think about.

GOD, THE SUPREME COURT AND PRAYER IN SCHOOL

The strict religionists get a severe twist in their knickers with the thought that it is no longer possible to pray in school. They have had anger over this for some time now. With some instigation from atheist Madalyn Murray O'Hair, The US Supreme Court looked at the issue of approved or compulsory prayer in schools and in 1963 decided to ban it in an 8-to-1 decision.

Thus, you can't pray in school! It is awful! And it is that awful Madalyn Murray O'Hair who caused all this! Well, that's not exactly right. Of course, you can pray in school, and it is a shame and tragedy that fundamentalists do not recognize this. It speaks of their poor mental faculties to even think this way and deprive themselves and their children of praying, if that is their wish.

What you can't do in school is pray audibly or pray when or where it might disturb others. You can't have an organized or rote prayer that would favor one religion to the rejection or exclusion of others. That is a big difference than not being able to pray at all. Or are they saying that only audible, approved prayer works?

You can think anything you want in school. You can think anything from good, kind, benevolent religious or non-religious thoughts through evil, illegal, sexual, malicious thoughts. No one will know about it.

There is no way that anyone or any authority can prevent you from thinking what you want to think. It's impossible.

In the same way, you can silently think evil or sexual thoughts while in church, Sunday School, during Bible study or anywhere else while with head bowed you are supposedly listening to the pastor or priest. Your thoughts, feelings, prayers, plans, hopes, wishes and desires are private. Period.

You can pray — silently — before school, on the bus to school, during breaks between classes, at recess or lunch hour, during quiet time in the library, etc. Similarly, anyone can pray silently at any time that is reasonable. This can include going to work, going to the water cooler, digging a ditch for a public utility, on a plane or bus or train — anytime.

In addition, these quiet inaudible prayers can be short or long. They can be one sentence such as "Lord, help me ace this chemistry test." They can be longer and for yourself or intercessory prayers for others and wished-for acts.

The sad thing is that Christians erroneously use this simple Supreme Court decision as a club by which to bludgeon the government, government officials, the secular world, religions not theirs, and others with their Christian faith and then try to foist their delusions on others. To insist on a state-sponsored prayer time for school or during any other state event only insists on pushing one religion over all others through a verbal and official proclamation.

And that is not right.

The Bible—There Can't Be Any Contradictions, Can There?

Many faithful Christians and Jews think that there are no contradictions in the Bible. The belief of many is that the Bible — or Torah (first five books of the Old Testament) in the case of Jews — is the inerrant Word of God, and thus cannot have contradictory statements. It cannot have errors. It is God's word — contradictions are thus impossible!

The easy way to check out some of these is to use the Internet to check out "Bible contradictions" or "biblical contradictions." You can find both short and long lists of them in many sites, with references to specific verses of the Bible that can be easily checked in the King James Version, New International Version or any other translation.

Some of these errors can be fairly descriptive and vivid in the mental picture that they create. For example, we all know that after Judas betrayed and identified Jesus by accepting 30 pieces of silver, he killed himself. In Matthew 27:5 you can find: "And he cast down the pieces of silver into the temple and departed and went out and hanged himself."

But you can contrast this with the description in Acts 1:18–19, presumably written by the same writer who wrote Luke. This states: "Now this man (Judas) purchased a field with the reward of inequity;

and falling headlong, he burst asunder in the midst, and all his bowels gushed out."

This is a little less exact than the alternate and totally different description in Matthew, but describes Judas as buying a field with his 30 pieces of silver. This would have taken hours or days. We just don't know. In also seems that the field must have been hilly or had a cliff on it. Otherwise, falling down would not have the cataclysmic bodily damage subsequently described. It would seem that Judas would have had to fall from a considerable height for his torso/abdomen to burst open and for his entrails and organs to "gush out" as described. A check with the CDC on how far one would have to fall for the abdomen to burst open as described in Acts 1:18-19 revealed no results.

Another very small example of contradiction can be found in instructions on answering a fool. "Answer not a fool according to his folly, lest thou also be like unto him."

"Answer a fool according to his folly, lest he be wise in his own conceit."

Those two contradictions can be found in order in Proverbs 26:4 and right after it, in Proverbs 26:5. With hundreds more contradictions — small and large — throughout the Bible, it gives one something to think about. With mix-ups like this, how right and inerrant is the Bible?

"Miracles" In Haiti Are Fortunate Circumstances — Not Miracles

Read the dictionary definition of a "miracle" and you will run into God. My Webster's says that a "miracle" is "an event or action that apparently contradicts known scientific laws and is hence thought to be due to supernatural causes, especially to an act of God."

Thus it sort of goes along the Christian lines of "God did it, God can do anything, God controls the whole world. God can do anything that he wants to do."

But just look at various past and present natural and man-made tragedies in the world. With the earthquake tragedy in Haiti January 12, 2010, supposed "miracles" were happening all the time. The TV reports at the time constantly referenced the words "miracle" or "miracles" — or a reference to God — in talking about these events and those saved or not injured or killed by the devastation.

For example, a man was pulled from the wreckage of a building after 15 days of being trapped. He had no broken bones and, other than being dehydrated, was in pretty good shape. It was a "miracle," or so the faithful proclaimed. No, it wasn't.

It was just the culmination of several things that are pure circumstance and that helped him to survive. First, he was a healthy active young man of 24. Second, he was trapped under a deck that prevented anything from falling directly on him. He had no injuries. Third, he found or had a bottle of soda that provided him with liquid hydration and nourishment prior to being rescued. He was also in a warm climate that would have prevented him from losing energy through hypothermia.

In short, being without food for the time trapped would not have been a great problem, given human biology and his general condition. The soda helped to sustain his bodily fluids until he could be pulled out.

People can survive on little or no food for weeks, and with little or no water (remember that he had a soda) for many days under the right circumstances.

Want a real miracle, accomplished by God? Without food or water, stick him back into his trapped condition in the building. Then wait 30 days or so before pulling him out again. If he is still alive at that point, then perhaps we can start talking about miracles and such.

In the meantime, despite this impossible and evil conjecture, we must assume that God did nothing, and that the circumstances of this healthy man and his condition allowed him to live. Let's be thankful for these circumstances and for the rescue team that pulled him to safety. No miracle here!

Of course — if there really is a God or if God really exists — perhaps could have arranged this earthquake differently, or changed the timing of it, or make those nasty tectonic plates in the earth to not move so disastrously. Now that would have been a miracle!

God's Omniscience Highly Questionable And Doubtful

From reading the Bible and following Christianity, we know that God is both omnipotent and also omniscient. God is both all-powerful and all-knowing. Let's stick to omniscient. God knows everything, what we think, what we have done, what we will do in the future, and future events that are beyond our knowledge or understanding.

With that in mind, one has to wonder about certain stories in the Bible. Take the one about God asking Abraham to kill his son Isaac as a burnt offering to God to prove Abraham's love for God. But we know that God is omniscient — all-knowing. God — through an angel — stops this terrible act before Abraham kills Isaac.

On the face of it, that's good, but it still leaves God at first insisting on this terrible act of asking a believer to kill his son. How could any of us deal with the anguish from this Godly command? Secondly, God, being omniscient — OMNISCIENT — would know that Abraham *would* do this and *would* be faithful to the Lord. Thus, why would God design this horrible test of something of which God already knows the answer?

The same thing applies to the idea of killing a lamb to have blood to put on the door posts and lintels of the Israelites homes during Passover. The blood on the lintel was to indicate to God the homes of Israelites so that they would not be killed when God was killing the first born of the Egyptians. Why? After all, God is omniscient. He would know all the Israelites, and would not need a bloody lintel as a sign of which homes to skip.

By the same token, God would and did know all of the first-born Egyptians to know who to kill, despite the fact that the average Egyptian had nothing to do with the Pharaoh and his captivity or release of the Israelites. Those first-born Egyptians were totally innocent. No bloody lintel needed here.

Similarly, God killed off all the inhabitants of the earth except Noah's family during the great flood. That also brings up an interesting question. If God made man in his image and saw that his work was good (Genesis) why and how would he then later find out that mankind had turned bad and needed to be destroyed? Being omniscient, he would have known that little fact long before and could have made man more perfect or without the flaws that God later "found." Maybe he could have put a "good gene" into our DNA to make us better and kinder.

Why would God make man as a flawed product? Why would God have made something that he knew in advance should and would be destroyed? Does all this — with Abraham, Moses with the Pharaoh and the creation of man — not question God's omniscience? And doesn't it raise questions about the idea of a God at all?

JESUS — WAS HE WRONG, LYING, MIXED UP OR CONFUSED?

It is an axiom among Christian fundamentalists that there are no mistakes in the Bible and that God cannot and will not make mistakes. That also means the Trinity — as in God, Jesus and the Holy Spirit — makes no mistakes, has no errors in anything said, done or prophesied.

Of course, that is not really so, as we find out in the sayings of Jesus concerning his Second Coming and his kingdom. It is a particularly vexing problem for theologians.

These sayings occur almost identically three times in Matthew 16:28, Mark 9:1 and Luke 9:27. They are easy to check in any Bible.

In these sections, Jesus is supposedly predicting his own death to his disciples and others (Mark), even though he gets the time of his Second Coming mixed up. In Matthew, the statement in 16:28 is: "I tell you the truth, some who are standing here will not taste death before they see the Son of Man coming in his kingdom."

This of course openly refers to the second coming after the crucifixion of Christ. It states that the youngest among the disciples to whom he was talking will experience the Kingdom of God and this second coming of Christ before they die. That would mean that second coming of Christ would come no later than fifty to sixty years from his statement, perhaps sooner.

The same thing is said almost identically in Mark and Luke. These both state as a quote from Jesus: "I tell you the truth, some who are standing here will not taste death before they see the kingdom of God come with power." Luke leaves out the end part "come with power" and ends with "before they see the kingdom of God."

Two thousand years later, the faithful are still waiting, not realizing that the time for the return of Christ has come and gone. That ship has sailed.

Thus, very simply, Jesus was wrong, lying, insane, mixed up or stating something erroneous. If the second coming had come within fifty — sixty years at most of Christ's death, then perhaps the Jews would have accepted him as their Messiah, the world would have been a wonderful place according to all Christian predictions, and the bad guys would have been dealt with accordingly.

The fact that three of the four gospels state this mistake as factual from the lips of Jesus, should make some people think about the truth of the Bible, the facts of the New Testament, and the veracity of their religion. Was Jesus wrong, lying, insane, mixed up or confused? Now that is something to ponder.

MARTIN LUTHER — ENEMY OF JEWS BUT SUPPOSEDLY MAN OF GOD?

Martin Luther, that stalwart of the Reformation, began the entire Protestant movement that continues actively to this day through many Protestant religions. He was followed by the likes of John Calvin, John Wesley, John Knox and many others in the further development of specific Protestant religions and religious beliefs.

The spark for all of this was Luther's development of 95 objections to Catholic belief and nailing these 95 theses to the door of All Saints Church in Wittenberg, Germany on October 31, 1517. It was not so much an act of defiance, but more an act of trying to reason with the Church and Pope and to state some objections to Catholic policy, doctrine and belief.

It became an act of defiance and one of the first controversial issues to be published in books using that new printing process developed by Guttenberg.

Less known about this man of God and Christian belief is his total lack of love, humanity, care, respect, and tolerance towards others, particularly Jews. He was virulently anti-Semitic and even wrote a 60,000-word book entitled *On The Jews And Their Lies*.

In these writings, he outlines in detail and obvious hatred his views of Jews, and what to "do" with them and about them. In some of his writings he stated, "We are at fault in not slaying them." This Luther diatribe against them later amounted to a blueprint for their destruction, imprisonment, slavery, concentration camps, gas chambers and death by the Nazi Third Reich. It was early-on the blueprint for Kristallnacht of November 9, 1938, in which Jewish businesses and homes were destroyed and Jews killed by the Gestapo and Hitler Youth. The Nazis would often use first editions of Luther's book in ceremonial presentations to high ranking party members and officers.

His writings called for burning all synagogues, with those parts that would not burn to be buried so they would not be visible. He also called for preventing rabbis from teaching and preaching, burning all Jewish prayer books and scrolls, burning Jewish homes and confiscating all property and valuables. He strongly suggested killing them or completely driving them out of the country.

The extreme irony is that the Bible, through the New Testament and Christ, calls for forgiveness, love, tolerance, forbearance, and compassion towards all peoples. And let us not forget that Christ and his disciples were Jewish.

Where is the love and tolerance in Christianity? You have to shake your head over biblical preaching and the hatred and venom of Christians, past and present. You have to be skeptical — terribly skeptical — of this supposedly man of God thinking and writing this way about his fellow man and yet becoming the stalwart of the Protestant Reformation. Doesn't his attitude towards the Jews make him far less than Godly?

WHO IS RIGHT ABOUT LOT — THE BIBLE, A MINISTER OR NEITHER?

The TV minister/evangelist/fundamentalist was in full voice. He was full of himself. He was exhorting about Lot, Sodom and Gomorrah, sin and all things evil.

But he had a new twist on the story of Lot other than that which we learned in Sunday School. His interpretation was that it was in part Lot's fault that Lot's wife was turned into a pillar of salt.

We all know the story of Lot (Exodus 19) and how the two angels arrived, Lot taking them home and saving them from the crowd by offering his two daughters to be gang raped (another story), the angels turning the crowd blind and then Lot, his wife and two daughters being led from imminent destruction by the angels.

But this minister had a new twist on this. According to him, Lot was partly responsible for his wife's turning around when leaving and becoming a pillar of salt. This man of God, this TV minister, taught that Lot liked all the immorality, lust, wanton sex, orgies and other evil goings-on in Sodom and Gomorrah. He seemingly did not engage, but he did like it. I guess that he was sort of a voyeur, enjoying the porn of the day without participating. He influenced his wife and she liked this also. She enjoyed it so much that she turned to see what was happening to this city as it was being destroyed.

So there you have it — straight from the TV minister. It was partially Lot's fault that his porn-loving wife looked back and died. He influenced her to do so through his — or their — interest in the soft or hard core porn of the day.

Of course, there is nothing in the Bible to support any of this nonsense. Read Exodus 19 in its entirety. It is not there. In fact, if you check 2 Peter 2:6–9 you will find the opposite.

"[God] rescued Lot, a righteous man, who was distressed by the filthy lives of the lawless men (for that righteous man, living among them day after day, was tormented in his righteous soul by the lawless deeds he saw and heard)."

Thus, the minister broadcasting to thousands, perhaps millions, for some reason made up this little bit of lying and subterfuge about Lot in order to blame him along with his wife.

When you can't believe what a minister says, and what a man of God states about the Bible — that inerrant Word of God — should you believe any of it? Should you look upon all ministers skeptically? Should you check their facts, their Bible and their fables and fiction? Is there any truth anywhere in religion? Are ministers and priests always truthful? Or are they always — or sometimes — lying to you? Those are good questions.

God's Creation Of The Earth And Universe — Fact Or Fiction?

We all know the story of creation as listed in Genesis in the Bible. We know the story of various creations over a six-day period with God resting on the seventh day. We know about, in order, the daily developments of light, day and night, land, seas, vegetation, the sun, the moon, fish and birds, land animals, and finally creating man and then woman, and God resting on the seventh day.

And by inference (Genesis 2:4), we also know that God made all the planets, stars, galaxies, solar systems, black holes, red dwarfs, comets, asteroids, etc. That's a lot of work, a lot of heavy lifting.

But wait a minute! If it took God a whole week to make the earth including the seas, land, flora and fauna, how long would it have taken God to make all the rest of the universe? That would have taken billions and trillions of days or weeks, even with the simplest planets, solar systems and galaxies.

If God had done this after making the earth, we would not have been around long enough yet to see the results and the Hubble telescope would not be recording pictures of the development of star systems as periodically described in the news media.

Also, we are told that God is omnipotent. He can do anything, any time, anyway, in a split second or over a thousand years. And even if God had created a planet or star each second, it still would have taken 32,000 of our years to make the first trillion of these separate masses. How come no one in the theological field ever tries to figure out all this? How come no one ever has the question, much less the answer to all this? How come no one ever does the math?

If God can and did do all the above to create the universe, but it took him a whole week to make our planet and contents, it puts God's omnipotence on hold, does it not?

If we compare God's ability to presumably make the whole universe instantly and yet take a week to make the earth including us, does that not lead to some serious doubts and questions?

Aren't there some inconsistencies in what the Bible says about creation and what really must have happened, if you assume the Bible is correct? Would not a reasonable thinking person figure out the inconsistencies and falseness of something here?

Holy Water And Swine Flu

Apparently Holy Water can cause sickness, or at least pass it on between various extollers of this holy and magical elixir in Catholic Churches. At least that is the conclusion that a skeptic might reach.

Holy water is water blessed by a priest and typically found in a font or stoup in various parts of a church. Often this font or bowl is located at the front of a church where Catholics can dip their fingers in it, wetting their hands with holy water, before entering a church or when leaving it. I guess that does something good for you. After dipping a finger or three in the Holy water, participants make the sign of the cross.

According to some definitions, holy water can just be water with the addition of salt for a preservative or with oil to be used in Baptismal rites. Wine, salt and ashes is added when priests use it to consecrate a church.

Of course, other religions use Holy Water of some sort, including religions that are decidedly non-Christian. The interesting thing about all this is that the water has been blessed by a priest, with this special water an example of the water and/or wine used in early Judaic and Christian rituals.

But if this holy water is special, blessed by a priest and presumably Godly, why would it have to have salt added as a preservative? Would not the blessing of this special water and its affinity with God make it immune from the growth of bacteria, microbes, and germs?

This doesn't seem to work, since Catholic churches world-wide have recently been suggesting that parishioners not do the traditional finger dip. An Italian inventor has also developed a touchless Holy Water dispenser. It works like a high tech soap dispenser in a fancy lavatory. The terracotta container of holy water works by waving a hand underneath a sensor to release a drop or two of holy water.

This is obviously to prevent the spread of swine flu through the common use font, with world-wide evidence of more deaths from this flu all the time.

Would you not expect that blessed holy water, special by its powers through priestly blessing, would not even need salt to make it pure? Would you not expect it to be immune from swine flu and other diseases? If Holy Water is not special and holy, what good is it and why have it? Couldn't this make a skeptic wonder about the true holiness of Holy Water?

God's Original Sin — Real Or Man-Made, Made-Up Fabrication?

The concept of original sin is basic to Christianity. It is the sin that Adam and Eve suffered from eating the fruit of the Tree of the Knowledge of Good and Evil that was prohibited by God. They did eat the fruit, with Adam having to work hard and Eve suffering pain in childbirth as a result.

These conditions were passed on to all mankind forever, and became the basis of original sin. However, "original sin" or "ancestral sin" are not mentioned anywhere in the Bible.

Admittedly, there are oblique references to this concept in Romans 5:12–21 and 1 Corinthians 15:22. However, the whole concept of original sin was nonexistent until a second century battle with Gnosticism, a Christian sect. It did not gain firmer ground until Augustine (354–430 CE). It was confirmed by several Christian Councils, but not completely accepted until the Second Council of Orange in 529 CE.

The irony of all this is that Christians are saying that we are all guilty of a belief of thousands of years ago, and of a philosophy that has nothing to do with any small child and the rightness or wrongness — goodness of sinfulness — of any decisions that he or she makes.

True, we ultimately do things that are against moral and societal law, mores and folkways and conventional social rules. Sometimes these are small such as hurting the feelings of someone, or physically hurtful or damaging another human being.

But all these basic societal rules and attention to good habits are things that we learn and hopefully adopt as we grow up. They are basic to humanity, not to religion. And they are and have been concepts of basic morality and societal rule for hundreds and thousands of years prior to Christianity and even predating early pagan religions. They are not dependent upon how or what our parents or anyone else living prior to us has done, good or bad. It is not dependent upon a flawed religious belief.

The sad thing is that so many children are brainwashed at an early age in Christian religion or faith and thus believing themselves inherently bad or evil. That belief is just because of the concept of this man-made "original sin" and the fact that their parents, Sunday school teacher or pastor/priest/rabbi have inculcated this into their curious and developing minds.

Now that is a shame. It should be a crime of child abuse to convince children of their inherent wrongness and "sinfulness" when they are just entering life. Christians and other religions teaching this should be ashamed of their teachings and belief in a figment of man's imagination and of his basic supposed sinfulness.

ARE MIRACLES STILL AROUND TODAY?

The list of so-called biblical "miracles" is long and fanciful. They include a talking snake, magical fruit (often called an apple), a floating ax head, sticks that turn into snakes and snakes that turn into sticks, walking on water, the dead coming to life, ill people being instantly cured, bushes on fire but not consumed, people who can withstand fiery furnaces, Jesus raising himself from the dead and going to heaven, Jesus reappearing on earth, parting of seas, city walls crumbling with the sound of a trumpet, instantaneous plagues on the Egyptians, making the sun "stand still," etc.

It is all quite remarkable — if you believe any of these. But let's assume that these "miracles" did occur during these times of the Israelites and perhaps early Christians. Remember also that the definition of a miracle is something that is attributed to God, supernatural and thus outside of known scientific laws and physical truths.

There is still a big question. "Why were there so many 'miracles' then and none since? In the past 2,000 years, why have there been no 'miracles'?"

These are good questions. Unfortunately for Christians, there are no good answers. The nonsensical answers are usually that God does things in his own time, it is a "mystery," miracles of healing have occurred by saints and saintly relics, etc. These are non-answers.

Could not God have saved his people — the Jews, the Israelites — from the Holocaust of the Nazi Third Reich? Could not 300,000 people have been saved by a slight warning of the tsunami in the Far East in December 2004? Could not a slight change of tectonic plate shifting prevented the several hundred thousand deaths and injuries in Haiti earthquakes in 2010?

The lists of these could go on for several thousand pages, but the answers are not there. There has been a 2,000-year hiatus since good old-fashioned miracles such as a floating axe head, walking on water, raising the dead, and turning sticks into snakes. Why? A really good solid "miracle" today should solidify Christianity or Judaism in everyone's mind, particularly with the international news media available. Call a Press Conference!

Then again, maybe early "miracles" never happened. Maybe they were stories made up by the winners and writers of early history. Maybe they were to try to prove that "my God is bigger and better than your god" in the God wars.

Maybe they are little more than early versions of the Land of Oz, Alice in Wonderland, or Winnie-the-Pooh in the Hundred Acre Woods. Maybe we should stop looking for present day miracles and start wondering if there were ever any at all. Or should we be putting the Bible on the same shelf and with the same importance as Winnie-the-Pooh and Alice in Wonderland?

CHERRY PICKING YOUR WAY THROUGH THE BIBLE

Not all religions in the broad-based Christian delusion choose to think that the Bible is the absolute, accurate, inerrant Word of God. Many pick and choose parts of this book, stating that one section or story of the Bible is absolutely accurate, while others are fables, parables, examples, or other ways in which the Bible or Jesus can make a point regardless of the veracity of the example.

Ironically, those who believe in the absolute of everything in the Bible still pick and choose although they often do not know it.

In any case, it all becomes a little difficult when you are picking and choosing parts of the Bible to believe or disbelieve when it is like picking pies in a bakery or the best marble out of a bucket full. Some examples of supposed fables or parables include Adam and Eve in Genesis, Noah's Ark flood story, Abraham and Isaac, Abraham marrying his sister, parting the Red (Reed) Sea, Egyptian plagues, Passover, the Ten Commandments, Samson bringing down the temple, making the sun to stand still, etc. Some of these should at least be considered fables.

Those that tie in with possible events and some additional documentation from history may at least have a basis of reality. But those that include so-called miracles such as the parting of the Red Sea, Egyptian plagues, floating ax heads, Jesus walking on water, Jesus ascending to heaven in the Ascension after his return to life following crucifixion, raising the dead, etc., are at the least highly questionable and of course physically impossible. They just can't have happened.

The point is that by choosing some parts of the Bible as literal, absolute fact and others as mere fables makes the whole document questionable. We have an individual human intellect and mind by which to choose what to literally believe and what not to believe.

Mankind is thus just arbitrarily accepting some things as real and true and equal to fictional fables or stories. For certain Christians, those things that they consider a story and not absolute God's truth are treated like a morality tale from Aesop's Fables.

Ironically, those that Christians accept as fables and morality plays are often those that sometimes could be true if modified and we only knew more about the actual documentation and history of the area and time. Thus, there could have been a small flood in place of the flood of a massive scale described during Noah's Ark, a few plagues in Egypt, or even a development of the Ten Commandments as per the known writings of Hammurabi's Code of 1760 BCE. Most likely, the Ten Commandments and much of Leviticus could have been plagiarized from Hammurabi's Code.

However, Christians seem to pick the impossibilities — listed previously — as those to believe as absolute truth. Isn't that more than a little strange?

THE GOOD AND BAD OF FULFILLED PRAYER

It is not uncommon for good Christians (or even not-so-good Christians) to pray for a nice, calm, sunny day for a summer picnic, church outing, outdoor Christian wedding, Christian camp retreat, etc. Something Christian, in any case.

What these shallow people do not realize is that there is hardly any prayer for something good that cannot also have very bad consequences in other ways or for other people. A hypothetical example would be the above prayer for a nice, relatively calm sunny day for one and all.

What could be bad about such a prayer, were it granted by God? Lots. Lots and lots. Suppose the weather turned dead calm, bad or windy? Suppose a young man had planned to take his girlfriend on a sailboat for a day-long adventure that would end with him proffering a ring and asking her to marry him?

He would have to delay or switch to "plan B," since a lack of wind would nix the sailboat ride. Plan B might see them out boating on a day when a dangerous wind came up..

Suppose it had been a long period lacking rain in that particular county? Suppose one more day without rain would be ruinous for a local farmer, struggling to keep his mortgaged farm, pay for his seed and planting costs, pay his farm workers, and continue to support his family?

Suppose this lack of a steady soaking rain on this day would finally ruin all of his crops, rending them as dry, brittle waste, lacking any value? Suppose this drought would result in his farm going into foreclosure and the farmer losing his life-long owned property?

What if it would result in no pay for his many workers, who worked on contract and thus were not eligible for unemployment benefits? Suppose it resulted in severe financial problems for the company who on credit sold the farmer implements, fertilizer and seed for his crop?

Suppose it forced those companies to fire workers as a result of the severe financial strain of lost profit, and lost payment for their seed inventory? That religious church picnic is not looking so good right now, is it?

The list could go on, but the point is made. The Christian hope and prayer for a calm, relatively windless, sunny summer day for a casual picnic and a day without a steady long-lasting rain could be the last straw for the financial well-being for a farmer and the many who directly and indirectly depend upon him.

What is a God to do? What should a God do? Is there a God who can make the right decision? Is there any right decision? That's something to think about. Maybe prayer is not the answer.

PRAYER CAN BE GOOD — BUT NOT IN THE WAY YOU THINK

Can prayer do any good? You bet. If it is personal prayer in which you pray for yourself to get better, do better or be a better person, it can make you satisfied in what you think will be God helping you achieve these goals. Even with a fictional God, that's good. It is not a bad deal. It is the Power of Positive Thinking.

If it is intercessory prayer (prayer for someone else or some extra-personal goal), it can also make you feel good in that you assume that you are aiding in the achievement of this beneficial act. In actuality, you could be fervently praying to God, Allah, Zeus, or a McDonald's Happy Meal to get the same results. But the fact that you think that prayer helps is beneficial to you.

It may also make the recipient of this prayer feel good if they know about it. It makes them feel as if you are thinking about them and praying for them, and that they are special to you and in God's eyes (if God has eyes). That's only if a fictional God has eyes.

Prayer in these senses can be a way of talking to yourself, a self-examination of your past life to consider whether you have strayed a tad from the straight and narrow. It is also a way of mentally convincing yourself that you are part of the solution/cure of something or someone with an illness, injury or problem.

Thus, if some loved one or friend is ill or injured and then gets better, you have the comfortable satisfaction of knowing that you prayed for this result, and thus you can think that you are at least partly responsible for the person's recovery. Thus, prayer — you think — works. This proves it, you think.

If you pray for some supposedly idealistic action — a law to be repealed (abortion) or passed (banning homosexual marriage), you again feel as if you were a personal part of the fervently desired result. Thus, prayer — again you think — works. This proves it, you think.

These are not proofs but only circumstances that happen to coincide. For anyone with this mental framework, switching from orange juice to grapefruit juice each morning, or stopping smoking, or giving up candy bars for this healing or change, would be the same thing. It is still only circumstantial, but the faithful believe it.

Subject all this to a truly scientific method of testing, with studies, test subjects, controls and double-blind tests to see what happens. I told you so — scientific studies show that prayer does not work other than the feel-good effect that you get that can also be attained by eating some chocolate or better still, petting a dog. Petting a dog, at least, will lower your blood pressure.

It Helps To Read The Bible Before Debating The Facts Of The Bible

The lady was sitting in our family room; an acquaintance, the friend of a friend. It was early spring, and conversations broke out about Easter. This lady is, so she claims, a good, life-long, devout, devoted, Bible-studying Christian of Protestant faith.

The subject of Passover arose, and how God saved the Israelites from the Egyptian Pharaoh. Included in the discussion was the killing of the first-born Egyptians. I couldn't stand it any longer.

"It's a shame that God had to kill all those innocent Egyptians just to make a point against the Pharaoh," I interjected.

"Oh, God did not kill the first-born Egyptians," countered the visiting lady.

"Yes, God did. God killed all the first born, including not only humans, but also all domestic animals," I corrected.

"No, no, God did not kill them," the lady ignorantly insisted. There was no doubt in her mind, and she did not question her erroneous beliefs.

"Well," I continued, "you had better read the Bible or that section. God killed the first born of all Egyptians."

"Oh," the lady countered, "I have read the Bible many times and that section many, many times. God did not kill the Egyptians."

"Well, Betsy (name changed to protect the ignorant), you had better read it again. God did kill the first-born Egyptians," I concluded. But if she was going to stay ignorant — willfully ignorant and stupid — there was nothing that I could do about it. I guess that anyone can be stupid occasionally, but Betsy was surely abusing the privilege.

Betsy turned her head away, with nothing to say to this skeptic contesting her knowledge of the Bible. Sadly for her, but good for truth, she was wrong. Just check out Exodus 12:29. Then check also Exodus 11:4, 12:12 and 12:23. Catholic and Protestant versions of various translations all say the same thing.

"At midnight the Lord struck down all the firstborn in Egypt, from the firstborn of Pharaoh who sat on the throne, to the firstborn of the prisoner, who was in the dungeon, and the firstborn of all the livestock as well." (Exodus 12:29) Prior sections in Exodus also state this. Note the part — "the Lord struck down all the first born in Egypt."

It's a shame that so many Christians are like this — with a faith based on a book that they never read. They have a faith based on what their minister tells them or what they wrongly think the Bible says, or what they want it to say.

How can they fervently believe anything when they do not really know what they believe? Their faith is based on wrong facts, erroneous ideas, happy conclusions — in short it is based on nothing. Now that is something to think about!

GOD DICTATING THE PHARAOH'S "FREE WILL" — WAS THAT FAIR?

We know from reading Exodus that the Pharaoh's heart was "hardened" to prevent the Israelites from leaving Egypt as the Lord and Moses — from the Lord — insisted. God was playing games — mean games — both with the Pharaoh and Moses and his Israelites.

This was followed by plagues on Egypt, each of them designed to make the Pharaoh release the Israelites. Ironically through the passages in Exodus it was God who "hardened Pharaoh's heart" to prevent him from releasing the Israelites. That's those games again.

Thus, if God, the omniscient, the all-powerful, created a situation whereby the Pharaoh would become stubborn and not release the Israelites, was this the Pharaoh's fault or was it God's fault for making the Pharaoh this way? The answer is obvious. According to these many statements in Exodus of God "hardening the heart of the Pharaoh," it can only be deduced that God wanted this stubbornness to continue to make for a grand ultimate plague in a final act of Godly circus showmanship.

The Pharaoh no longer had free will in choosing whether or not to accept the insistence by Moses of releasing the Israelites, but instead chose the promised plagues and disastrous outcome for the Egyptians. The Egyptians had no choice in any of this, since all the decisions were made by the Pharaoh, even though it was the Egyptian population that suffered the plague consequences.

That God hardened the Pharaoh's heart and was ultimately responsible for these plagues — not the Pharaoh — can be found in many passages that refer to the hardening of Pharaoh's heart by God. These include Exodus 7:3–4, 7:13, 7:22, 8:15, 8:19, 8:32, 9:7, 9:12, 9:34–35, 10:20, 10:27 and 11:10. So don't pretend that this is a mistake or misunderstanding! Don't pretend that there are different ways to "interpret" it.

All this was a set-up con job by God to create a Pharaoh without free will, and the Pharaoh doing things as ordered by God, almost like a puppet on a string. The cards were marked for a non-acceptance by the Pharaoh for releasing the Israelites until after the final plague of Passover in which the first born of all Egyptians — man and animal — were killed, including the first born of even cattle and those humans lacking the ridiculous but prescribed blood on the lintel and door frame of the Israelites.

Sadly, this was and remains markedly unfair and cruel to all those Egyptians who had no decision in any of this, any more than the Pharaoh had any decision after his free will was removed and his actions dictated by God. Was God being fair to others? Was God being tolerant to those who were innocent? Imagine yourself being an innocent Egyptian commoner and then consider these questions. God really is not a very fair game player, is he?

GOD'S PUNISHMENT AND THE EXECUTIONS OF INNOCENT CHILDREN OF WRONG-DOERS

Those who follow TV and movies know the name Woody Harrelson. He played the hapless and helpless bartender on Cheers and also has been in a bunch of movies. Those who follow actors more deeply may know that Woody's father, Charles Harrelson, was a freelance contract killer who in 1979 was tried and convicted for killing federal judge John H. Wood, Jr. He spent the rest of his life in prison.

Should Woody Harrelson be executed or imprisoned for the crime of his father? The answer is obvious and the question ludicrous, ridiculous and shameful. Of course not — Woody Harrelson had nothing to do with his father's criminal activity.

Now let's take Achan (Joshua 7). When God ordered all the population of Jericho to be killed and certain items of pillage saved for the Lord, Achan stole some of these items. These stolen items included an ornate robe, two hundred shekels of silver and a wedge of gold — all taken as booty from the innocent Canaanites who were killed when their city Jericho was invaded by the warring Israelites.

These stolen items marked for the Lord were hidden under Achan's tent. After Achan confessed this to Joshua, runners were dispatched to Achan's tent. These messengers found the robe, shekels of silver and wedge of gold. They brought them back and presented them to Joshua and all the Israelites and spread these stolen items out before the Lord. (Joshua 7:19–22).

These items along with Achan's sons and daughters, cattle, sheep, donkeys, tent and other belongings were taken to the Valley of Achor. There, not only Achan was stoned for his theft, but also his sons and daughters and all property including cattle, donkeys, sheep, tent and other items were stoned and destroyed. (Joshua 7:24–26).

What did Achan's sons and daughters have to do with Achan's crime? There is absolutely no indication in the Bible of any involvement of Achan's children in this crime of theft. Since we would rightly be appalled today at any hint of involving Woody Harrelson with his father's crime of murder, why are Jews and Christians not equally appalled by the punishment of innocents in this Old Testament crime of theft?

What is there about Achan's crime of theft that makes his sons, daughters, cattle, sheep, and donkeys culpable and thus killed? Why should any of us be punished by society for any crime of a father, mother or any other close or distant relative?

If nothing else, shouldn't this story should make us wary of facts, fairness, faith and biblical justice of the Old Testament God?

Picking And Choosing God's Law In Leviticus

God's Bible states specific rules by which to live, with a preponderance of these in Leviticus. Ironically, with the cherry-picking Christians, there are some interesting choices which echo philosophies and controversies of today.

Some of the biggies among these prohibitions are homosexuality and adultery, or having sexual relations with a family member. Another is abortion.

You can find these prohibitions (except abortion, which is not mentioned anywhere in the Bible) very specifically described in Leviticus 18, 19 and 20. Other early prohibitions relating to clean (allowed) and unclean (not allowed) foods are discussed in Chapter 11.

The irony is that most Christians of today are vehemently opposed to adultery, abortion, and homosexuality, but they completely ignore or are ignorant of other prohibitions which, according to God and his Bible, have equal standing.

Admittedly, a prohibition of adultery is good for society, and such a ban is generally practiced even in primitive religions and early tribal societies. Such rules tends to minimize jealousy and bloodshed and help to maintain stable families.

There is no reference to abortion in the Bible. As fundamentalists like to preach, there are references to "child sacrifice," which is a totally different critter and which should be abhorrent in any culture, religion or society. The fact that such offerings were made during biblical times to the gods Molech and Baal has nothing to do with abortion. The fact that it happened among the Israelites and other primitive religions is not discussed by religionists of today.

Similarly, the fundamentalist-stated "shedding of innocent blood" against battles or assaults is a general admonition and prohibition, not one specific to abortion, as they would like you to think. Certainly abortion is always better avoided, for instance by using good birth control methods, but nowhere is it mentioned in God's Bible.

Homosexuality is and often was culturally acceptable, as per the early Romans and Greeks. It was known and had its place. According to many pastors, the statement about tattooing is related to grief ceremonies along with other bodily mutilations of early cultures only upon the death of a loved one.

Ironically, those Christian fundamentalists believing in and adamant about the above biblical rules have no compunction about planting gardens with many types of seeds, despite the specific prohibition of this in Leviticus 19:19. Nor do many of them have compunctions about eating crabs, lobster, shrimp, clams, oysters, abalone, other non-finned seafood, or tender ham and crispy bacon, despite Leviticus 11.

Also, they have no problem wearing clothing woven of two different materials, cutting the hair on the sides of their heads or clipping their beards, despite the specific prohibitions against these in Leviticus 19:19 and 19:27 respectively.

Since religionists pick which part of a faith they wish to follow and which they choose to ignore, doesn't it seem that they really have no faith at all?

CAN WE TRUST A GOSPEL HISTORY WRITTEN DECADES AFTER THE EVENT?

Historical analysis can often determine when an ancient text was written. This is done by comparing it with the known history of other works, comparing the dates of events, wars, reigns of kings, years of famine, etc. written about in the questioned texts. The origin of the four vitally important Gospels in the New Testament — Matthew, Mark, Luke and John — was well after the death of Christ (in about the year 29 to 33 CE).

The four gospels were written over a period of approximately half a century, supposedly ranging from about 30 years after the death of Christ (for Mark) to about 50 years after his death for Matthew and Luke, to about 70–80 years after Jesus' death — for John.

Other than oral history and the writings of Paul, there was no basis on which to write a history of the life of Jesus. Even Paul's writings were set down after the death of Christ, and again probably only from oral history. Studied analysis by experts leads one to the belief that Mark read the writings of Paul, that Luke and Matthew relied on Mark and other texts, and that John would have had access to all these earlier writings. Despite this, only Matthew and Luke narrate the genealogy and birth of Christ, with Mark and John dealing mostly with the adult life of Christ.

It is also important to consider the accuracy — or lack thereof — of this history and also the various direct quotes of Jesus in all four gospels. Most verses in the Bible are only a sentence or two. Consider the number of direct, Jesus-quoted verses in these documents. If my counting is correct, for Matthew, 654; for Mark 277; for Luke 575; and for John 411. How many direct quotes could you remember exactly, if you were you working from an oral history by a person 30 to 80 years after his death? How accurately could you remember any history?

It would be like asking me — were I Mark — to write a history of Operation Desert Storm of George H. W. Bush, that continued from August 2, 1990, through August 17, 1991. That war ended 26 years ago as I write this. If I were John, it would be similar to having me write a history of World War I that ended 99 years ago, long before I was around.

To put us in the place of 2,000 years ago, realize also that that for many centuries after the year we denote for Christ's death, there was little recorded history. There was very little writing going on, few people were able to read, and there was no news media. At best there would be some manuscripts attempting to trace basic history, all based on oral history — that is, something like story telling.

It sounds like an impossible task. And it undoubtedly was. Now that is something to think about.

Does The Old Testament God Differ From The New Testament God?

When someone brings up the Old Testament in a debate about God or Christianity, some people point out that the Old Testament was prior to Christ and thus null and void in any argument about Christianity per se. Certainly, the Old Testament was written prior to the times of Jesus and the formulation of the Christian belief system. No question about that. And we are often looking at an Old Testament God of wrath and evil as compared to a New Testament God supposedly preaching love and mercy.

There are several possible answers to the question of whether it is legitimate to involve the Old Testament God in a discussion of Christianity and Jesus. First, the speaker or writer (me in this case) might be totally wrong in this comparison, since obviously these are two different parts of the Bible. But in what way is this wrong? That is never explained.

Second, if the Old Testament is null and void, why include it in all Bibles used in all Christian churches? Why don't Christians leave the Old Testament to the Jews and use only the New Testament? Once I see pastors of the Christian churches tearing the Old Testament out of all the Bibles in the pews, I might believe that it is not relevant in discussions of Christianity. Once I see Sunday School teachers no longer teaching the Old Testament stories about Adam, Eve, Abel, Cain, Moses, Abraham, David, Solomon, Samson, Joshua, Jacob and others, I might accept this fiction.

If the Old Testament is so bad, wrong, or not applicable to Christianity, why do most if not all Christian ministers and priests use it repeatedly in their sermons and Sunday School? Sometimes I attend a nearby church just for ammunition for my next essay, and for amusement. At various times in this church, there have been prolonged Sunday School lessons, small group Bible studies and serious sermons on Exodus, Job, Genesis, Joshua, and other Old Testament books. In addition, most of these same sessions contain references to virtually every other book of the Bible, both Old and New Testament. Why include the Old Testament if it is not applicable or acceptable to Christianity and if Christians dislike it so much?

Maybe there are separate Old Testament and a New Testament Gods. Maybe the Old Testament God had an epiphany with the birth of Christ and changed his Godly philosophy at that time. Maybe there is no God and these ramblings are just fables told by the winners in any Old or New Testament dispute or story.

Even if the Old Testament does not apply to Jesus and the New Testament, does that justify God doing the evil things he did in Joshua (killing all Canaanites), during Passover (killing all first-born Egyptians), and in the great flood (killing all throughout the world except Noah's family), or killing Job's or Achan's (Job and Joshua) children?

There's an awful lot to think about when considering the Old Testament and New Testament and the mating of the philosophies of the differing Gods of these two texts. Isn't it possible that all this is just fiction?

GENESIS IS NOT JOURNALISM — THE FACTUAL BASIS FOR EVOLUTION

The subject of evolution had come up, raising its ugly head in the family home of some staunch evangelical fundamentalists. "It's all ridiculous. There is no proof of evolution. It's rubbish," the head of the household said, thinking that he had just hammered the final nail into the coffin of evolution and into Darwin's massive and definitive study.

The irony is classic. Here, a man with a belief in a religion for which there is no proof at all scoffs at the truth of evolution with thousands of books and tens of thousands of research projects explaining the massive studies that demonstrate the theory's validity. He believes in his Bible, the one and only document that he has for "proof" of Christianity and "proof" that evolution did not occur.

He believes in the Bible, despite the fact that it took hundreds of years to write, and that there are no additional secular documents of the time to back up the so-called "truths" of the Bible. He believes the Bible, despite the fact that Genesis is not journalism.

It took hundreds of years for early religionists and scholars to argue over which books were to be included in the Bible. These arguments determined which books were to be "canonical," which translations were considered authentic, which biblical statements were to be interpreted to become dogma, doctrine and Church law.

In evolution we have the monumental works of Charles Darwin starting with his book *The Origin of Species*, published November 24, 1859, and his slightly later *The Descent of Man* in 1871.

But it does not stop there. In the ensuing 150 years we have the equivalent of whole libraries of books with all the "ologies" and related works continually confirming the theories posited by Darwin. We have confirmation and refinements in cosmology, astronomy, geology, fossil studies, anatomy, comparative anatomy, histology, paleontology, embryology, radiometric dating, zoology, entomology, ichthyology, herpetology, genome studies, taxonomy, DNA studies, basic biology, archeology, physiology, and more. Much more.

The interesting aspect of all this is that as with other works on both sides of the religious fence, Christians do not read anything contrary to their hide-bound belief in the Bible. With that kind of philosophy, Copernicus and Galileo would not have discovered the heliocentric nature of our solar system, and the Flat Earth Society would be holding monthly meetings in your neighborhood.

With that kind of thinking, Charlie Darwin might have stayed with the ministry studies with which he started life and not contributed his definitive and monumental work to the world. The lack of basic scientific and biological knowledge by fundamentalists is both interesting, and depressing for those seeking scientific truth.

Jesus Genealogy — Fact Or Fiction?

One would think that reporters and historians would have their facts straight in any story. Not so in the Bible.

Look at the genealogy of Jesus, as reported by Matthew and Luke. Mark, from which much of Matthew and Luke were taken or plagiarized, has nothing to say on this, nor does John, the last of the four gospels to be written.

Both of these genealogies report the ancestors from Jesus back to David, this to prove earlier Jewish prophesies as to the coming of the Messiah and his lineage from David.

However, in Matthew, counting David but not counting Jesus, we have 27 male ancestors from David up through Joseph. In Luke, we have a listing of 42, more than half again as many as listed in Matthew. In fact, counting backwards, once we get past Joseph, the two historical accounts immediately diverge. In Luke, Joseph was fathered by Heli, while in Matthew, Joseph was fathered by Jacob. Who is right — or is neither of them right?

When I asked a minister about this conflict, he explained that of course both are correct, since Heli had no sons and thus the genealogy had to continue through his daughter to Mary. This is total nonsense, and that preacher should have known better. He probably did know better, but did not want to admit it for fear of losing his job. The Bible in these sections constantly references "son of," not "daughter of." That is pretty clear. In fact, my King James Bible even italicizes "*the son*" in each of these geological stepping stones.

The minister also contradicted himself by explaining that under Jewish law, genealogy had to be through sons only. In addition, among two Bible concordances checked, there is no reference to Heli having only daughters. Where do ministers get this stuff? No cigar for that minister's weak — and erroneous — answer! In addition to that, the numbers just don't add up, or add up too much in Luke with 42 ancestors of Jesus.

The real fly on the wedding cake is the statement about following the line of David through males to Jesus. Breaking news! Joseph was NOT the biological father of Jesus. To believe the Bible, you have to believe that Mary was a virgin and that at best Joseph was only a step-father.

There was no direct line from David to Jesus. Maybe they were hoping that people would not catch this major flaw or that readers would just overlook it. There are nothing but questions here, nothing but false so-called proofs as to Bible validity and Jesus' ancestors. This lack of proof is one more reason why the Bible, Judaism and Christianity should be questioned. Fortunately, more and more thinking people are questioning it.

Did Righteous Lot Really Offer His Two Daughters To Be Gang Raped Or Worse?

The story of Lot is well known. He and his family were supposedly the only good people in Sodom and Gomorrah, and were to be saved by God, as per pleas by Abraham, Lot's uncle. According to the story, God would have saved everyone if as few as ten righteous people could have been found among the wicked who lived there.

Only Lot's family was determined to be "righteous," and thus they were the only ones to be saved as described in Genesis 18:16–19:29. The story is that two angels showed up at the city gate, were met by Lot and went with Lot to his house to stay overnight. Men from all over the city gathered outside Lot's house to demand that the visitors be handed over. Genesis 19:5 states: "They called out to Lot, 'Where are the men who came to you tonight? Bring them out to us so that we can have sex with them.'"

Lot refused this and then offered a strange proposal that would be considered criminal or child abuse today. "No, my friends," says Lot in Genesis 19:7–8 "Don't do this wicked thing. Look, I have two daughters who have never slept with a man. Let me bring them out to you and you can do what you like with them." Do with them what you like??

Ultimately, the angels struck the crowd blind as the crowd was planning to break down the door to get at the men/angels or Lot's daughters. Thus, neither the angels nor Lot's daughters were ever attacked. Lot's daughters were not gang raped by the crowd despite Lot's offer.

The question here is not whether the daughters were, in the end, saved by angels or other means, but only what their father offered to do with them or would have allowed to be done to them. Had the daughters been released to the crowd as Lot offered, they would have been savagely raped, possibly even killed, as occurred to a concubine in a very similar tale in Judges 19.

What kind of a man, highly favored as righteous by God, would commit such a heinous act as to "give" any young girl — much less his daughters — to a crowd for a sexual attack?

It makes one seriously wonder about God's goodness, planning, and love. It makes one seriously wonder about the "goodness" of Lot when his plan — obviously known to an omniscient God — was to allow his daughters to be raped and worse.

Lot's Daughters And Incest With Their Father — How Righteous Was This Chosen Family?

The story of Lot — the only "righteous" man and family in all of Sodom and Gomorrah — is well known. We previously discussed his role in offering his two virgin daughters to a crowd outside his house to be gang raped. This was to prevent the crowd from breaking in and taking his two guests for the night. Not nice at all.

But the story does not end there. (Genesis 19:30–38) Lot and his family escaped the fire and destruction of Sodom and Gomorrah, but Lot lost his wife, who disobeyed God by looking back towards the cities. Lot and his daughters first went to Zoar and then moved to the mountains to live in a cave. The daughters did not know whether any other men had survived and thus planned to continue their biological line by having sex with their father.

"Our father is old and there is no man around here to lie with us, as is the custom all over the earth. Let's get our father to drink wine and then lie with him and preserve our family line through our father," said the older daughter to her sibling (Genesis 19:31–32).

This they did, taking turns, with the older daughter first getting her father drunk and then having sex with him, even though he was so drunk as to not be aware of it.

The younger daughter followed with the same practice the next day. "So both of Lot's daughters became pregnant by their father. The older daughter had a son and she named him Moab; he is the father of the Moabites of today. The younger daughter also had a son, and she named him Ben-Ammi; he is the father of the Ammonites of today." (Genesis 19:36–38).

Two thoughts occur. One, if the father Lot was as drunk as suggested, so that he did not even know that he was having sex with his two daughters, would sexual intercourse have been possible?

A more important question revolves around this so-called "righteous family," the only one worth saving by God. With Lot offering his daughters to strangers for gang raping, and later his daughters plotting to have sex with their father, how "righteous" could this family have been?

What were the standards by which God was governing this immoral family to be ranked so highly above all the other families of Sodom and Gomorrah? It makes one wonder. With these "good" people, who did God reject?

Do Ax Heads Really Float?

Axes are made to cut with more force than a knife and are tools and weapons of early man. Over the centuries, they have been made of stone, bronze, iron and steel. They are weapons for primitive warfare, tools for cutting trees and wood for construction and — as with a fireman's ax — devices for entering buildings to save trapped residents.

In all cases, ax heads of stone, bronze, iron and steel are heavy and sink like an anchor when dropped into water. Physics tells us that, in fact insists upon it with the periodic table and weights of elements. But not so in the Old Testament.

In 2 Kings 6:4–7, an ax head sinks in water, but the prophet Elisha causes it to float so that it can be retrieved. We all know that this is impossible, in the same way that the Cheshire cat in Alice in Wonderland talks, or that the stuffed bear Winnie-the-Pooh strolls around the Hundred Acre Woods.

That does not stop the floating ax head story from being accepted as gospel truth (pardon the pun) by those who literally believe every word of the Bible, this inerrant Word of God. "They went to the Jordan (river) and began to cut down trees" starts the story listed above. The reason was to fell trees to make poles to construct a dwelling where the students of the prophet Elisha could meet. Where they had been meeting was too small for all of them.

"As one of them was cutting down a tree, the iron axhead [*sic*] fell into the water. 'Oh my lord,' he cried out, 'it was borrowed.'" (2 Kings 6:5) "The man of God asked, 'Where did it fall?' When he showed him the place, Elisha cut a stick and threw it there, and made the iron float. 'Lift it out,' he said. Then the man reached out his hand and took it." (2 Kings 6:6–7)

Obviously, while accepted by many of the fundamentalist Christian genre, this is a physical impossibility with the known facts listed in the periodic table and with our understanding of the atomic weights of the components of iron, of the known facts regarding whether iron does or ever could float, or of anything else in the comparison of weight, water and specific gravity.

Knowing this, the impossibility of this story, and the time frame in which this was transposed, translated, copied and changed, does it not make one wonder about the truth and accuracy of all other stories in the Bible?

WHO IS AT THE TOMB AFTER THE CRUCIFIXION OF JESUS? CAN'T ANYONE GET IT RIGHT?

Let's assume that some important event occurs, or some important person needs to have his life recorded for historical posterity. Let's also assume that four credentialed newspapers — the New York Times, the Washington Post, the Atlanta Constitution and the Chicago Tribune — send out their top reporters to cover this.

Naturally, the basics of journalism are to get and record the who, what, when, where, why and how of each event, to the extent possible. The who, what, when and where are a must in this recording journalistic process, and are usually included in the first line or first paragraph of any major news story. The how and why might be a little iffy, depending upon what occurred and how it was discovered.

A very important event in the four gospels is the trial, crucifixion, death and resurrection of Christ, as described in all four gospels — Matthew, Mark, Luke and John. The interesting thing is that while most Christians believe each and every word of each gospel on this, each gospel has different descriptions, events and people, all different, and described in different ways. Does that make sense? Could that be real? Is there any accuracy to any of this?

Let's start with the ladies who visited the tomb of Christ after his death on the cross. Visitors listed in Matthew are Mary Magdalene and "the other Mary" (not named or otherwise identified) who visited the tomb. (This "other Mary" may have been Mary, the mother of James and Joses, mentioned elsewhere.) In Mark the women were Mary Magdalene, Mary the mother of James and Joses and Salome. Luke refers to "the women also, which came with him from Galilee, followed after, and beheld the sepulcher and how his body was laid." There is no listing as to the names or numbers of women. John records Mary Magdalene alone as visiting the tomb and sepulcher.

Why could not all of these four important reporters of the basis of Christianity recorded the straight story — the same story? Was it two named women, three named women, a bunch of unnamed women or one named woman alone? Why could not these four vitally important writers of the four gospels of Jesus life and death get it right?

If you read something this disjointed, disquieting and inaccurate in four separate major newspapers, would you not begin to wonder about the truth of all of the story, or of all of the report? Would this not make a questioning, critical reader of these four important gospels wonder about the accuracy of everything written? At the least, it is something to arouse curiosity.

GOD'S CRUELTY VERY EXPLICIT DURING PASSOVER AND THE KILLING OF INNOCENT EGYPTIANS

A pivotal example of God's cruelty occurs with Passover in Exodus 12:12. There God speaking (as prefaced in chapter 11:4) says: "For I will pass through the land of Egypt this night, and will smite all the firstborn in the land of Egypt, both man and beast; and against all the gods of Egypt I will execute judgment: I am the Lord." Check also Exodus 13:15. "And it came to pass, when the Pharaoh would hardly let us go, that the Lord slew all the firstborn in the land of Egypt, both the firstborn of man and the firstborn of beast."

This comes after a detailed condemnation of the Pharaoh, of Egypt and instructions that the blood of a lamb shall be used to mark the lintel and two side posts of each Israeli household so that the Lord would pass over (thus the name) the homes of the Israelites. This follows with the firstborn (or firstborn males, later in this chapter) of all in Egypt, man and beast, being killed by God.

There are several monumental evil acts with this. First, God had "hardened Pharaoh's heart" so that Pharaoh no longer had true free will to choose what he would do with the Israelites and was acting only as God willed him to. Thus, God was the cause of the Pharaoh not releasing the Israelites from Egypt as requested by Moses. It was not Pharaoh's fault.

Second, it was the Pharaoh who was "wrong" in this story — not the many unknowing, uncaring and innocent firstborn of Egypt. A corollary of this would be as if some world or US leader had done something horribly evil and all our first born children in each community, city, state or country had to pay with their lives. The uproar, riot and rebellion from this would be unstoppable. Yet this is exactly what God did as he killed the innocent Egyptians who played no part in part the Pharaoh's decisions.

Also, there was no need for the Israelites to use lamb blood on the lintel and door posts to signal God. God is God — presumably all powerful, all knowing. God being God, he would in his infinite wisdom have known which households were those of Israelites and which were those of Egyptians.

To unjustly kill the Egyptians as he did, he had to know in his omniscience which of the men, women, children and babies were not only Egyptian but also firstborn. This gives one something to think about when it comes to evil and justice.

ARE ANGELS MEN? ARE MEN ANGELS? WHAT IS GOING ON AT THE TOMB OF JESUS?

The Gospels of Matthew, Mark, Luke and John are decidedly different in the stories of Mary and various women going to the tomb of Jesus after his crucifixion as reported previously. The four writers of these four most important gospels just can't seem to get their stories straight.

Are they any better with what these women saw when they got there? You would think that any good reporter, journalist or historian would be fairly clear about the facts in cases of reportage like this. Not so. In addition, the facts about the tomb would also turn out to be slightly different in different reports.

In Matthew, Mary and Mary the mother of James and Joses saw a single angel come down from heaven and only then roll back the stone blocking the tomb. Then this single angel sat on the stone he had just rolled back. Thus, we have not only one angel, but also some action in the stone being moved.

In Mark, Mary Magdalene, Mary the mother of James and Salome (different from those in Matthew) went to the tomb and on the way worried about who among them could roll back the stone. When they arrived, they saw that the stone had already been rolled back and saw a young man sitting in the right side of the tomb when they entered it. The same thing happened in Luke, except that the one man in the tomb had now become two men.

In John, Mary Magdalene was alone and upon entering the tomb (the stone had been rolled back before this) found two angels sitting where the body of Jesus was previously lying. In all this, you have four stories, all of the same event, in which you have the stone being rolled back or already rolled back. You also have differences of who was there to greet the women. Take your pick. Was it one angel sitting on the stone, one man, two men or two angels sitting inside the tomb area? Inquiring minds want to know.

The point is that with this much disparity of a simple act, it makes one wonder about the rest of the gospels — their truth, veracity, and their accuracy of the life of Jesus, his direct quotes, "miracles," works, acts of faith, crucifixion, death, resurrection, etc.

The devil (no pun intended) is in the details and if you can't get accuracy out of the details, can you really, really believe the rest of the story? Maybe not.

BELIEFS AND DISBELIEFS OF VARIOUS RELIGIONS — WHY
CHRISTIANITY IS NO MORE REASONABLE THAN OTHERS

The idea that Muhammad flew to heaven by riding on the back
of his winged horse Buraq is ridiculous. Just ask any Christian about
this Islamic belief. The idea that Alexander the Great was born after
his mother was impregnated by a snake is equally ridiculous. So is the
idea that Minerva sprang fully formed from Jupiter's head, as per the
Roman myths.

Realize also that most of the early mythic gods were born of a virgin
birth of some sort. Also, many early CE or BCE religions had beliefs
later taken over by and plagiarized by Christians. The Christians
adapted them for their use while discounting and condemning the
earlier pagan religions from which these so called "Christian" beliefs
came. But check out the idea that Christ was killed by a hideous
Roman method of execution and then three days later rose to fly off
into the sky. That's believable, Christians say, that is real, that really
and truly happened and that is something which we must believe to
get to heaven. Just ask any Christian. But you can't believe the story
of Muhammad riding Buraq to heaven and Allan.

The point is that every religion has major, important aspects of
that religion that are totally ridiculous to all other religions. And
with 10,000 different religions and variations in the past and present
world, it is only natural that everything is false except for the one
"true" religion in which you believe. Just ask your fellow believers.

Then check out all the various Christian "faiths" which differed
from each other and how the winner took pains to rid the world of
all evidence of the other "Christian religions" or early pagan religions
from which the Christians plagiarized. Check out the Gnostic texts,
why certain books of the Bible were excluded and not considered
canonical for present day use and why parts of the Vatican were built
on the rubble of early pagan religions, most likely Mithraism.

Study enough and you come away with the strong feeling that
it is all smoke and mirrors, that it is all discounting the obviously
ridiculous claims of one religion while believing and accepting
different, equally ridiculous, claims in Christianity — claims that you
have to believe to get into heaven.

It is surely all pixie dust, the weak superstitions of the First
century while we live and try to exist in a technological 21st century.
That's something to think about.

Should Abraham Have Been Pimping Out His Wife? Is It OK To Marry Your Sister?

"If a man marries his sister, the daughter of either his father or his mother, and they have sexual relations, it is a disgrace. They must be cut off before the eyes of their people. He has dishonored his sister and will be held responsible." (NIV Leviticus 20:17). But don't tell Abraham (Abram) or Sarah (Sari), his wife/sister.

The irony is that there is a specific prohibition against this, as noted in Leviticus 20:17, which was ignored by Abram (Abraham) and Sari (Sarah). Abraham married his half-sister, an abomination. He also used this double definition of sister/wife when trying to gain favor. When going into Egypt, Abram told his wife to tell the Egyptians that she was Abram's sister. She did and was taken to the Pharaoh to be his wife. That was half true of course. She was Abram's half-sister but she was also his wife. The Pharaoh found out after taking Sari to be his wife and then banned both Abram and Sari from the land. (Genesis 12:11–20)

This happened again with Abraham and Sarah (note name changes here) dealing with Abimelech, king of Gerar. Abimelech took Sarah to be his wife, but he never touched her after a dream from God warning him that Sarah was already married. Abraham again waffles out of this bit of difficulty by explaining again that Sarah is really his sister (half-sister) as well as being his wife.

Abraham explains his offering his wife Sarah to Abimelech. "Besides, she really is my sister, the daughter of my father though not of my mother; and she became my wife." (Genesis 20:12) The disturbing aspect about all of this is the prevaricating, side-stepping, lying and justification that takes place with God, Genesis, Leviticus, Abram (Abraham), Sari (Sarah), Pharaoh, Abimelech and others in this story of deception, dishonesty and duplicity. And you can't blame Abimelech or the Pharaoh.

Sadly, this is just like small children making up a game and then changing the rules as they play to justify the role and advantage of some in the game. It is like the bullies making rule changes to their advantage. That is really the only way that an attempt of explanation can be made, by claiming that the rules of marriage and sibling relationship had changed from the time of Abraham and Sarah to the time of the rules and admonitions of Leviticus.

But aren't basic rules basic rules? Shouldn't the basic rules have applied to all of early mankind if this fable is correct? Did God forget about this in his plan for a perfect man made in his image?

THE FICTION OF NEAR DEATH EXPERIENCES AND THE CONCEPTS OF HEAVENLY VISITS

Christians and perhaps others place a lot of stock in the concept of heaven and an afterlife through the so-called Near Death Experiences, or NDE's. Unfortunately, all that stock in NDE's is misplaced, misguided and nonsense. One pastor has even made a lot of money (we won't mention his name or book title for fear of giving him more publicity) from such a book about his NDE.

The fact of the matter is that an NDE is just that — a NEAR death experience — not death. Near death might be some synapses going haywire in the brain for a while, a coma, some brain chemistry going wild or something else that medicine and science has not yet completely figured out. It is not death. It is not wandering around heaven for a while and then coming back and giving a nightly news report on what heaven is like.

Death is death of the brain — nothing more, nothing less. Sure, other accidents, illnesses and dysfunctions can cause this brain death, but it is still the brain and only the brain that makes each of us "us."

Let's take a horrible-to-think-about but still possible example of all this. We could have a human with both arms removed at the shoulders, both legs removed at the hips, genitals removed, removal of one lung, removal of one kidney, part of the liver removed, a few feet of large and small intestine removed, blinded, deafened, sense of smell destroyed, lower mandible and upper teeth removed. What would you have?

In this horrible, unthinkable example, you would have a biologically functioning living human being, albeit one that would have to be cared for the rest of his life. You would not have anything like death or a NDE. You would not have any wandering through heaven hand-in-hand with God or Jesus.

Take a healthy vibrant youthful individual and destroy the brain, and you would have death. We are our brains and our brains are us. The concept of finding pearly gates, golden streets, gorgeous robes and constant singing from a heavenly choir is a figment of the imagination or some crossed-up brain cells and wiring. It is fiction. It is not a real concept of heaven, no matter how much we want to think so or want to wish that this fable would or could happen.

NDE's as "proof" of heaven are no more proof of heaven than a "near miss" of an airplane in flight is a real crash. You can sleep through both without consequence.

WRATH OF GOD AND A PROPHET TOUGH ON KIDDING, JEERING YOUNGSTERS — THEY GET A KILLING PUNISHMENT

The punishment should fit the crime, at least as we see crime and punishment today. Today we would not execute someone for stealing a loaf of bread or jeering at someone. You would not expect such draconian punishment in the past either, since it often seemed that God was a little emphatic about having the Israelites do the right, Godly thing. That was seldom the case, but that was often the pretext of Judaism and later its offspring Christianity.

Take the story in 2 Kings about the parable (or true story — you take your pick) of the prophet Elisha being jeered by some youths. This can be found in 2 Kings, 2:23–25 immediately after Elisha purified some water while at the same time making a land area productive (2 Kings 19–22).

In this story, Elisha, apparently bald or balding, is jeered by some youths. The story does not identify the youths as boys (likely) or a mix of boys and girls. "From there Elisha went up to Bethel. As he was walking along the road, some youths came out of the town and jeered at him."

"'Go on up, you bald-head!' they said. 'Go on up, you bald-head!' He turned around, looked at them and called down a curse on them in the name of the Lord. Then two bears (or she bears) came out of the woods and mauled forty-two of the youths. And he went on to Mount Carmel and from there returned to Samaria."

This prophet of the Lord thus asked for and got from God a terrible punishment for some not nice but childish jeering by some kids. It was a punishment far exceeding any appropriate penalty for just jeering at an old, balding man.

Furthermore, it does not say that Elisha did anything to help these injured forty-two youths after this bear mauling that must have been pretty bad to put forty-two of them down. Were they killed? Were they just badly injured? The Bible does not say. And Elisha continued on his way, leaving the bear mauling behind him.

Be this a story, true rendering, fable, fiction, parable or absolute fact, nothing more is said and no preamble explains it. This leaves the reader with the disquieting belief that this is OK, that this is a fitting punishment for these jeering boys, and that God approved it by sending along two bears to literally tear to pieces forty-two children.

This is just one more example, whether possible or parable, that makes one wonder about this caring, loving God. Doesn't it make prophets and God seem highly capricious as to how they choose a punishment to fit the crime?

ARE ALL BABIES ATHEISTS? ARE THEY BETTER OFF BY LEARNING ABOUT RELIGION AND CHRISTIANITY?

The concept of Christianity is that original sin inhabits us all, that we are born sinners, and that even a fetus (most Christian religions) is guilty of original sin. Never mind the fact that the concept of original sin was not codified until the Second Council of Orange in 529 CE. It was thought and written about earlier by St. Augustine (354–430 CE), but not decided upon as good or bad, true or false, until about 500 years after the death of Christ.

Nonsense. We can't be held responsible for those things good or bad of our ancestors. I don't care what Adam and Eve did with the magical apple and as a result of the talking snake. When we are born, we are needy little parasites, but that is all.

Oh yeah, we are also atheists. When born, we have no concept of a god or gods, morality or immorality, or good or evil or anything else. As far as we're concerned, there is no god, no God, no religion, no heaven, no hell. We don't believe in a god or God, since we have no reason to do so.

We stay that way in some sort of happy bliss until we are brainwashed and abused, coerced and threatened by religious teaching, often as early as age one or two. Check most church bulletins and you will find notes as to where and when the various Bible classes are for the babies (one to two years old), toddlers (three to four), children (five and six), etc. The ages and groups might differ, but you get the idea. They also give the older children and youth groups fanciful names to make them feel like "warriors of God," "crusaders for Christ" or some such hype. This continues up through high school years and then goes into the various regional, religious denominations or national youth groups.

The bottom line is that babies are atheists. They can and should learn morals, mores, folkways, regulations and laws as they grow up, but these are and should be all separate from religion. Morality does not require God or religion. God and religion do require morality to make them seem important and necessary to live a good life.

That connection of God and morality is not true, never has been and never will be. Babies start out as atheists. Left alone, many of them would stay that way without the necessity of inventing religion. Doesn't it seem shameful that some people warp small brains with concepts which at best are speculative, suspicious and questionable?

FOR APPLE EATING, GOD PUNISHES EVE AND ALL WOMEN

When dentist William Morton decided in the early 1840s that he needed some way to alleviate the pain of dental surgery and tooth extraction, he turned to Dr. Charles Jackson who suggested ether.

Previously, nitrous oxide (laughing gas) had been tried, but without total success.

Morton tried ether, first on a patient on September 30, 1846 and subsequently in a public demonstration on October 16, 1846. The public demonstration was with Dr. John Warren who removed a neck tumor while a patient was under ether anesthesia.

Thus Morton introduced anesthesia to the world. Without it, the long and complex operations common today would be impossible. Patients would die of shock from horrible intractable pain with small operations, much less heart surgery, knee replacements, back operations and bowel retractions.

Of course, women could not get, and should not receive any anesthesia during childbirth. That was the learned opinion of clergymen, pastors, ministers and some religious doctors during this time and occasionally into the early 1900s. After all, it is pretty clear that granting women alleviation of pain during childbirth would be a complete violation of God's law, God's wishes, and Genesis of the Bible, that inerrant Word of God.

After Eve toyed with the talking snake, ate the magical apple and convinced Adam to snack on the apple also, both were subsequently banished from the good life in the Garden of Eden. And Eve got the pain punishment from God.

In Genesis 3:16 God says to Eve, "I will greatly increase your pains in childbearing; with pain you will give birth to children."

So during normal births, breech births, Caesarean sections, anything, women had to have pain. After all, as they say, the Bible tells us so.

You would have to wonder about anyone who would deliberately deny an innocent fellow human being any possible alleviation from pain. You have to worry about clergymen — with emphasis on "men" who never have to experience the pain or difficulty of childbirth.

You have to be appalled about those clergy who would preach this from pulpits or write about it in religious tracts. You have to be appalled that they claimed to be religious, Godly, loving and caring about their parishioners, yet still insisted on no pain alleviation to approximately half of their flock.

While this sad stage of religion ultimately gave way to science and common sense, there are still those around today — clergy and parishioners — who insist on the ridiculousness of religion rather than the marvels of medicine to solve medical problems and to prevent pain, debilitation, disease and death.

Today, they are called faith healers.

SKEPTICISM AND QUESTIONING OF CHRISTIANITY OBVIOUS JUST BY READING THE BIBLE

In the New International Version of the Bible, the preface states that "the translators were united in their commitment to the authority and infallibility of the Bible as God's Word in written form." The King James Version suggests the same thing, particularly in reference to the exact quotes by Christ.

That puts believers in a tight spot with no wiggle room, and leaves skeptics with a lot to think about, wonder about and question. This, by the admission and pronouncements of the translators, leaves the Bible open for skeptics to question the very words of the Bible, that inerrant Word of God.

Thus, Bible contradictions, absurdities, atrocities, condemnations and laws are subject to be picked on and torn apart by a little thinking and comparing. Ironically, Christians cherry-pick the Bible to find only the good and acceptable to them, ignoring the bad or questionable.

Take contradictions. In Genesis 1:3–5. God created light on the first day. In Genesis 1:14–19, God created the sun and the stars on the fourth day. God is making light on different days in different ways? This sort of thing continues throughout the Bible to near the end. In Revelation 8:7, you read that a third of the earth was burned up, a third of the trees burned up and all of the grass burned up. In Revelation 9:4, an army of locusts is told to not harm any grass or tree. How can locusts harm grasses when they have all been burned up?

The religionists never answer questions like this, nor do they want to be confronted with this kind of critical thinking or questioning.

For atrocities, you can pick almost anywhere in the Bible. For a major event, read all of Joshua where God directs Joshua to kill everyone in all the 30-plus innocent cities and peoples conquered by the Israelites. Realize that includes every innocent person — man, woman, child, baby, pregnant woman, boy, girl, grandparent, etc. And all were innocent.

Or look at Psalm 137:9, where approval is expressed for those seeking vengeance: "happy is he who repays you for what you have done to us — he who seizes your infants and dashes them against the rocks." I always thought that in war, soldiers were supposed to fight soldiers, not deliberately harm innocent civilians. I guess that God did not and does not think that way.

The horrors of the Bible, carefully read and critically examined, leave one with real concerns over the "goodness" of this Good Book, the "love" of God and Jesus, the "fairness" of religion and the "justice" enacted throughout the Bible. You have to wonder about all those imbued with Bible stories, yet ignoring the horrors accompanying those stories.

Cheap Tricks On The Christian Science Front

During my college days, several of us science majors decided to go to the religious/Christian club meeting for a film showing on Christianity and blood. We — all with majors in biology, chemistry, physics — were truly interested to see what religion could add to the text material we had learned in class.

The film (no video then) was on red blood cells, variously called erythrocytes or RBCs. These are critical to the absorption of oxygen and expelling of carbon dioxide in any vertebrate with a circulatory system.

And RBCs are interesting. In a cubic mm of blood (measure that on your ruler), women have about 3.5 to 5 million RBCs while men have about 5 to 6 million per cubic millimeter.

The film went into great detail about how the shape of the blood was perfect — no doubt due to God. It has no nucleus (non-nucleated) and has no appreciable other cellular aspects. It is round and flat with depressed centers; a biconcave disc. This, the film noted, is the perfect shape for the mass of the cell, designed by God of course for the maximum absorption and exchange of oxygen and carbon dioxide. This red blood cell, with a life span of about 120 days and made continually in our bodies, could not be better designed by God, or better made for us. We create about 2.4 million RBCs per second in our bone marrow.

With this information, you had to believe that there has to be a God and Jesus. How else could we have such a perfect cell, this but one example of our perfect bodies made in God's image?

The film left one with the distinct impression that there must be a God. It left one with the knowledge that God was omniscient in knowing how to make this important cell for humans and that God was omnipotent in perfecting it for us.

But the film left out one small tiny bit of important information. This same non-nucleated biconcave disc red blood cell is also found in every other mammal on earth, with the exceptions of a few ungulates and camels. Biologists think that the camel has a nucleated red blood cell so that it can make through cell division (mitosis) other RBCs, necessary for the camel and otherwise impossible to make as a result of drought and heat conditions where it lives.

Is this lack of information a sin of omission by the film makers, or did they forget to check basic biology? Were they deliberately trying to convince the unknowing fence-straddlers and make the devout more fervently believe? One can only speculate — and be skeptical. But leaving out information to make an erroneous point is a cheap trick. You would not expect that of honest people. Were these film makers and Christians honest?

GOD, JESUS AND PLANS A, B, C, AND D FOR MANKIND

Today, Christians look upon Christ's crucifixion and resurrection as the saving grace of God, the key for believers to open the door of heaven and jog up to those golden streets past the pearly gates. Not so fast, Bunky.

Salvation as preached today was God's Plan D. God's Plan A, B and C did not work. In simplest fashion, Plan A included Adam and Eve, who were to live in and enjoy the Garden of Eden forever, never dying, never filling a 9 to 5 work schedule, never suffering any pain or discomfort. Then they were banished by God for believing the talking snake and eating the forbidden fruit.

Thus, mankind, this imperfectly-made perfect example of God and made in the image of God, could not keep his hands out of the fruit bowl and thus — if you believe all this — condemned all of us to ultimate death unless there was a back-up plan to save us.

You could look upon the birth of Jesus as Plan B. There is certainly ample evidence of this belief in Matthew and Luke, the only two of the four gospels that address the birth of Jesus. Jesus was considered the King of the Israelites, which (in Matthew) frightened King Herod who in turn demanded that all boys in Bethlehem two years old and younger were to be killed to destroy this royal interloper.

Plan C could be considered Jesus returning from Egypt to which his parents had taken him with the Herod threat. He was found by his parents in Jerusalem in the temple, listening to and teaching the rabbis. In the words of Luke to his anxious parents, he said, "Didn't you know that I had to be in my Father's house?" That seems to cement the idea that Jesus was/is the Christ, the King of the Israelites, the son of God, etc.

You might want to also segue a few other plans in there, with Jesus performing miracles by walking on water, feeding thousands with a few crusts of bread, healing lepers, raising a few people from the dead, etc. Thus, crucifixion could be Plan E, F, G, etc.; however you want to play with it.

The bottom line is that the understanding among some — certainly not all — was that Jesus was the Christ, the son of God, the secret key to salvation that was not expressed sufficiently in biblical times until his crucifixion and subsequent resurrection and ascension to heaven. By our accounting above, that would be Plan D.

However, it does make one think that if God in his omniscience had figured out how to make a better prototype human than the flawed Adam, we might all live forever and been fine with Plan A. But then, you have to be a little skeptical.

If Your Kids Die, Can They Be Replaced? God Says So! — Really?

In the book of Job, Job loses everything as a "test" of his Godly ways and stalwart faith. In this story, Satan and God discuss the faithfulness of Job and how Job might be tested.

As part of this test, God allows Satan to test Job by causing a loss of all of his property and belongings as a result of this betting game between Satan and God. The only stipulation was that Satan could not harm Job. But in the process (Job 1:9–22) Job lost all of his oxen, sheep, camels, donkeys and servants. A tribe of Sabeans stole the oxen and donkeys and killed the accompanying servants.

Fire from the sky — from God — fell on Job's sheep and accompanying servants and killed them. This was followed by the Chaldeans who stole all Job's camels and killed his servants. Finally, a mighty wind storm swept in to collapse a house and kill all seven of Job's sons and three daughters who were feasting there. All of his children died!

In all of this, including the death of his ten children, Job did not blame God but only praised him. This follows with Satan (with God's permission) affecting Job with boils and sores all over his body. This is followed by a long series of thoughts or ramblings by Job and his three friends who visit him.

The end — or epilogue — of all this is that because of Job's faithfulness to God and not condemning him, God restores Job to double the property he had before — to fourteen thousand sheep, six thousand camels, a thousand yoke (two thousand) of oxen and a thousand donkeys. God also "restored" Job's children, allowing Job and his wife to have seven more sons and three more daughters, just as he had before all his first ten children were killed. Isn't that great?

Does Job's ability to have more children make up for the ten children that God allowed to be killed? If someone were to kill your children even though you could have more children later to "replace" them, would that make you feel good? Would you be happy with that? You would certainly love the "replacements" but would that make up for the other children who died? Do "replacements" make up for children who have died?

Would you consider this as fair? Do you value your children this poorly? Would you consider your children as replaceable — like replacing a tent or a sheep? Or today, replacing a toaster oven with a new one from Wal-Mart? Does this book of the Bible prove or disprove that God is or was fair to Job? On this basis, would you trust God to be fair with you? That's something to think about.

WHAT HAPPENS IF SOMEONE LIKE JOSHUA MAKES THE SUN STAND STILL — REALLY STILL?

Check with Joshua 10:12–14 for something else that ought to perk our curiosity and skepticism. This is the famous scene from Sunday school class when Joshua asks God to extend the day, to make the sun stand still, so that Joshua and the Israelites can defeat their Amorite enemy in Gibeon.

Naturally, as little kids in the middle of religious brainwashing, most of us were or are astonished and amazed that God can stop the sun. That, after all, is some pretty heavy duty magic, some pretty major voo doo or ju ju. But as we know from Galileo in the early 1600s, the sun does not really revolve around the earth. That is even something that the Catholic Church finally realized. Some 359 years later on October 31, 1992, the Church "forgave" Galileo for Galileo being right.

The earth revolves on its own axis, so for the sun to appear to "stand still," for the sun to stay in place, in the middle of the day (as stated in the Bible), the earth would have to stop spinning. That would create problems. Big — very big problems! For example, our day and night combined is 24 hours. That means that the earth spins around full circuit on its axis once per day.

The earth is about 7,917 miles in diameter, or 24,901 miles circumference at the equator. Do the math, and the earth is spinning at the equator at roughly the rate of 1037 miles per hour. Naturally, the closer you get to the poles, the slower is this spinning effect. At 30 degrees latitude, where Israel is located (along with Jacksonville, FL, and Houston, TX), the spin rate is about 902 miles per hour.

Next, think what happens to a car when it hits a brick wall at 65 mph. With the "sun standing still" we are thinking of a speed of 15 times that car wreck. True, there is no brick wall to hit, but people, horses, armies, houses, castles, churches, cathedrals, synagogues, wild animals, domestic cattle and stock, uprooted trees, water out of rivers, loose rocks, etc., would all be flying off into space tangentially to the curvature of the earth.

In Israel, they would be flying at an initial rate of 902 miles per hour. And that says nothing about the damage that would result to habitats, the environment, etc., left in the hot sun for a full day as described in this Bible, this truthful, inerrant Word of God.

The point is that it could not happen; would not happen. A screeching braking by the earth is impossible, much less the problem of immediately starting up the earth at 902 miles per hour afterwards.

Is this one more little tidbit of information and a "fact" from the Bible about which we should be skeptical? You betcha!

PREGNANCY, GOD, RELIGION, CHRISTIANITY, BELIEFS, AND STORIES TO COVER THE TRUTH

One of the myths of the Civil War was that during a May, 1863 battle in Virginia (or Vicksburg, MS — the myth varies), a Union soldier was shot, lost his left testicle and at the same time, a young girl watching the nearby battle from her front porch was hit in the groin by a bullet.

You guessed it — the bullet that partly emasculated the Union soldier lodged near the ovary of the girl. Both were treated — so the myth goes — by the same battlefield surgeon, who some 278 days later (the story is very specific here) delivered a son to the groin-injured woman.

The story, first printed as a joke of poor taste in a medical journal, made the point that sperm was carried by the bullet striking the Union soldier to impregnate the woman.

One can see a young woman of the period making up a story like this, particularly if she received a slight wound from a battle, and particularly a wound in the groin area, and particularly if she was diddling with a boyfriend (soldier or not) and particularly with the morals and religion of the time and the admonitions of her parents.

You can check this on Snopes.com, and it is false, sometimes elaborated upon from the medical journal joke. While less likely today, you do not have to go that far back in history to find similar fanciful tales of a young "virgin" girl becoming pregnant without her knowing it or without her becoming pregnant normally. After all, becoming pregnant before marriage was proof of having sex before marriage and that was immoral, sinful, ungodly, against the Bible, and saddened the baby Jesus.

But explain it away with a tale, however fanciful, and all is well again. This beat the other practice of some years ago (and likely practiced today also) of a young girl going on a "vacation" or "field trip" for some months and upon returning home bringing with her a baby birthed by an "aunt," "sister of her mother or father," "distant cousin," etc., none of whom could care for the child, and thus accepting the offer of the girl's mother to take the child and raise it. Sure. And I have a nice bridge for sale in Brooklyn. This is not new. Studies about pregnancy in Puritan times indicate that up to 30 percent or more of young women were pregnant when they married. The studies supposedly discovered this by comparing marriage dates with dates of the first born child.

Could not this also be the case, 2,000 years ago, with Mary and Joseph making up a story about her pregnancy? Lacking Pennsylvania rifles and Minie balls as ammunition, the next best thing in those times was to blame it on God, to say that it is God's child, etc. Maybe,

maybe not. But it is something to think about, possibly with the biblical story made up afterwards to fit the earthy prevarication.

Food For The Animals On Noah's Ark Might Have Been More Of A Problem Than The Animals Themselves

Food would have been a major problem for Noah in stocking his millions of animals of the Ark that would not hold all of the animals anyway. It could not hold all the necessary food either.

Also, most people in thinking of food for animals probably think of a sack of Purina kibbles or a couple of cans of Alpo, as we do for our dogs. But that won't work.

A quick look at a few species just begins to broach the problem. First, food takes a lot of space, particularly for some animals and for the 190 days necessary for the rain to fall and for the Ark to float around.

We are not just thinking of a few bales of hay for a goat or some grass for a groundhog. Some ant colony species need constantly fresh leaves to carry back to the nest to feed the fungus that in turn becomes their food. Much vegetation for most herbivores would or could become stale, moldy, mildewed, and rotten in the time on the Ark.

Many animals are carnivores including lions, tigers, wolves, hyenas, cheetahs, bears, shrews, fox, mink, anteaters and aardwolves. They eat meat — ranging from ants and termites to impala, wild boar and fish.

And no, you can't substitute vegetation for meat for the time aboard the Ark. The gastrointestinal system, stomach and digestion process of carnivores vs. herbivores is completely different. Their teeth for tearing meat or grinding grain are completely different as are their intestines down to the length and type necessary to digest their given food. Substitute food will only kill them.

For shrews you would have to have mice and live insects. Boas will only constrict and eat live rabbits and rats. Lions would eat only gazelles and impala, cheetah perhaps smaller springbok, while aardwolves require termites. Termites might be bad for the boat, but definitely a must for aardwolves.

Nor could you substitute meat for the vegetation needed by insects and herbivores. Monarch butterflies need milkweed. Zebras, wildebeest, impala and others need African savanna grasses. Elk, deer, moose and caribou need native vegetation with moose eating underwater plants. Caribou eat lichens.

Naturally, Noah would have to have aquariums. They would not be needed for pairs of fish (they can swim) but for the fish, minnows, crayfish, frogs and such that would be necessary as food for mink, otters, water voles, anacondas, etc.

This is getting to be a big, big — let's face it — impossible problem. It is a Gordian knot that cannot be sliced, diced or untied. Think of all the things possible that are necessary for a task as described in the Bible and you have to come to the conclusion that this impossible task is indeed, well, truly impossible. With these impossibilities, is the Bible really the inerrant Word of God?

NOAH HAS MORE PROBLEMS WITH ANIMALS, LOADING ANIMALS AND THE NUMBER OF ANIMALS

We have previously covered some of the problems of loading animals onto the Ark and that it would take a couple of years if loading them at a rate of a pair a minute, around the clock.

But there are more problems. Assuming that the Ark contains 1.5 million cubic feet, and you had two million animals (probably very conservative), it would leave each pair of animals with ¾ of a cubit foot of space. That is for a "voyage" of 40 days of rain plus 150 days of just floating around (calculations on this vary based on who is doing what calculations — from a total of 267 to 370 days). The space listed above would be a problem for anything larger than a tiny shrew.

Today scientists do not even know how many animals that we have on the planet. Estimates range from about five million to 100 million different species.

We do know that there are taxonomic collections of about 350,000 (and counting) beetles, 150,000 species of flies, 200,000 species of moths and butterflies, 20,000 each of species of ants and bees, etc. It is starting to look as if Noah would need a whole fleet — a very large fleet — of ships of the size of the Ark — 450x75x45 feet — to even begin to accomplish the task at hand of saving pairs of all the animals on earth.

But there are even more problems than the one pair of each species to be collected and loaded onto the Ark. You would have to have more than one pair for some species to mate and repopulate the earth once this flood ends. A prime example is with our native American passenger pigeon. Never heard of them? No wonder — they are all extinct, with the last one dying in the Cincinnati Zoo September 1, 1914.

They were an extremely plentiful species with John James Audubon and others describing migrating flocks of one mile wide and 300 miles long and consisting of two billion birds. Populations were estimated at up to five billion birds. They were no match for humans. They were clubbed out of trees as food for hogs and slaves.

They are extinct today because they would only mate in a huge, large flock and with many, many additional pairs of birds all around them. They needed a mating orgy. Thus, for Noah to have saved passenger pigeons and other animals like them that need numbers to mate, he would have had to have stocked dozens or hundreds or thousands of them on board.

All this is starting to look like an impossible task, not only for one man and his family, but even for an entire modern civilization. But there is even more . . . even though this is enough to disprove the Noah's Ark story, along with it much of the truth of the Bible.

FLOODING AND WATER VOLUME DURING THE NOAH'S FLOOD? I'LL BET YOU CAN'T EVEN GUESS, BUT IT IS A LOT

Many religious believers do not calculate the immensity of the flood during the Noah's Ark story, or the total amount of water involved or the rate at which rain fell and water gushed from the earth. It is just accepted on face value that that the entire earth was flooded to 20 feet above the highest mountain as per the inerrant Word of God, the Bible.

For some facts, do the math and try a flooding rate of 30.25 feet per hour, or 726 feet per day!

To put this in perspective, realize that maximum torrential rain reported in the US was 474 inches (39.5 feet) in one year at Mount Waialeale on Kauai, Hawaii. That's just about one-third more than would occur in one hour during the flood at Noah's time. And that rate of participation would continue for 40 days and nights!

If the Bible is accepted as the inerrant Word of God, as it is with most fundamentalist protestant religions, then you have to believe the words of Genesis 6 through 8.

These words include the basic facts as follows. All of mankind in the world was evil and God wished to destroy all of mankind with the exception of Noah and his family, considered righteous and holy. Noah and his family were to build an Ark to hold two of all the animals in the world.

Dimensions of the Ark as described by God were to be 450 feet long, 75 feet wide and 45 feet high. (300 cubits by 50 cubits by 30 cubits.) Noah built the Ark, loaded the animals and feed as directed by God and the rains came.

The rains and flooding covered the earth to 20 feet above the highest mountain (NIV translation — 15 cubits or 22.5 feet in the King James Version) or a height of 29,055 feet. This is 20 feet above the highest mountain; Mount Everest at 29,035 feet.

With flooding/rainfall of 30 feet three inches per hour, the 40 days and nights of flooding would cover all mountains, as per above.

The average rainfall in a rain forest is about 68 to 78 inches *per year!* Whether or not there would be enough water falling and in the earth to accomplish this worldwide flood is a serious question. Many experts believe that there is not enough water in the world to reach the top of Mount Ararat where the Ark supposedly rested, much less reach the height of Everest.

It is a difficult — no, impossible — question to answer when considering the supposed inerrancy of the Bible. Serious thinking can't lead to this ridiculous biblical conclusion.

They Found Noah's Ark — Or Did They? The Jury Is Still Out.

The big news is that Noah's Ark has been found. But not so fast, Bunky. First, history and science and facts proceed on the back of testing, retesting, examining, and caution. History does not proceed with the "findings" of an admittedly calculating group called the Hong Kong based Noah's Ark Ministries International.

Immediately, the group announced to the world that they are not 100 percent, but at least "99.9 percent sure" that their finding is the Ark. This Ark was found at a height of 13,000 feet on Mount Ararat in Turkey.

They state that the wood brought down from the structure found has been carbon 14 tested and found to date back to 4,800 years, or the right timing for the biblical Ark of 2,888 years BCE. But there were several tests done, and there are rumors and suspicions that some earlier tests indicated wood dated much later.

But there are some questions. Could this be a boat from the earlier flood description in The Epic of Gilgamesh? That boat was also large, as a cargo ship to carry animals. It was 180 feet high, (length and width not noted) with six decks and seven levels, and was sealed with copious amounts (amount not noted) of raw bitumen.

If the found structure on Ararat is truly a boat instead of a hut for climbers as postulated by others, how do we know that it is or could be the Ark? Could it not be just another boat that lasted this long in the ice and snow? How come everyone is making a light-years leap to make it the Ark?

Is there any real evidence that there was a catastrophic flood that reached the 13,000 foot level of this structural find? What is necessary to prove this to historians?

For starters, proof would include evidence of a flood. It would include accurate, reliable carbon 14 dating that the wood of this structure is from the time period postulated for the Noah's Ark as described in the Bible. It would require that the structure is or was a boat, with measured dimensions and indications that it was made to float. It would require that there are pens or bulkheads that would be used to separate animals and the food necessary for the 40 days of flooding and the 150 days (or more) of floating around, as per the Bible.

That's a lot to think about, a lot to prove or disprove and a lot to conclude with any bias for or against a conclusion of this as "THE ARK." I think that the jury is still out on this one, but I am placing my money on it not being proven as the Ark.

How Did Noah Solve The "Bathroom" Problem On The Ark For All Those Animals And During All That Time?

While feeding the animals is a problem with the Noah's Ark story and fable, literalists also have to contest with another little glitch. What goes into an animal — any animal — must come out.

To put it delicately, the "bathroom" problem for all those animals numbering in the hundreds of thousands and millions would be huge. And remember that Noah had only eight people for this monumental zoo-keeping task. He had his wife, and his sons Shem, Ham and Japheth and their wives. That's eight people for all this work.

Horsemen call this work "mucking the stalls" and mucking is a good word, considering that the first dictionary definition of "muck" is "moist manure." We don't have to spell it out more than that.

One creationist site described a possible solution for this problem — the decks on the Ark were all sloped, allowing the urine and feces to slide off or drain away easily. Admitted, a slight slope might be a slight help, but a severe slope to make this an automatic task would require hand rails, safety ropes and mountain climber's crampons to get around the decks. And this says nothing of the animals falling and rolling around deck, quite possibly in their own muck. Want to wash off a mucked-up wild animal?

The next time you go to a zoo, realize how many people it takes to muck the stalls of the very few animals that they have on hand compared to the impossible task of cleaning and caring for hundreds of thousands — or millions — of animals.

A zoo could not accomplish its commitment to the animals with eight people. Noah could not accomplish this task with 80 or even 800 or more people, considering also that they would have to feed and water the animals. It's just impossible.

Elements like this, which few people ever consider in this story from the inerrant Word of God — the Bible— make this tale not only suspect but laughably impossible. The numbers just don't add up in any part of this equation with this being perhaps the final straw to break the camel's back.

Regardless of how you postulate the poop and pee problem, the food and water problems, years of loading animals problems, the lack of staff with only eight people, the volume of water required for the flood, and perhaps even the vindictiveness and evil of God in killing everyone else on earth, it does not add up.

There is more to come, but already we have far more than enough to attribute this Noah's Ark tale to nothing more than the scribbling of a non-thinking child or a primitive fiction writer in postulating this ridiculous literalist story that facts just can't support.

Noah Contends With God's Flood — Water, Water Everywhere And Not A Drop To Drink

With the literal interpretation of the biblical Noah's Ark story, we have to somehow figure out how all that water got there to flood the whole earth (Genesis 7:19 and Genesis 7:24, etc.) and where it went later. Experts say that there is not enough water in the world to accomplish this.

Creationists say that there was and is enough water, with some saying that the earth was covered by a high humidity mist prior to Noah and the flood and only since do we have rain. The Bible says that the rain fell for 40 days and nights and that water also gushed from the earth, just as it does now from springs and artesian wells throughout the world.

Still you have to go back to the math that calculates that the water during those 40 days and nights was rising at a rate of 30.25 feet per hour, continuously. For the earth to be completely covered by water to a level of at least 20 feet over the highest mountain, water would have to rise 29,055 feet during that time. After all, Everest is at 29,035 feet, unless the creationists plan on somehow changing that biblical "fact" to fit their agenda and story.

Geology and hydrology experts emphatically state that there is not enough water in the air, on the ground, in the oceans, and under the earth to accomplish anything like this. Even so, with excessive amounts of water drawn from the ground, would it not be likely that the whole earth would be covered with sink holes as Florida suffers from now and again with the draw-down of the water table?

If creationists and literal believers somehow suspend their literal belief to suggest that this flood only happened in one area, or one valley or on one river, then they have abandoned their belief in the Bible as being the literal, absolute, inerrant Word of God.

Where do they go from there? How do they pick and choose what is right and what is a fable or story when examining the rest of the Bible?

Similarly, the water sloshed around for 150 days and then started draining, this taking another 75 days for the tops of the mountains to become visible. Where did the water go?

Water would not evaporate this fast, and it would not all go back underground. Yet if we can't believe the literal statement of the water rising and falling again, can we believe anything about this tale? Can we believe anything in this Bible, this inerrant Word of God?

God, Genesis, Noah, Journalism, Truth, Logic, Facts And Science — What Works?

Genesis is not journalism. When journalists start their career, they are taught to get information on the Who, What, When, Where, Why and How. This applies to any assignment, from a PTA cake sale to a City Council meeting to a heinous multiple axe murder. For the Noah's Ark story, these just do not add up.

For "Who," we have Noah and his family, eight in all, working to build a huge boat, then gather and load animals. The loading of the animals alone would take years. That's impossible.

"What" is the flood, courtesy of God. Yet could not God in all his omniscience just miraculously saved a few pair of every animal on earth and avoided all this nonsense? After all, according to the literalists, God can do anything.

"When" is a little unclear, but it was obviously after the Epic of Gilgamesh with its own flood story and from which the Noah's Ark story could have been plagiarized. Suggestions are that Noah's story occurred about 4500 years ago, or around 2500 BCE.

"Where" the Ark was built and the flood occurred is a little more vague, but Israel is close enough for building the Ark, a task that took up to 100 years or more. We "know" that the Ark supposedly ended up far from Israel on Mount Ararat in eastern Turkey.

"Why" is the big question, since we have to credit/blame all this on God. God of course created the flood to get rid of all the wicked people on earth, with the exception of righteous Noah and his family.

But God is omniscient and omnipotent. Would not God have known that the world would become wicked? Was his prototype of Adam and Eve a little off in the morality department to create people worthy of killing? Could he not have corrected this with a gene implant or modification? Considering the deadly Egyptian plagues and Passover first-born edict, could not a simpler solution been found that would negate the entirety of the Ark story? Is this not like running around the house and repeatedly firing a shotgun to kill a mouse that could be taken care of with a trap?

Answering the "How" question is equally ridiculous. Take a small family and have them impossibly build a boat as protection against an impossible flood, then impossibly gather a few million animals from all over the world and over many years of time, impossibly load them and an impossible variety and amount of food. Then care for these animals for a few hundred days on a boat.

Any way you look at this, you have to laugh — or perhaps cry for those people still literally believing it this fable.

God's Land And Sea Animal Transportation Not Explained And Thus Unlikely To Have Happened

With the Noah's Ark and flood story, the elephant in the living room (no pun intended) is how did all the animals get to the mid-East, and get there in time for the Ark sailing date? How did they cross oceans? And how did they get home after the rude disembarkation on Mt. Ararat?

No creationist or literalist wants to touch this one. Yet the Bible says clearly (Genesis chapters 6 through 8) that ALL animals were taken into the Ark to be saved. Specially, check out a quote from God — yes God — in Genesis 6:18–22.

In this literal interpretation of the Bible, we are looking at the earth in terms of Africa, Europe, Asia, North and South America, Australia, the Arctic and Antarctic.

Thus, to believe God's dictates, we have to get animals from all continents and crossing all oceans such as the Atlantic, Pacific, Indian, Arctic, etc. In addition, we have to figure on latitude. The polar bears of the Arctic require different climate and living conditions on the Ark than the lemurs of Madagascar or the penguins of the Antarctic. And how would they get there? (And please don't answer me about the Coke ad of Arctic polar bears and Antarctic penguins as BFF's.)

The Bible does not explain this, other than requiring that they all must get to the Ark and all must be saved in pairs. Creationist literature suggests no answer other than the idea of a "kind" of animal as mentioned in the Bible being a genus and thus all the evolution taking place at a really, really rapid rate in the last few thousand years after getting a few (4,000,000 or so?) of the animal "kinds" on board.

Even without the ocean problem, some animals are not that speedy. A South American sloth zips along at the breakneck pace of about a mile a month. Even with a bridge between South America and the mid-East (which dos not exist and never has existed), he could not cross an ocean. Forget the sloth, two-toed or three-toed.

You just can't get animals to the mid-East and the Ark construction site in any reasonable way, in any reasonable time frame, with any way to cover huge land masses and practically limitless oceans. It just won't work, despite the dictates of God in his absolute Bible, this inerrant Word of God.

For the creationists, this has to be a sad story and a sad time with the current emphasis in some quarters on "finding the Ark." Creationists keep trying to find or cobble together facts to fit their fairy tale, and always falling flat with their explanation, or just ending up as a laughing stock for anyone critically thinking about this. Isn't that both ridiculous and sad?

How Come God Can't Figure Out Pi, The Mathematical Constant For The Circumference Of A Circle?

Since the Bible is looked upon as God's inerrant word, it ought to be accurate in all things. It isn't. For a good example, look at I Kings 7:23. This was part of a passage of Solomon on making a large cylindrical container, almost like a giant tin can or round swimming pool.

The passage states: "He [Huram — a worker for King Solomon] made the Sea (the container) of cast metal, circular in shape, measuring ten cubits from rim to rim and five cubits high. It took a line of 30 cubits to measure around it."

A cubit was 18 inches in length, or the length from the elbow to the fingers. However, the writer — a messenger from God — of this passage obviously did not make accurate measurements or did not know the concept of pi. He should have known, even if it was many centuries before this aspect of Euclidean plane geometry was developed, named and worked into mathematical formulas in the Western world. A simple piece of string would have helped him out.

Today we all know that pi rounded off is 3.1416. Thus with even a piece of string in biblical times, they could have easily figured that with a diameter of 15 feet (10 times 1 cubit or 1.5 feet), the circumference would not be 30 cubits or 45 feet, but instead be 31.416 cubits or 47.1240 feet. The extra measurement beyond the biblical 30 cubits (45 feet) would be respectively 1.416 cubits or two feet, one and one-half inches.

With a piece of string, I just measured a four-inch diameter food can from the kitchen pantry and found the circumference to be approximately 12-1/2 inches — not 12 inches or 3x4 inches. That is a close approximation, assuming the accuracy of the four-inch diameter can to the actual 12.5664 inches circumference when calculated with pi. But the fact that pi was not a simple and exact "3" was obvious.

If you are looking for inaccuracies in the Bible, check this section, since it is mathematically proven to be wrong. And there is no reason for this. While ancients might not have been able to figure the exact formula for pi, they could have at least approximated. In fact, just the word "approximately" in this biblical section, along with a close-as-possible correct reading, could have prevented this biblical and Godly error.

You have to wonder what other passages are wrong, and how a change or addition of words might have brought about different meanings to the Bible, this supposedly inerrant Word of God. This is pretty sloppy writing and pretty sloppy calculations. It's pretty sloppy religion also. Since God was dictating the Bible to humans, does this mean that God flunked the 6th grade?

"Heaven — I'm In Heaven. . ." But What Do We Really Know About It? Is It Real?

The word "heaven" in our language comes from roots in English meaning the sky, firmament, and similar words from Old English, other old Germanic languages and some from Icelandic, Gothic and Old Saxon.

The term developed from the concept of where God lived or dwelt, God's house, God's kingdom, life everlasting, the house of God, heavenly Jerusalem, the holy place, etc. In fact, many of the biblical references to heaven use the above appellations or variations as to the place where God resides and to where we go upon death, with a big "if" in that trip.

Varietal concepts of heaven are Tian (Chinese), Jannah (Islamic), and Summerland (Wiccans). The concept of heaven or an afterlife of the Egyptians, Canaanites and Israelites has been lost or is yet to be found by archeologists.

The big "if" is of course the acceptance of Jesus or God in the Christian religion, although there are many variations of this in many other religions and sects throughout the world.

Ironically, the Bible does not say much about heaven, other than preparing a place for you, or the statement about many mansions. And, other than the mystical references to it in both the Old and New Testaments, there is little information to glean. And this in the face of 606 or 662 references to heaven, the number of references dependent upon which translation of the Bible you read.

The idea of "pearly gates" "golden streets" and similar earthly materialistic appointments and accouterments is strictly a man-made fabrication and fiction, nothing more.

In addition, there is no information about heaven elsewhere, or in any other documentation, although there are references to various heavens in the religious rites and documents of religions around the world, each of which has its own belief of a heavenly life after death and how to best get there.

In short, there is absolutely no proof of any heaven of any type or design. It seems to have crept into beginning civilization as a concept, in the same way that early peoples conceptualized tools as a need before they were made for a specific task.

Note also that no one has come back from heaven, including the master magician Houdini who would have seemed to have had the best chance of doing so.

Even among Christians, the concept of heaven and of our spirits going to heaven varies widely from an almost completely materialistic concept to that of a spiritual belief only.

One would think that with the importance of heaven in many religions, and as a basis of Christianity, we would know a lot more about it, including the design of the toothbrush holders in the bathrooms and the Wednesday cafeteria menu. Why don't we know anything about heaven? Is it a myth like so much else in the Bible?

MINISTERS AND THE MOB — ARE THEY RELATED IN THEIR DEMAND FOR PROTECTION MONEY?

We know that tithing is basic to both Judaism and Christianity. It is one-tenth of everything "earned," before taxes or any other expenditures. It goes, so they say, to the Lord.

But wait a minute! If it goes to the Lord, how does it get there? How does the Lord have it delivered? How does the Lord use it? Why would the Lord need money?

God is a spirit. He (she, it) does not need a Posturepedic bed, Armani clothing, silver or gold, dead or alive sheep, goats, cattle, wine, a Lexus, IBM computer or grain.

In the Old Testament, these tithings go to the Levites, the priestly clan of the Israelites. But that is not giving the tithes to God — it is giving tithes to people who are claiming some Godly or religious entitlement at the expense of their fellow man.

This presumably all began in Genesis 14:18–24, when Abram gave to the high priest Melchizedek, king of Salem, one-tenth of everything. Presumably this means a tenth of everything that Abram owned, or perhaps a tenth of everything that he had with him or his yearly earnings, or something. We really do not know.

It is a morally forced or expected payoff to the religious leaders, just as the Mafia requires paid protection money to keep a dry cleaner or sub shop from developing a severe case of arson.

One of the tithing sites on the Internet (www.answers2prayer. org/ Bible_questions/Answers/law/tithing.html) indirectly states this relationship to Mafia protection payoffs. "The children of the Kingdom cannot do anything less today to guarantee our blessings," it says of tithing. That "guarantee" on tithing parallels mob protection money. Pay up and get blessed. Don't pay and you get tough times and the fire department.

Bible believers making $50,000 per year "have" to give $5,000 to the church before taxes. The same ten percent of forced giving applies to any income from any means.

But you still have to ask the question — where does it go and why it is a dictate from God? God does not use it, will never get it, has no need for any material objects, be it money, grain or a goat.

All churches which have flourished like weeds in a garden have used these statements to guarantee protection money. For the various church officials including priests, pastors, rabbis, ministers, bishops, and other clergy, it gives them a comfortable guaranteed income for little work — a sinecure.

Would you not be better off staying home and from the library or book store reading books on religious history? Would you not be better off reading the works by religious and ancient-text scholars? Would you really rather pay for someone else each Sunday to admonish you about religion when you can read the factual accounts from trained scholars? Check your library or book store. Start reading. It will pay off so that you don't have to pay out.

Is God Good When He Asks Abraham To Kill His Own Son? Would You Do This? Could You Do This?

In Genesis 22:1–18, the story of Abraham and Isaac is told. In this, God asks Abraham to sacrifice his only son Isaac in a burnt offering to God and then gives him instructions on how to do this.

(While the Bible says "only son" this is really not true — a mistake in the Bible. Earlier Abram (Genesis 16), (with Abram the early name for Abraham) was given Hagar by his barren wife Sarai (early name for Sarah). With Hagar he had a son Ishmael prior to having a son Isaac with his wife Sarah.)

Abraham follows the instructions of preparing and traveling with Isaac to make him a burnt offering to God. He is stopped from killing him at the last minute by an angel of the Lord. This story is considered a great story of the faithfulness of Abraham to the Lord in following all of God's instructions.

This is to prove that Abraham loves God and will do anything to please him. But wait a minute. Is not God omniscient and knowing everything, past, present and future? That being the case, God would know that Abraham would do this and thus "prove" his love of God. Pretty ridiculous and pretty evil, isn't it?

Now, let's jump ahead to today. Let's say that I have a ten-year-old son John and he has a pet dog Skippy that he adores and loves. As a test of my son's love for me, I ask him to kill Skippy as an example of his great love for me over that of his dog.

Suppose that John, my son and very obedient to me, gets his dog and, as per my instructions, gets a sharp hunting knife by which to slit Skippy's throat. This would be as per my instructions to prove John's love for me over his dog. But as he holds the knife to kill Skippy, I stop him, stating that I know by his actions and intent that he truly loves me.

What would you think of me? What kind of horrors would run through your mind about a father who would commit this child abuse — I don't know what else to call it — by asking his son to kill a living, loyal pet that the son loves? If you knew about this, would you not call the authorities? Would you not hope that I would be arrested for child abuse and hauled into a court room for some punishment and justice?

The big question — would you ever compare this fiction to the supposedly real life Abraham and Isaac story? Would you ever think of the abuse by God and God's insistence on Abraham killing his son, even though stopping this awful deed before the finality of Isaac's death? Now that is something to ponder and think about long and hard. Is God really good?

Can Jesus Make a Thirty-Eight Year Invalid Walk? I Don't Think So

Among the many so-called miracles that Jesus performed, you find the one of "curing" extreme muscle wasting disease, muscle atrophy, and cachexia in John 5:1–15. Cachexia and atrophy are catch-all medical terms dealing with the loss of muscle tone, loss of muscle mass, general atrophy and complete weakness often associated with cancer, AIDS, congestive heart failure, renal failure, burns and pulmonary disease.

This tale of Jesus healing involves a man at a "healing pool," one of five in Jerusalem. According to this story, you have to be in the pool "when the water is stirred" to be healed. This occurs (John 5:4) when an angel of the Lord occasionally stirs the waters. The first to enter the pool during this period of rippling waters is healed of whatever disease that he had. A crippled man is not able to get to the pool in time during these short periods of activity, and no one will help him.

Jesus finds out how long the man had been an invalid. Earlier, in John 5:5, it is noted that the man had been crippled for thirty-eight years. Any doctor will tell you that you begin to get muscle atrophy in only a few days or weeks, and that this can happen with prolonged bed rest or even with a cast on a broken limb.

But Jesus, finding out the length of the man's invalid state, orders the man to get up, pick up his mat and walk, (John 5:8). Naturally, the man does so. "At once, the man was cured; he picked up his mat and walked." Naturally, this would have been impossible. When you have lost muscle tone over 38 years, you can't walk.

Contrast this to modern medicine. Those in hospital beds for a week or two or who have limited mobility due to disease or surgery, will all almost immediately notice a loss of muscle tone. Prolonged inactivity leads to complete weakness and loss of muscle. Continue this way and a patient becomes a non-mobile invalid, unable to walk.

This story is obviously a fake, a sham, a con, a fiction. Of course, the Christians, fundamentalists and religionists will say that "God/Jesus can do anything that he wants to do!"

OK. Then to be completely fair, caring and loving of his fellow man and flock, perhaps Jesus should have cured everyone at the pool. Perhaps today there should be some proof of this, other than a fanciful tale of the distant past, no different from childhood fiction stories.

Perhaps Jesus or God could do just one thing today that would be provable, demonstrable, and without doubt a Godly miracle in the dictionary sense of the word. Perhaps this and other tales of the Bible are just shams, with the participants no different from the shills or the gullible that populate the audiences of TV evangelists during their "healing" conventions.

Is Slavery OK With God And Jesus? Is It OK As An Aspect Of Society Or Religion At Any Time?

"Slaves, obey your earthly masters with respect and fear, and with sincerity of heart, just as you would obey Christ. Obey them not only to win favor when their eye is on you, but like slaves of Christ, doing the will of God from your heart."

This is from Ephesians 6:5-6, that is, from the New Testament. Religionists often counter complaints about slavery references and how to treat slaves, by stating that it is all in the Old Testament. The argument is that is the old times, the old ways, the old laws are not applicable with or after the coming of Christ.

Guess what? With Ephesians, it is applicable to the New Testament and the stories, religion and philosophy of Christ. It still doesn't fly. And yes, you can find numerous references to slavery in the New Testament and of course also in the Old Testament.

Unfortunately, prohibitions *against* slavery are not mentioned in the Ten Commandments of the Old Testament, nor are they alluded to in the Golden Rule of Jesus or Confucius. Instead, in the Ten Commandments, we have four Commandments dealing with God, one with honoring parents and one on coveting.

These are all ridiculous. The other four against adultery, killing, stealing or lying are pretty good and should stay in place. But there should also be a commandment against slavery.

Instead of an admonition against slavery in general, we have in Ephesians and elsewhere an insistence that slaves obey their masters, how slaves should act, or how masters should treat slaves for various offenses to them and by them. Of course, in the Old Testament, you can find in Exodus (Exodus 21:7) references as to how to sell your daughter into slavery. How's that for good and Godly?

A slave, by dictionary definition, is "a human who is owned by and absolutely subject to another human being as by capture, purchase or birth; a bond servant divested of all freedom and personal rights." (Webster's New World Dictionary)

Thus slavery robs a person of the most basic of rights, the right of free will to do what they want, when, where, how and with whom they want, within the constraints of a civilized society.

For the Bible, in either the Old Testament or New Testament, to approve of or not disavow any such practice of slavery makes it as a religious work totally reprehensible to any thinking person. Is this Bible really the work of a loving, caring, benevolent, responsible, tolerant, kind, fair, just God?

Did God forget about or not know about some of the basic societal rules and conditions of fairness for all people? Are people not to be free and have free will? Are slaves of any type acceptable and to be treated as property as the Bible suggests? Think about it.

An Overview Of The Ten Commandments. Or Is It Four? Or Two? Or Only One?

You can find the Ten Commandments most clearly in Exodus 20. But this collection of social mores can be reduced to four. George Carlin in a funny shtick reduced it to two and the Golden Rule of Jesus, Confucius and others whittled it down to one. Carlin figured that, "Thou shalt always be honest and faithful, especially to the provider of thy nookie. Two, thou shalt try real hard not to kill anyone, unless, of course, they pray to a different invisible avenger than the one you pray to." Confucius used a variation of the Golden Rule, stating "Do not impose on others what you do not wish for yourself." The Ten Commandments of the Bible get a little more complicated and varied.

First, "Thou shall have no other gods before me" sounds like a god who is a little afraid of his position in the god contest. He wants to make sure that you keep him first and only.

"You shall not make for yourself an idol. . ." is further indication that God wants you thinking of him, not a hunk of manufactured metal, wood, or clay.

"You shall not misuse the name of the Lord your God . . ." is more indication that God takes himself pretty seriously.

Of course people do, including Christians who are constantly saying casually and without thought, phrases such as "Lord help me," "Oh Lord," etc. Their kids are into the constant "Oh my God" or an extended "Oh----my----God!" as a part of their juvenile language about anything that is within their tiny frames of reference.

Keeping the Sabbath holy is another and a further indication that God wants your full attention, all the time.

With these four, it sounds as if God has some serious insecurity and self-esteem issues. "Honoring your mother and father" as a Commandment is very weak, since some terrible parents do not deserve respect or honor.

Those Commandments on murder (killing), adultery, stealing and false witness (lying) are all good for any society, predate religion and important to help us get along with each other without anarchy or revolution. These are OK.

"You shall not covet your neighbor's house" which goes on to include his wife (covered already by the adultery clause) manservant, maidservant, ox or donkey, or anything. Today, most of us do not have servants, and we can switch the ox to a John Deere farm tractor and the donkey to a Ford F-150 pickup truck.

This is patently foolish, since we all want things that will improve our lives, be it a better plow, pencil, car or computer. The error of coveting is when you do things (murder, steal, lie, etc.) to obtain those things that you want, rather than gaining them by legitimate means.

Thus, it looks like four of these edits are OK, two are foolish and four are in the "my god is better and bigger than your god" category. That leaves a skeptic a lot to think about.

Did God Goof When Making Man In His Own Image?

Did God goof when making man? That might be the conclusion of many when critically reading stories in the Old and New Testaments. Checking Genesis, we find that Eve in the Garden of Eden was tempted by Satan, posing as a snake, to eat of the Tree of Knowledge of Good and Evil.

We all know the story of how the snake (Satan) convinced Eve to eat fruit of the tree and that she also give some to Adam. Later God found the two walking in the Garden and asked them about eating from the Tree of Knowledge of Good and Evil.

God, obviously displeased, then told Adam that he would have to toil the rest of his life and would then die and return to dust. Eve was told that she would experience pain in childbirth.

But wait a minute. Is not God, according to the inerrant Bible, omniscient as well as omnipotent? Is God not all-knowing as well as all-doing? That being so, would not God have known the future and that this scenario would happen?

The answer is obvious. Yes, of course God would have known the outcome. That being the case, could not or would not God have started over with his game plan and made man and women with a gene or DNA code where they would not want to disobey him or eat from the Tree of Knowledge of Good and Evil? God, as described by most Christians, could do that to make man a perfect example of his work. However, it seems as if he chose not to and then later blamed us for a lot of things.

Would any of us, as inventors, want to make a car with square wheels? Or a cell phone that would not transmit higher pitched female voices? Or a pencil that would not write?

Since God would know how to make a perfect man and woman, his failure in this regard can only be calculated as a deliberate attempt to make a defective product that would fail. The result of a flawed man "made in God's image" leaves one with disturbing choices of God not being quite as omniscient as Christians would like, God as a jokester who likes to play around with human lives or God as malicious in making a flawed product and then complaining that the product does not meet God's quality standards. Which choice do you like?

Just think, couldn't there have been other ways by which God should have known better about the humans that he was making?

What Is First On Your List Of "Needs" For An Impoverished War-Torn Country? How About A Bible?

Amongst the constant mailings from religious groups seeking MONEY, is a recent one that points to "God has opened an unprecedented window of opportunity." Send MONEY and this group can convert it into a great event for Christianity. Sure.

They refer to and are working in an African country, one (as with many) rife with civil war, hunger, disease, violence, corruption, kidnappings, mutilation, Al-Qaeda, genocide, tribal warfare, etc. One of the tactics used by these thugs in their own country is to summarily amputate a hand or foot of those who do not believe in the Koran or do not "live" as a Muslim.

So what would you think that this Christian ministry group might do to help the poor people of this impoverished devastated country? Would they send in support teams to help back up the UN peace keepers trying to maintain order?

Would they set up schools for both boys and girls to further their learning? Would they build small clinics to solve health problems and help those attacked and hacked up by Al-Qaeda thugs? Would they finance a major hospital in a large city? Would they drill wells in villages for clean pure water to protect these people from water-borne disease?

Would they send in food supplies? Or agricultural specialists to help grow better and more bountiful crops? How about engineers to help them construct simple yet sturdy homes in protected areas? Could we expect clothing, or a treadle-operated sewing machine by which native women could make their own clothes and start a small tailoring business?

Sorry, but you would be wrong on all of the above. Send your bucks, send this religious group MONEY that they claim to need for this ravaged area of Africa filled with the desperate and the dying, and you get something else. Instead of clinics, hospitals, better crops, wells, sewing machines, protection, schools, food, better engineered houses, basic supplies of need, you would get — hold on — a "permanent translation center."

That's right, a center whereby the Bible of the Western Christian can be translated. Plans are to translate the Bible into five new languages, to provide God's word (their words — not mine) for 1.6 million people, to get "The Word" to distant parts of this scarred and damaged country and its people.

Well, if I were lying in the hot sun with no shelter, owning only the clothes on my back, with no education, vomiting from bad food and e. coli-contaminated water, and with a right hand missing courtesy of a machete and local thugs, I don't think that a translation of a foreign Bible would be first on my list of needs. I think that I might want some good basic food, pure water, shelter, basic clothing, and some antibacterial salve and dressing for the stump of my missing hand. I don't think that I would care about a Bible.

You really, really have to wonder about the thinking — or lack thereof — of some missionaries. Isn't it time to be a skeptic?

How Many Deaths Are Necessary To Prove That Faith Healing Doesn't Work? It Never Did And Never Will Work

Some time ago, a case of childhood death through faith healing was playing out through the courts in Oregon. This is not uncommon on the left coast, where the ignorant, delusional and gullible seem to think that their prayers and faith healing can cure their Godly flock of disease, injury and prevent death. Jeff and Marci Beagley were being tried for the death of their son Neil for not taking him to the doctor or a hospital.

Neil had a treatable bladder infection, and he was sick for much of his 16-year life. His parents are members of a Followers of Christ church which, according to reports, believes in faith healing and does not rely on medicine or doctors.

Sadly, much of the testimony — on a following "In Session" TV — involves the parents on trial stating that Neil did not want to go to the doctor. Instead, he wanted to rely on God, praying and laying on of hands for healing. Naturally. That was apparently all that he was taught for his entire short life.

His parents considered his objection to getting medical help and did nothing medically to help him. He died. The sad thing about this is that parents are morally and legally responsible for children under the age of 18. Thus, you do not have to buy your child a cell phone, but you do have to provide them with nourishing food. You do not have to buy a child Nike shoes, but you do have to buy them shoes, other necessary clothing, provide a bed, housing, and an education.

Constant statements in the broadcast referred to the parents allowing Neil Beagley to decide if he wanted medical treatment.

The problem is that Neil at 16 was not an adult and should not have been able to make decisions about something this important. You allow kids to make decisions as to whether they want to eat a hamburger or hot dog. You allow decisions as to which family TV show to watch, perhaps which pants to wear to school, whether he wants a thick or thin pillow for sleeping.

You do not allow kids to decide whether or not to get medical help, to get vaccinated, to go to school, to do their homework, to ride their bike on the Interstate, to jump off the roof or get involved in other concerns of health or protection.

If an adult wants to rely on prayer, laying on of hands, anointing, and other rites of faith healing for themselves, that is up to them. They are responsible for the ultimate outcome of their life or death. But it is not right for kids under our legal and moral control to decide.

The sad fact is that prayer and faith healing does not work. Time and again, tests have shown this. The fact that some faithful and foolish parents want to impose this on their children is a tragedy. Isn't it time to be skeptical of all religion, especially when it involves children?

"Thou Shalt Have No Other Gods Before Me" Seems Pretty Silly

The first of the Ten Commandments states that "Thou shall have no other gods before me." It does not say, "Thou shall have no other gods" or anything similar, or with a similar meaning of an absolute rule. It uses a statement — or command — that suggests that you can have other gods, just as long as they are not the main god, the head guy, the major leader.

This suggests a closer adherence to many other pluralistic god religions of the world, in which there are several or many gods. Some variations of Buddhism and Hinduism are prime examples of this, with many gods or minor gods, sometimes numbering into the thousands.

The interesting thing about all this is that Christianity or Judaism is supposed to be a one-god religion, or in the case of Christianity, a three-in-one deal with God, Jesus and the Holy Ghost or Holy Spirit.

Under this wording of "no other gods before me," it would seem that God is saying that he is the main god, the one like the president or CEO of a company, ultimately responsible for everything with the company. Or it could be like the president of the US under which various levels of importance and position exist. These include a vice president, speaker of the House, Congress with the Senate and House of Representatives, and the various cabinet secretaries responsible for specific federal agencies.

With our governmental system, there are no other leaders ahead of our president, or on an equal level with him, even though there are various individuals with authority in their specific areas of responsibility. In this, it would be like having a main god, and under that many lesser gods.

This makes this First Commandment sound like it is dealing with a god with severe insecurity problem and major self-esteem issues. A god without these concerns, or not making a statement about "no other gods before me" would not need to make a declaration like that to assert authority and power or prove that he is the biggest boy on the block.

It seems as if the God of the Old Testament — the God of the Christians and Jews — has a few problems to work out if he really wants to be the main sky guy without equivocation or expressing personal doubt as to his god-position that might be contagious with others.

Thus, the First Commandment seems to waffle a little on the importance of a god or God, with much of this — as with the three following commandments — working on the idea of "my god is better than your god" or "my god is bigger and stronger than your god." Does that make sense?

THE SECOND COMMANDMENT IS DIFFICULT TO FATHOM, DIFFICULT TO INTERPRET

A graven image, according to the dictionary, is one that is "engraved, carved, sculptured." And that ties into our look at the Second Commandment.

This commandment states, "Thou shalt not make unto thee any graven image, or any likeness of anything that is in heaven above or that is in the earth beneath, or that is in the water under the earth."

It follows with instruction of not worshiping these things, or bowing down to them, or serving them. In other words, you can worship the real thing, the real god, but not any man-made imitation of wood, metal, plastic, paper or anything else.

This creates a bit of sticky wicket for those studying the Bible, whether that study is to more closely worship God or to prove the ridiculousness of much of the Bible. If the object or image is that of a figure, then it is understandable that worship of a thing is not worship of a god or God. That image could be a human, human-like god, animal or combined parts of a human, god and animal.

If it gets into something different than a recognizable bodily form, then it gets difficult. In some cases, and more with some religions than others, you find worshipers honoring, venerating and seeming to worship objects of their religion, rather than the god or gods of that religion. In some cases, this could be an image of Christ on the cross, or just the cross itself, a small pendant of Christ or the cross in a picture, necklace, key chain or wall hanging, or something similar.

Of course, honoring and venerating is just respecting someone or something, not necessarily worshiping it. Thus, it is hard to tell what an individual adherent of a particular religion is thinking or doing with a given object in terms of respect or true worship.

In many cases, with those flocking to, bowing in front of and praying next to strange images, you have to wonder. These are often strange apparitions of something religious such as a reflection in a store window of Jesus face, of a cross and Jesus somehow burned into the toast of a grilled cheese sandwich, a potato chip that resembles Mary's face.

Of course, the fact that we have no earthly idea of what the face of Mary, Jesus or anyone else in the Bible looks like does not enter the mind of those worshiping (if they are) or just venerating this image aberration.

All this makes this religion thing, with all the symbols, images, statues, carvings, and paintings, somewhat suspicious and perhaps subject to a lot of supposedly good Christians violating the Second of the Ten Commandments. That in turn, makes one wonder about a lot of things with religion, doesn't it?

CHRISTIANS, SORT OF, ALMOST, SOMETIMES, FOLLOW THE THIRD COMMANDMENT. BUT NOT ALWAYS

The Third Commandment, about using the Lord's name, seems to be a biggie for Christians. And no, for the sake of sensibilities and censorship, we will not get into trouble here.

This Third Commandment specifically states: "Thou shalt not take the name of the Lord thy God in vain." The NIV version of the same text says: "You shall not misuse the name of the Lord your God."

Either way, you can't use it the wrong way, regardless of what that wrong way happens to be.

Do that, and some nearby Christian is likely to admonish you. "Don't take the name of God in vain. The Bible tells you that." Well, if you don't care or follow the Bible, why shouldn't you? Naturally, you do have to be aware of and follow local customs, legal regulations about speech and such, but other than that you are free to do what you want and say what you want.

"Vain" in this sense means "fruitless, hollow, without value, empty, idle," etc. In this religious sense, it is OK to talk seriously about God or the Lord, OK to pray using his name, but not OK to use it in any other sense such as "God damn it or "Goddamn it."

By the same token, the youth of these same good Christians are constantly using terms such as "Oh my God!" in anything and everything that — pro or con — affects their petty lives. Sounds pretty frivolous to me.

In some cases, for even more emphasis, they expand this with pauses into an "Oh-------My-------- God!!!!" seemingly to lend more importance to their response. With young people, this could be a response to anything from the enormity of the 9/11 disaster to the fact that they lost their mechanical pencil. It is all equally important to them. This can just be a rapid "OhmyGod" or even an "OMG" in a text message.

Sometimes youth and adult alike will just use the deity expression in conjunction with some frivolous expression. "God, I could sure use a drink!" "God, it's hot!" "God, I'll be glad when Junior gets out of my hair this summer and goes back to school!" Naturally, these and a thousand other expressions are not respectful as per the Third Commandment.

You can also hear adult Christians with venom and malice in their tight-lipped voices utter, "God *bless* this . . . ," with the rest of the exclamation referencing something, someone or some situation about which they are particularly vexed. It is an obvious curse under the guise of a blessing. But that is really not nice, and presumably God knows what they mean.

It is funny and strange that good Christians and their obedient offspring use these expressions but are not condemned for this. But again, Christians make up the rules as they go along, perhaps only so that they can condemn the rest of us for not being like them. Very interesting! And why would I want to be like them?

More On That Pesky, Inflammatory Third Commandment
Do We Ever Pay Attention?

The Third Commandment gets more difficult with the use of words other than the oft-condemned and criticized "God Damn it" or "goddamn it." Today and for a few hundred years in the past, we use and have used words to get around this. It is the same as using words and strange spellings and pronouncements with other curse words — mostly four-letter, and now we find these strange new words semi-acceptable in print and in TV. To go to cursing extremes, we currently have a TV cooking show featuring Gordon Ramsey, with the show called "The f Word". Things have changed and are changing.

Today we get around the "Lord's name in vain" rule and cursing condemnation by referencing "goldurn it" or "gosh-darn it," with other alternatives to damn becoming drat, dang or similar mild words.

Many of these words and others were developed in the 1700s, mostly as a way to use close substitutes for the really bad words but in a new light and in a way less punishable or not punishable as the original referencing God.

Etymology teaches us that "gosh" as a substitute for God dates to 1757, "dang" in place of damn to 1793 and "darn" for damn to 1781.

Even today, the first part and often both parts of the common "God damn it!" is muted on TV shows to avoid troubling the general populace, upsetting the TV censors, and annoying the Christian right.

In addition, "Oh my God!" is an interjection with no grammatical relationship with other words in a sentence. It could obviously include a completion to this thought. "Oh my God, it's raining and I don't have a raincoat." "Oh my God, I have to make cookies, and I'm out of sugar." "Oh my God, I broke a shirt button!" It could also be the acceptable "Oh my gracious" or "Oh my goodness" or something similar.

All of these are frivolous, of course, but all correct in the context of complete thoughts. In being frivolous, these referencing "God" violate the Third Commandment, although most Christians never see it this way.

Sometimes we just find the word "God" or "Lord" used by itself, or with a strange request that would seem out of character for the Lord to worry about. "Lord, I hope that the Orioles win this baseball game!," would be one example. Personally, I did not know that God cared about this or any other sporting events.

We could use the single word when faced with a difficult brain-twisting problem, or an arduous physical effort, a moral dilemma, or some anguish as per a family member problem or job related difficulty.

Ironically, Christians get squeamish about the words used for their God and about the usage others might make also, even though the non-religious are not the least upset or fearful of a god or god word. Isn't it interesting how Christians try to force their delusion on everyone else?

The Fourth Commandment, About Keeping The Sabbath Holy, Has Some Serious Flaws

The Commandment about keeping the Sabbath holy seems to be pretty simple upon first reading. "Remember the Sabbath day, to keep it holy," says the King James Version. Similar wording from the New International Version reads, "Remember the Sabbath day by keeping it holy."

This an admonition to not only rest, but to spend the day honoring God and reflecting on holy things, committing holy acts and worshiping God.

In referencing it to the Ten Commandments, it seems to apply only to the Judeo/Christian religions. The Ten Commandments are best represented from Exodus 20:1-17 where it is specifically outlined. But you can also find these Commandment basics in the Qur'an of Islam, although not codified in one place as with the Bible.

In the Qur'an, you find an admonition to drop all business activities on the Sabbath, and "hasten to the commemoration of God." The problem with all of this is which Sabbath are we to follow or to believe? Naturally, people follow one faith, so the Sabbath would come on Friday, Saturday or Sunday, depending upon following respectively Muslim, Jewish or Christian religions. Each religion has its own Sabbath.

In the Bible, the admonition against doing any work applies to the entire family (except perhaps the wife who does the cooking, etc.) and even to cattle (and presumably other domestic livestock), along with visiting strangers and guests. The Bible also relates this to God making the "heaven and earth" in six days and resting on the seventh — "the Lord blessed the Sabbath day and hallowed it."

Just how severely and faithfully this is followed depends upon not only the religion, but also the degree of belief by individuals. On the Sabbath, Orthodox Jews usually walk to synagogue to avoid using a car. They will not turn on electricity for light, heat or cooking and today often use timers to adjust such "work." Often Orthodox Jews do not cook, do any household or garden work or other daily chores on their Saturday Sabbath in respecting this belief.

Naturally, in practice, this degree of honor and worship of God or a god varies. For some it can be an all-day long practice of worship attendance. For others, it can be an hour of church service, perhaps with a Sunday School lesson added, followed by a golf game.

The Qur'an seems a little more lax in this, only insisting that no business should be done, but without time guidelines and restraints or a definition of "business."

All this leaves a lot of wiggle room in what should be a day of worship. That leaves the skeptic seemingly a little concerned about a

Godly ruling which only seems to glorify the god creating the ruling and for no other earthly — or heavenly — purpose.

Strange, isn't it?

The Fourth Of The Ten Commandments Can Involve Rest — But Does It Have To?

The idea of a day when you can rest after six days of work, in emulation of God, is patently ridiculous. This comes in the Fourth Commandment, which commands keeping the Sabbath holy for worship of God.

But you have to wonder about the whole concept of this, and the origins of this Sabbath day of rest and worship. Sure, we can take this back to Genesis and making the various parts of the universe and the earth over the six-day period described.

This is an admonition to not only rest, but to spend the day honoring God and reflecting on holy things, holy acts and worship of God. The curious thing about this Genesis-based law or Commandment is that it is based on the six-day work week of God and the fact that from a religious standpoint we should subscribe to this and to a day of rest and worship, especially worship.

But why would God need to rest, as per Genesis and the Ten Commandments? Note that a literal belief of the Bible states that God whipped up the universe in a few days at most. In this, we know today that there are billions and trillions of galaxies and trillions of planets and stars. This sounds like a lot, but most people do not know how many, or the differentiation between millions, billions and trillions.

As an example, if we were to count seconds, we would reach a million seconds in twelve days. To reach a billion, we would have to wait for 32 years. A trillion seconds would take 32,000 years. Think that I am wrong and that it could not be? Do the math. Think of all this the next time they talk about these figures with the national debt or deficit. If this were numbers of planets and stars and such, this would be a lot of stuff floating around out there.

A literal interpretation of the Bible would be God creating billions and trillions of planets and stars in a few days. Surely, an omniscient and omnipotent being would not — cannot — be tired after making all this even though it does seem to involve some heavy lifting. Ask any Christian — God can do anything, any time, in any time period and any way he wants. There are no limits, he cannot get tired. He is God.

The idea of a "time out" for God is strictly a man-made convention designed to keep the faithful and the gullible in check, in-line and under control with this system of regular worship organized to keep preachers in business and almost — that's almost — gainfully employed.

Some Additional Thoughts On The Fourth Of The Ten Commandments

The fourth of the Ten Commandments requires a day of rest and reflection. But why? It seems that it is a man-made ruling and convention, following the supposed "rest" of God after whipping up the universe in six days. But God the omniscient, the omnipotent, would not require any rest at all. He can keep right on chugging along.

But there is another way of looking at this as a rest period of one day per week being necessary biologically for us to recharge. But this is not necessary as per basic biology.

Admittedly, carnivores will often take a few days off to digest after a big kill. Lions do this all the time. They will take down a foraging animal or prey, eat their fill and then lounge around for a day or three until it is necessary to make another kill. Foraging animals — herbivores — do not take time off, but forage constantly during waking hours.

Today, we consider or think of our "right" to a day or two off on a weekend, and even then often try to extend it with a Friday off or Monday holiday to make for a three-day weekend and more leisure time.

But that is all just recent in society. Less than one hundred years ago, at the beginning of the 20th century, steel workers manning blast and Bessemer furnaces often toiled 84 hours per week. That's a 14-hour day, six days a week. In the rest of the steel industry at that time, 12-hour days were common.

Naturally, there was no time off and little disposable income for recreation such for baseball games, golf and fishing that we enjoy today, and whole careers revolved around these working hours. But even then, Sundays were kept for worship and many were expected by society, ministers or convention to go to church.

Today, that separation of a six-day work week and one worship day has eroded a little with the repeal of the blue laws of the early and middle 20th century and the rejection in part at least of the Puritan philosophy that it is sinful to have fun anytime, and particularly on weekends and Sundays. The blue laws legally prohibited sales and certain activities on the Sabbath — the Christian Sabbath, naturally.

Unfortunately, among the faithful and the habitually guilted, the idea of a weekly reminder of God is necessary to stay in line and be good with God. And oh yeah, be sure to keep on tithing so that the preachers, priests and church can continue building churches in an architectural circular argument for religion. The bigger the church, the more important the religion and the greater need for money and tithes; the more important the religion, the bigger the church and necessity for tithes and money to keep it all going. And so on.

We might want but do not need the time off to rest and reflect and worship God. We might not even believe in a god or God or need to believe in a God or god.

Does Honoring Parents As Per The Fifth Commandment Require Stealing, Killing And Lying? Yep!

"Honor your father and your mother, so that you may live long in the land the Lord your God is giving you," So it says in Exodus 20:12 of the New International Bible, with the King James Version almost identical.

That's the fifth of the Ten Commandments, and one that also creates a lot of anguish. I know people who feel religiously bound to honor their parents even though those parents are not really worthy, deserving or due any honor or respect.

Sadly, we read in the newspaper or see on TV cases where parents have not only not cared for their children, but actively abused them. Are they worthy of the honor and respect that God wants children to give parents? We hear or read of children who have died or remained seriously ill as result of the terrible, useless and abusive faith healing practices of their parents. Those people are not parents worthy of respect and honor. They are child abusers who deserve jail time.

In many other situations, children are not cared for or about, with little that the parents do for them including even the basics of food, clothing, shelter, heat and schooling. Those parents are also not fulfilling their societal role — forget about God's wishes — in caring for their offspring. They are not worthy of respect and honor, but only scorn and shame from both society and their children.

This also does not seem to be important enough for a commandment, when compared with the biggies of no stealing, killing, adultery or lying. We are talking about being nice when compared to killing and stealing? This mild exhortation is along the lines of a number of admonitions and guidelines useful through life.

Examples of life guidelines would be:

"Be nice and talk to grandma when she visits today."

"Be sure to walk the dog before it starts raining."

"It's a school night — remember to be in bed by 9:30." You could go on with a few hundred other suggestions for living that also don't make the Big Ten list.

The irony is that the latter part of this Fifth Commandment promises that "you may live long in the land that the Lord your God is giving you."

It takes another couple of Bible books to get to Joshua where God gives the Israelites their "promised land" of Canaan, first referenced in Genesis 12:7 with God speaking to Abraham. The irony is that God and Joshua and the rest of the Israelites wanted this land that was not theirs, but belonged to the innocent Canaanites.

But to get this land, God and Joshua had to kill, steal, rape, lie, covet, and totally disrespect and dishonor the gods and beliefs of the Canaanites, as per Joshua 6:20-21. How many of his own Godly Commandments did God break or have Joshua break just to steal the lands promised in this Commandment? It can only disgust a thinking skeptic.

"Do Not Murder" Is Basic Social Morality, Not A Commandment Handed To Us By God

Killing or murder is bad. Just check the Sixth Commandment. The King James Version says, "Thou shalt not kill." The New International Version says, "You shall not murder."

The distinction between the two is the use of the words "kill" and "murder." Presumably, both apply to only killing people. After all, we kill lots of things, necessary for survival. We directly kill animals of all types for food, for sport (hunting or fishing — also for food), for utility use such as hides for clothing, horns or antlers for tools and other uses and hooves for glue.

We also kill animals indirectly, such as often happens today with increasing human population. This occurs through destruction of natural areas for houses, shops, roads, timber for building, mining operations, etc. and the loss of animal habitat. If animals do not have a place to live and a place to find their food, or the food itself, they cannot live. They starve.

The difference between the two translations of "murder" and "kill" might also be why some religions and members of specific beliefs become conscientious objectors and will not fight in the military. The term "killing" is broad enough to include war. Murder would only include an individual wrongly — in societal terms — taking another human life.

The important thing about all this is that Christians always insist that our morals and ethics come from God and from the Ten Commandments as per the above. They do not. Laws such as the admonition against killing or murder predate the Ten Commandments and most certainly predate recorded history.

These laws, along with the following Commandments against adultery, stealing, and lying (false witness) are a way for large and small groups such as families, tribes, villages, communities, and other groups to get along without complete anarchy.

Among the earliest of rules for society is the Code of Hammurabi, set during the reign of this king from 1795 to 1750 BCE. This code includes 281 rules for the functioning of an early society including in many variations the moral rules involving killing and murder. (The Code lists 282 numbered laws, but there are only 281 because even then, the number 13 was considered superstitious and evil with no law listed for this number.)

The point is that there is and was no definitive religious, Jewish or Christian-precursor series of laws or morals on which to give God the credit for presenting it to mankind. Surely, mankind developed this and other early rules and laws through experimentation with societal relations, and without any help from a God or gods. Chronology and common sense cannot come up with any other explanation. Considering the role of God as a murderer throughout the rest of the Bible, it definitely takes God out of the caring, good and beneficent morals equation.

PROHIBITION OF ADULTERY IS A GOOD BASIC RULE FOR SOCIETY, BUT IT DID NOT ORIGINATE FROM GOD

"You shall not commit adultery." That's the Seventh Commandment of the Bible. Again, this is not morality handed down by God through the Ten Commandments. Instead, it is a basic rule of society that existed for years prior to the writing of the Ten Commandments.

You can find this in the Code of Hammurabi along with many (281) rules that formed the basis of society hundreds of years prior to the writing of the Ten Commandments. The important thing to realize again is that like the prohibition against murder, it evolved in society without the help of God.

While Christians and many religions like to believe that all morals came from God, that is patently untrue. In this case also, there are notable exceptions. This basic rule against adultery also tacitly endorses the concept of marriage and a marital commitment between those involved.

But in some early societies, polygamy (one husband, two or more wives) was common. Less common was polyandry (one wife and two or more husbands). Also common among some religions was temple or religious sexual intercourse, or temple prostitution, these as religious rites and devout worshiping practices.

All this is not unlike the animal kingdom, of which we are a part. In some species, random sex is practiced while others have a single male with a large harem (elephant seals), or many males following one female (fish), or a pair mating exclusively for a long time or even for life (some birds). Date rape is often involved in the animal kingdom, despite what you might see on the Disney channel as animations or anthropomorphic stories.

And there are some human exceptions that existed until recently, such as the practice of some Inuit (Eskimos) sharing their wife when greeting guests to their dwelling. It was rarer than commonly believed, and primarily a practice between extended family and community groups, often to cement relations or partnership/business opportunities.

The fact remains that men, women and societies — not God or gods — decided on useful ways to arrange their family groups. These admonitions were not handed down by God, but developed for practical purposes by man.

The fact also remains that in modern society, the prohibition against adultery is a good rule. This rule when broken can lead to all sorts of other bad things such as divorce, broken families, lying, stealing, property distribution problems, distress amongst children, and even murder. And some of these are listed in the Ten Commandments, and thus for the Christians, would be a sin. And that's bad, even for a skeptic.

Not Stealing A Good Societal Rule, But Not Religious In Origin

Not stealing as per the Eighth Commandment is another good rule for all societies, starting with early man in tribes or extended families. It is good, but not Godly, or at least does not come from God as a moral rule and as head-bobbing sycophant Christians would like to insist.

As with adultery, stealing can lead to all sorts of societal problems, many of which lead to terrible consequences. Countries can steal land, peoples, ideas, food seeds, trade routes, etc. Small groups of people and individuals can steal anything from the identity of another as per current society, including property, money and even intellectual property, ideas and inventions.

As with the admonitions against adultery, murder and lying, this is a good rule for societies, and one that predates recorded history and certainly religion including Judaism and Christianity. In religious and fundamentalist commentaries on the Ten Commandments, you find a lot of wiggle room, phrasing and parsing about Commandments One through Five and number Ten. There is little wiggle room or juggling about numbers Six through Nine.

Admittedly, in primitive society there was probably little concern about this, since most people and families had little in property and most had no more or less than their neighbors. In that case, what is there to steal?

This Commandment has played into the Bible, with one example by Achan in the book Joshua. Achan was stealing from the spoils of war that was to be given to God. Achan stole a robe, two hundred shekels of silver and a wedge of gold.

Achan paid in a big way when caught, since he was stoned to death. His family also paid, since Achan's children — completely innocent according to the Bible — were also stoned to death, just for their genetic association with their father. That's a tad extreme, since we today do not execute anyone for stealing anything. And we certainly don't deliberately execute innocents, as God and Joshua did. We don't and should not execute the next generation or innocents just because they are related to the accused and convicted.

When practiced properly with appropriate punishment, this Eighth Commandment, is another of those few among Ten that are good for society. But it is not from God as a morality rule or edict from a deity.

Along with the next Commandment on lying, we are whittling down the list to the Four that are useful for society and which predate any religion or religious concept. And that's good — provided everyone understands it and gets away from the pixie dust of religion and the excesses of religious edicts and religious punishments.

Ninth Commandment On Lying One Of Four That Is Worth Something For Society

When kiddies are little and being brainwashed about religion and the Bible, they often do not understand the Ninth Commandment. "Thou shalt not bear false witness against thy neighbor," it states.

What is false witness? How many neighbors are applicable or how far out in the neighborhood does this edict apply? Children might ask these questions, not understanding that "false witness" is lying and that "neighbor" applies to anyone and everyone.

In interpretation, this basically means that you should not lie and that this applies to anyone and any situation. It applies mostly to various legal or judicial proceedings, along with a basic rule as a good way to live.

It does not have to apply to the "little white lies" we tell all the time. It would not apply when telling a woman relative that her dress does not make her look fat when it does, gushing to a neighbor that her meal is delicious when it isn't, or that your home looks beautiful painted bright pink when it looks terrible. You can tell the truth in these situations, but at your own risk of hurting someone for no real gain or positive effect.

In legal proceedings, lying is illegal, is called perjury and does have associated punishments if the court decides to enact them. Lying in a court or judicial proceeding creates a miscarriage of justice when a wrong doer is unjustly found innocent, or when an innocent person is punished with fines and/or prison.

But as with other rules from the Ten Commandments, edicts against lying can be found in the much older Code of Hammurabi of 1760 BCE Babylon in which 281 rules for society are listed. Even that is recent when compared to Egyptian laws that can be dated back to 3000 BCE.

The Sumerian king Ur-Nammu developed societal laws around 2200 BCE. These included two laws relating to lying in judicial proceedings, with perjury punishable with fines.

The Ten Commandments — from God according to the religionists — did not exist until about 1280 BCE. These moral laws and edicts were predated by earlier laws in several countries, with those in turn probably predated by laws and rules covered only in oral tradition by the ruling class of more primitive societies.

The lateness of the religious Ten Commandments from the Torah, compared with the earlier laws of Ur-Nammu or Hammurabi, means that these moral laws of the Jews and Christians are late comers to the laws of jurisprudence and justice of human societies. God did not develop our morals and ethics. They have been around since civilization began to be developed. Skeptics know this. Shouldn't religionists learn and respect it?

TENTH COMMANDMENT ON COVETING RIDICULOUS AND FOOLISH

Not coveting is another biggie in the Ten Commandments, presumably equal to not murdering, not stealing, not working on Sunday, etc. But coveting is really a plus in the commercial field, keeping the machines of industry humming; the business trades flowing, people working and societies thriving.

When looked at in a biblical context, when the Ten Commandments were created (1280 BCE), there was not much to covet. The Israelites were just a step or two out of the Stone Age, nomadic wanderers of the mid-East, early purveyors of that new funny religion of Judaism.

Almost everyone had the same things, although some may have had more primitive items than others. Today, there is much to covet, need and want, if you have the money and ability to honestly get it.

The Bible in this section is also very specific, mentioning not only general coveting, but also specifically your neighbor's house, wife, manservant, maidservant, ox, ass or anything that belongs to your neighbor.

Translated to today, a house still means a house, a wife still means a wife and that ox and ass can be translated into your Hummer, Honda or Hyundai. Everything else still means everything else.

Taken to an extreme, coveting can be wrong. If I covet your new huge flat screen TV and am so envious about it that I break into your house to steal it, that is wrong. It suddenly jumped from coveting to stealing, something wrong not only in the Ten Commandments, but

in laws everywhere. My coveting and then stealing your big TV can —
and should — lead to my arrest in this hypothetical case.

Coveting per se to buy or honestly acquire something is not
wrong. If we never aspire to something new or better, we would
never advance and gain the benefits of new inventions and ideas.
Satisfied with no insulation in your house? No need for new fiberglass
insulation to keep warm in winter. Satisfied with a wood stove and
the necessity of splitting wood all year? No need for a gas or electric
range. Satisfied with a quill pen? No need to buy a new ball-point.
Satisfied with a horse? No need for a car. It goes on and on.

The Ten Commandments rule about coveting is another of
those foolish rules along the lines of excessively respecting your
parents, or the foolish rules about honoring God with those first
four Commandments. These, from a narcissist God with serious self-
esteem and insecurity issues are ridiculous.

You can break down all the important stuff in this biblical section
to the Golden Rule, as espoused by Confucius and a few hundred
years later by Jesus.

The big question is whether or not Jesus stole this from Confucius'
earlier writings. That of course, would be a violation of one of the Ten
Commandments. And Jesus would not like that.

Was Jesus A Socialist Or Communist? He Had To Be One Or The Other!

The Berlin wall is gone now, but just think of past Socialists and
Communists. We had Stalin, Engels, Marx, Lenin and Jesus. Oh yeah
— Jesus fits the category also, although not often credited for his
communist or socialist leanings.

Just think of it — Jesus did not aspire to or preach about great
wealth. He was not a farmer with huge fields, a shepherd with many
flocks of sheep or cattle, a widely and wildly popular tent maker. He
presumably was trained by his step-father Joseph as a carpenter or
maybe a stone cutter, but we know little of his life. The Bible states
that he was born, preached in the temple at age twelve and was a
rabble-rousing activist during the last three years of his short life.

But he never owned anything of value other than his clothes.
When he died, he did not even have a tomb or cloth for wrapping his
body. These came from "a rich man from Arimathea named Joseph,"
who provided the wrapping linens and also his own tomb cut into
the rock.

You can check many biblical references about Jesus that prove
that he was not about wealth or possessions.

Luke 6:20 says, "Blessed are you who are poor, for yours is the
kingdom of God. Blessed are you who hunger now, for you will be

satisfied. Blessed are you who weep now, for you will laugh." It continues in this vein.

The same thing is found in Matthew 5, 6 and 7 in the Sermon on the Mount, including this section from Matthew 6:19. "Lay not up for yourselves treasures upon earth, where moth and rust doth corrupt, and where thieves break through and steal."

Or check Matthew 6:24, "Ye cannot serve God and mammon." These references continue throughout the four gospels of the life of Jesus.

The references are obvious. Jesus did not aspire to own something, to buy or trade anything, or attempt to expand an ambitious carpentry business. He was a socialist or communist. He was sort of like a bum or beggar on the street.

His complete philosophy was barely that of communism or socialism. That is the philosophy that each must work and contribute what he has with communistic ownership of everything by the state or community, or socialistic distribution of goods or services by society rather than by individuals. Jesus did not work, at least not in the sense of what most of us consider work.

Many would not consider Jesus a communist or socialist except by reading and critically understanding his life and philosophy. Would that not upset many who look to Jesus for continued material prosperity and wealth through a belief in him and his inerrant word, the Bible? Would they give up their belongings to follow Jesus as Jesus suggested on many occasions? Would the TV preachers have to stop their pleas for money for "seed planting"? We could only hope.

No Spare Ribs In The Biblical Story Of Making Eve From Adam's Rib

The two missionaries walked up my driveway with a purpose — to make me understand and join their particular brand of religious delusion. I was delighted. It would be like a cat playing with a mouse. Except that I had two mice.

We somehow got onto Genesis. Playing dumb, I asked about Eve being made from Adam's rib. "Since Adam's mistakes created original sin for all mankind, causing death and pain as a result of his action in the Garden of Eden," I asked, "does it also follow that men today would have fewer ribs than women, since Eve was made from one of Adam's ribs? Wouldn't men have one less rib than women?" You could see the immediate smiles among the happy proselytizers. They had me, they thought. They really had me.

They could see that I was getting it — "it" being the basic, literal, ultimate, actual, inerrant Word of God story and understanding of the

Bible in their choice of religion fiction. "You've got it!" one exclaimed. He was happy. Very happy. He shouldn't have been.

Then, suddenly tiring of playing, I told them the truth. There is no difference in the number of ribs between men and women. The numbers of ribs on both sides of the bodies of both sexes are identical. Check Gray's Anatomy.

And how and why would I think of this preposterous idea in contrast to "the truth" of the Word of God? "Because," I told them, "in a former life, I worked as an instructor in the Anatomy Department of a major medical school and taught human gross anatomy to first-year medical students and third-year physical therapy students. I have dissected more bodies and studied more skeletons than there are residents on the next few blocks of this street."

They looked crestfallen about the truth that confronted their false belief. I could have also told them that they could check any copy of Gray's Anatomy, the Bible in the medical world.

Telling this bit of truth gave me great joy, since I felt as if I had stamped out just a tiny bit of ignorance and stupidity. Hopefully, they would spread to others this bit of information of their false belief and maybe spur a few believers to more critical thinking, research and reading.

Also, you don't need to be a former medical school instructor in human anatomy to find this out. A simple check of any number of medical and anatomy books — available in any library or on the Internet — would divulge the same truth to anyone.

Shortly thereafter, the two mice wandered down my driveway. They had more important things that needed their immediate attention, they said. I waved "goodbye "and told them to come back anytime. I hoped that they would return soon. Sadly, I haven't seen them since.

The Logic? Of Original Sin And Salvation From Jesus' Resurrection? Wait — Does This Make Sense?

The reason for Jesus' birth is that we needed a Savior so that we can go to heaven instead of hell, and eliminate the original sin caused by Adam and Eve. Yep, it defies any basic logic, but hang on as we trace this story.

Jesus had to be born so that he could save all from eternal hell and damnation through his crucifixion. Jesus had to be born of a virgin to prove his validity as the son of God. We certainly would not want two people — a man and a woman — to be messing around with that untidy sex to create our Lord, would we?

Of course, Jesus is not only Jesus, but also part of the Trinity of God, the Holy Spirit and Jesus. Thus each of these separate entities is not only itself, but also its son and father, all at the same time. That, of course, makes it easier to talk to yourself or either of the other two of you.

Approximately thirty-three years after his birth, Jesus was killed by the Romans with a little encouragement from the Jews, according to the stories in the New Testament. He was crucified with this act and his later resurrection "proving" to mankind that Jesus died for our sins so that we would not die and rot, or go to an eternal hell, but instead go to heaven.

What? What was that?? Say that again??? Of course it makes no sense — it is a non-answer to a non-question. The problem and solution are not logically connected in any way. The so-called solution is not connected in any way to the causation-problem.

The reason that we otherwise would go to hell without this act of Jesus is because of "original sin." This is a made-up man-made fiction stating that everyone is "bad" — sinful — as soon as they are born. It started with St. Augustine, lurched into codification with the 529 CE Second Council of Orange and continued on until today.

That of course is because Eve was convinced by a talking snake (a lizard that subsequently lost its legs through an act of God) to eat a magical fruit that God had forbidden to Adam and Eve.

Since Adam along with Eve also ate the magical fruit, both were charged with "original sin" for themselves and all of subsequent mankind. That is mean of God — to blame us today for something that some ancients did. In addition, Adam had to work hard all his life and Eve was subject to pain during childbirth.

Just ask — it says so in Genesis. It was because of this talking snake convincing Adam and Eve to eat the magical fruit that all mankind is "bad" and subject to original sin. No logic there. That, Christians say, is why we needed Jesus to die and be resurrected to take away that original sin. No logic there either. Make sense? Any logic to any of this? That's what I thought — I don't think so either.

A Free Thinker Is Satans Slave — So Say Some Fundamentalist Churches

A friend emailed me a photograph of a marquee-type sign, as many churches now use, the marquee in front of a fundamentalist church. "A FREE THINKER IS SATANS SLAVE!" proclaims the sign. Yeah, shame on them. I know, I know — they left out the apostrophe.

Now that is a sure way for any person to be rounded up, roped in, saddle-cinched, tamed down, hog-tied, corralled, fenced-in and convinced that the truth of science is a lie, and that the errors of the Bible are truth. You just have to wonder...

My Webster's Dictionary defines a free thinker as "A person who forms his opinions about religion independently of tradition, authority or established belief." And what, I may ask, is wrong with that?

If this is wrong, and makes one "Satan's slave" (with the proper apostrophe here), then the concept of Big Brother is in full force. In this case it is just in the religious field rather than in politics, governmental regulation and law. Sadly, some people think this way (provided that it agrees with them), or are convinced that this is the way that the world should work. They want a theocracy, provided that it is their theocracy, not that of somebody else with a different religion. They want to tell all of us how to think, how to believe, how to live. Shades of Iran, Iraq and the Muslims!

Just think of this — "A free thinker is Satan's slave." The whole aspect of this is to suggest that one should only listen to and believe in the minister (as in this case of the sign on a fundamentalist church) or the Bible. Never mind what reality, facts, newspapers, magazines, books, TV, Internet or anything else tells you or suggests for thinking and analysis.

We know better. Were people to follow this scurrilous dictate, we would still "know" that the sun goes around the earth, that the earth is flat, that you can't be protected against disease by some silly thing called a "vaccine," that climate change is false, that there is no such thing as genetics, that we should not develop anesthetics, that the internal combustion engine is Satan's work and a million more things. These "errors" were all disproved respectively by Galileo, many scientists, Pasteur, Mendel, Morton, and many automotive engineers. Were all these people working for Satan? These erroneous "facts" of history were disproved by free thinkers and through independent thoughts and ideas.

Similarly, those who stamp out their own and others free thinking presumably don't think of or accept the errors, contradictions, mistakes, impossibilities, improbabilities, immoralities, evils, etc., of the Bible. They only keep their eyes on searching out and destroying any possibility of truth, logic, science and facts.

Now that is frightening. It only leads to a parody of an old saying. "You can lead a horse to water, but you can't make it think."

Here's for free thinking — or for that matter, any kind of honest, careful, considerate thinking, analysis and logic using the Scientific Method.

Discovering The Truth About The Bible And Religion Demands Careful, Critical Reading And Thinking

Christian believers always like to scoff at skeptics, questioners, atheists and agnostics by picking out one little verse in the Bible that will counter or squash (they think!) anything that a skeptic says. In short, they pick and choose ideas to make things fit, bouncing around in the Bible like a bumblebee in a mayonnaise jar.

What these believers can't get around are the facts that the skeptics bring up, the verse or quote that makes the Bible questionable, if not completely false.

In this, you can look at big things or little things, but the total of it all leads — or should lead for thinking people — to serious questions and skeptical thought. Big things can be the resurrection of Jesus, crucifixion, walking on water, feeding thousands with a few food scraps, calling down plagues on the Egyptians, the flood and Noah, creating the universe, making Adam and Eve, etc.

Little things can be items such as floating axe heads, killing Israelites as a result of David fouling up a census, withered fig trees, putting demons into pigs, and the many, many contradictions and errors found throughout the Bible.

Almost any one of these, big or little, should be enough to make most consider this nothing more than a tale of Toto, Dorothy, and her collection of friends going to and cavorting in the land of OZ. There could be lots of questions there in that story, one of many on the subject by Frank Baum.

The difference is that we all know that this Oz story is a fiction for children, a fanciful tale of another unreal world. So is the Bible, but far too many people read it and think of it as factual and absolute truth. But Genesis is not journalism.

Read the Bible critically, and you can't help but come across errors and contradictions that have to — or should — make you think twice. Unless. The "unless" is only if you are taught — brainwashed really — into not accepting anything from facts, logic, truth or science.

If you only believe what a minister, priest, rabbi, imam or other religious type says and dictates, you're probably doomed without a critical transplant of critical thinking. But to be a truly, thinking believing person in anything, you have to critically consider all aspects and nuances of everything written, including the Bible.

You have to be a free thinker, careful critic and analytical of anything written or spoken. To be anything less is to blatantly believe in fairy tales, the possibility of fiction, or to follow the mental gymnastics of some very creative writers of fairy tales or 1960s science fiction by the likes of Bradbury and Asimov.

Little Things Mean A Lot When It Comes To Proving Evolution And Disproving Creationism

In the evangelical fundamentalists fight against Darwin's Theory of Evolution, they miss one tiny but important fact of evolutionary evidence. They miss a lot — a whole lot — but let's stick to one little fact for right now. While there are encyclopedias of information about the absolute scientific proof of evolution, you seldom hear about the small proofs that we carry with us all the time.

The basic truth is that there is no reason to create man in God's image (according to the Bible) if it includes something that man does not need. If we have something that we needed in an evolutionary past and that is still with us in vestigial form, then that would be a small but continued proof of evolution.

All agreed? Then let's look at the following.

This small fact or bit of evidence is the arrector pili muscles found over most of our bodies on all of us. Never heard of them? Think goose bumps. "Goose bumps" are nothing more than a series of these tiny muscles that are attached between the base of the skin and the base of a hair follicle. When contracted, these muscles dimple the skin (the goose bump) and also cause the attached hair to rise as the hair follicle is pulled straight up. This is most commonly found in the forearms, but can occur anywhere on the body of an mammal.

This is caused by the autonomic or sympathetic nervous system, which means that we cannot control it directly the way we can an arm or leg muscle. This system is in part controlled by adrenalin in what is commonly called a "fight or flight" response. More primitive animals (and primates/people years ago) use this to protect against cold by increasing the insulation value of fur fluffed up, or to make themselves seem larger when cornered or in a "fight" situation. You can see both responses in your pet dog.

People do not need it now, and it has evolved into markedly diminished form over millions of years. Today, we have no appreciable hair, just a remnant of fur, that in much earlier evolutionary times would help insulate or to make us seem bigger to enemies.

Would God, in his infinite wisdom, include this on our bodies if there is currently no need for insulation or fight/flight protection? Would our sympathetic nervous system and the smooth involuntary muscles involved still be in effect were it not a remnant of a long-past evolutionary step? Would we still have this tiny ineffectual muscle if it were not a leftover from earlier evolution?

While we did not evolve from current ape species, we are in essence a form of an evolved almost-hairless more primitive ape or primate from a more primitive primate.

All this makes one wonder about the opinions of the evangelicals vs. the truth of science. But check out those encyclopedias for more — lots more — evolutionary evidence. Take that, Creationists!

THOSE WHO DO NOT READ OR THINK ABOUT RELIGION ARE NO BETTER OFF THAN THOSE WHO CANNOT THINK OR READ

Those who do not read are no better off than those who cannot read. This seems to particularly apply to religious fundamentalists and fanatics who refuse — absolutely refuse — to try to learn anything other than what their minister, priest or rabbi teaches them, or has taught them in the past.

This came to light a few evenings back when we had a few couples over for a light dinner. Some in this group knew of my thoughts and disgust with religion; others did not. I don't make it a practice to beat others about the head with the fact that I used to write an Internet religious skepticism column or that I now write books and articles on atheism and that outline the problems and failures with religion and Christianity.

One such friend, Sally (names changed to protect the guilty), did know and has had severe problems with this, stating that I am writing trash, that I had better stop writing anti-Christ material, that I am wrong and evil, etc. She pounced on this again during the evening in question.

She hates it when her husband Jack (name changed) talks to me about religion or asks a question. We usually have a cordial conversation until Sally chimes in with her vindictive, hateful wrath about my "trash," my horrible writing and my awful thinking. She is Catholic and of course racked with a lifetime of abuse, misinformation, fear, guilt and shame.

The irony of all this is that she is not familiar with my writings, has read none of them, and has not read nor will she ever read my book or books or anything that is a work-in-progress. Her complaints would be like my complaining about her food without ever having smelled, tasted, or eaten any of her meals. In truth, Sally is a good cook.

Sally is a devout Catholic and yet can't see the error of her ways. No — not the error of Catholicism — but the error in not considering the possibility of studying further, reading the works of theological scholars, learned atheists such as Christopher Hitchens (*God Is Not Great*) or Richard Dawkins (*The God Delusion*), or studying and critically reading the Bible.

I think that there are several possibilities here.

    1. She is scared to death to even think about believing anything other than the Catholic brainwashing that she received as a child.

2. She is scared to hear about anything other than what she has been told and taught, even if that information is from accredited theological scholars.

3. Her fear is palpable to the extent that she cannot even entertain the idea of discussing thoughts other than those that have been parroted to her by priests.

4. She is totally afraid to learn anything new that might call into question her "faith."

5. Sally has an investment of time, energy and perhaps money into her beliefs and can't stand the idea that these beliefs or some of them might be wrong or in error. Better to continue to believe in her girlhood fables.

6. That she is not interested in anything other than a very casual, shallow explanation of religion from very cursory Bible reading and reading only superficially and without any depth, detail or understanding.

7. All of the above.

Me, I am going with number seven. And what is your take on all this?

Were Adam's Sons Having Sex With Their Sisters Or With Their Mom Eve, Or Both?

According to the truth of the Bible — this inerrant Word of God — Adam and Eve were the first two people on earth. We can leave out all the evidence for evolution, since fundamentalists "know" that the Bible – the Word of God - is right and that the evil, secular, ungodly atheists have it all wrong.

We also know that Adam and Eve had three sons, Cain, Abel and Seth. After Cain killed Abel and was driven away to Nod by God, Cain had children with his wife.

But wait a minute! Since there were only two people — Adam and Eve — as the first people of the earth, where did any other women come from to be wives to Cain and Seth? If we accept the "fact" of first people as Adam and Eve, then there are no possible women, unless Eve had more children including or exclusively being daughters.

But there is a problem there also. If the only other women on earth were the unnamed and unexplained daughters of Eve mentioned in the Bible, that still leaves a biological and social problem. The only possible wife of Cain or Seth would be their sisters. In Genesis 5:4, it is stated after describing Seth's children, that Adam had other unnamed sons and daughters. But that is also well after Genesis 4:17 when Cain had a wife and sons, starting with Enoch. Thus, the only possibility for wives for Cain, Seth and their sons were their own sisters or for the second generation offspring perhaps their aunts.

Biologically, this is very dangerous, since close family inbreeding leads to damaged offspring with deformities and disease. Socially, it is not acceptable and never has been, with early Egyptian royalty one rare exception accepted culturally if not biologically.

The only other possibility is that Cain and Seth or their sons could have had sex with their mother (or grandmother) Eve. Similarly, the daughters and granddaughters of Adam, Cain, Seth and their male offspring could have had sex with their brothers, fathers or grandfather. Regardless, it is still inbreeding and not even condoned in animal husbandry because of potentially adverse biological effects.

All this makes one wonder about the truth of the Bible, the inerrant Word of God. With no other choices in the inerrant Word of God as written and believed by millions, it gives one the squeamish thought of Adam, Cain, Seth and their offspring having sex and procreating with their sisters or mother/grandmother Eve. Now that doesn't make for a pretty biblical picture, does it?

God's Gospels In The New Testament Very Questionable At Best

One would hope in reading the New Testament with a current translation (King James, New American Standard, New International Version or other) that the text would have been made directly from the original documents written or ordered by God. One would be wrong.

For now, let's just stick to the four New Testament gospels, since these, with the story of Jesus, are the basis of Christianity. In biblical order, these are Matthew, Mark, Luke and John.

In all of these four, the originals have been long lost and what we were or are translating from are copies of copies of copies of copies.

The original documents, such as they were, are long lost and we cannot be exactly sure as to what was said in them. Copies are fine, but in the early centuries after the death of Christ, there were no copy machines, no printing presses, nothing to make an exact, verifiable document of anything on paper, papyrus or velum. Copies were all made by man — scribes and monks of various Christian sects and cults.

Thus there is and were distinct possibilities of accidental errors in transposing something incorrectly, missing a line or two of text, spelling a word wrong, etc. Just look at the following two statements, both identical, other than the presence or absence of a space between letters.

"God is now here." "God is nowhere." This minimal change from "now here" to "no where" reverses the meaning of the sentence completely. One sentence refers to the presence of God; the other to the complete absence of God. But these statements have the same letters in the same order. Only a space between words is missing.

This could be a mistake, missing or adding a word here or there, misunderstanding a dictator reading a document to a scribe, or other forms of written and copied error.

In addition, it has to be realized that history is written or modified by the winners. In the case of these copies presently used by scholars, documents could have been deliberately modified to espouse the case for the then-new Christianity cult.

For this, verses could have been left out, modified, added, or with just a slight word or letter shift as above, completely changed as to meaning. The results could be that the entire basics of Christianity were changed, modified, adjusted or promulgated to make the text into the Christianity desired by the writers and promoters of a particular sect or cult.

Doesn't this make you think long and hard about the accuracy of the early Bible, and the effect of translations of copies to our present day religious beliefs? Doesn't this make for a lot of thought and skepticism about the divineness of God? Doesn't this make for some real concerns about the dogma and dictates of the early Church and the Church of today?

Have You Checked Luke 14:26? Are You Still So Sure That You Are — Or Really Want To Be — Christian?

We all know that Christians, particularly Christian ministers and priests, hop-scotch around the Bible, cherry-picking those verses that will "prove" their valued religious points. These points are usually that you have to believe in Christ to gain salvation, and that Jesus and God and the Bible are just chock-full of love, family devotion, kindness, caring, brotherly love, and all that warm fuzzy stuff.

Somehow, they never seem to get around to a few verses in Luke. These verses from Luke 14:26 are particularly telling and important in light of the love, family devotion, brotherly love, care, kindness, and all the above as often espoused by the religiously deluded.

It is an interesting series of verses, and a direct quote from Jesus, in quote marks or in red for those Bible editions in the red letter (for Jesus' sayings) printings.

Jesus, in commenting to the large crowds traveling with him, says, "If anyone comes to me and does not hate his father and mother, his wife and children, his brothers and sisters — yes, even his own life — he cannot be my disciple."

Do you love your father and mother? You do? Do you love your wife and children? You do? Do you love your brothers and sisters? You do?

(And by supposition, do you wives love your husbands? The woman's role again is often left out — since women in the Bible were treated only a tad better than stray dogs. In any case, a wife loving her husband is also important and axiomatically follows in this verse.)

But realize that if you do love any of these family members — mother, father, wife, husband, sons, daughters, brothers, sisters, etc., you cannot be a Christian and follow Christ. It is impossible. After all Christ says so, right there, big as life, in Luke 14:26.

This section concludes with the saying, "And anyone who does not carry his cross and follow me cannot be my disciple." There is more wiggle room in this sentence. Carrying a cross could be a figurative term of speech, and "following" could be interpreted in a lot of ways other than a literal marching down the trail following in someone's path.

But there is no wiggle room in a straight and literal reading of Luke 14:126. You have to — have to — hate your parents, children and siblings to get anywhere close to being accepted by Christ and Christianity. And yep, Christianity is a two-way street. Sure, you have to accept the dictates of the faith as to belief in Christ, resurrection and other aspects of the faith of your cult, but without accepting all of it — such as Luke 14:26 — you really can't be a Christian. If you are loving normal member of society, I guess that you can't be a Christian.

Sorry — you will just have to wait for the next religious delusion to come down the pike. Are you going to wait?

JESUS IS NOT REQUIRED TO FOLLOW THE TEN COMMANDMENTS? THAT SEEMS STRANGE AND UNGODLY!

Previously we commented on Luke 14:26 and how this states that we all must hate our parents, siblings and children to be followers of Christ. You can find a statement similar to that of Luke in Matthew 10:37. "Anyone who loves his father or mother more than me is not worthy of me; anyone who loves his son or daughter more than me is not worthy of me . . ."

Not mentioned in that column was that by hating our parents as per Luke and Matthew, we are totally disrespecting them and thus completely violating the fifth of the Ten Commandments. You can't hate or not love your parents and at the same time respect and honor them.

But as they say on the TV commercials — wait, there's more!

Jesus' violations of the Ten Commandments continue throughout the New Testament. In Matthew 12:46–50, you find the following. "While Jesus was still talking to the crowd, his mother and brothers stood outside, wanting to speak to him. Someone told him, 'Your mother and brothers are standing outside, wanting to speak to you.' He replied to him, 'Who is my mother and who are my brothers?' Pointing to his disciples, he said, 'Here are my mother and my brothers. For whoever does the will of my Father in heaven is my brother and sister and mother.'"

Jesus brushed off his mother and family dismissively, not talking to them and not even really recognizing them, according to what we find in the Bible. That is totally, totally, totally disrespectful and a complete violation of honoring his parents as required by the Fifth Commandment.

Check out also Luke 9:59–62. "He (Jesus) said to another man, 'Follow me.' But the main replied, 'First let me go and bury my father.' Jesus said to him, 'Let the dead bury their own dead, but you go and proclaim the kingdom of God.' Still another said, 'I will follow you Lord; but first let me go back and say good-by to my family.' Jesus replied, 'No one who puts his hand to the plow and looks back is fit for service in the kingdom of God.'"

This is insisting that a follower of Christ totally disrespect his father and family by not burying him and a family by not recognizing them.

Then in Luke 8:19–21, find the following quote, similar to the earlier-mentioned Matthew quote. "Now Jesus' mother and brothers came to see him, but they were not able to get near him because of the crowd. Someone told him, 'Your mother and brothers are standing outside, wanting to see you.' He replied, 'My mother and brothers are those who hear God's word and put it into practice.'"

Again, similar to Matthew, this is total disrespect by Jesus of his mother. There's more, but this is proof that Jesus violated the vaunted Ten Commandments or did not think that they applied to him.

Do we need any more to be skeptical, wondering and dismissive of the Word of God, Jesus' role as Christ or the validity of the Bible? I think not.

Needed Separation Of Church And State Clear With President Obama/NY Mosque Controversy And Dinner

A clear example of why there should be a complete separation of church and state occurred during the Obama administration and some flack with Muslims and zoning laws. The brouhaha at the time was over a proposed mosque in New York planned for an area near the ground zero site of the 9/11 World Trade Buildings attack. That ground zero site is where the two World Trade Buildings were brought down by those cowards flying planes into them on September 11, 2001. We all know what "9/11" means. We don't have to say anything else.

The brouhaha was over the building of a Muslim mosque near this now-hallowed ground of the trade buildings. It was ramped up with comments from President Obama who seemed to try to state that while the Muslims have a right to build the mosque, dependent upon local zoning laws and regulations, perhaps it was not wise. No kidding!

Naturally, the Constitution provides for the right of this construction, but the wisdom of this from and for all sides is at the least highly questionable. Then Friday night, there was a White House after dinner celebration of the Muslim fasting holiday of Ramadan. President Obama was presiding and made some additional comments about the right (remember — the Constitution!) of such a building. News reports noted that since the President was honoring the Muslim religious holiday, he felt that it would be perhaps disingenuous to not mention the continued controversy and the constitutionality (only!) of building the mosque.

The point is that if there was a clear — absolutely clear — separation of church and state, then the president — any president — would not have a celebration or recognition of any religious date or holiday of any religion, there would be no White House dinner, there would be no various Prayer Breakfasts, and there would be no need for anyone in the government to say or post anything about any religion.

The whole New York mosque controversy could be handled by the appropriate permits and licenses for zoning of such buildings, and hopefully by wise heads on both sides of this dispute deciding what is best for further understanding and healing.

The same could and should apply to other aspects of church/state dealings. We should remove the statement "In God we trust" from money, abandon starting and ending governmental meetings with prayer of any type, remove quotes of the Ten Commandments from courts, governmental buildings and publicly owned property, keep vocally "approved" prayer out of schools, take "Under God" out of the Pledge of Allegiance (the 1892 pledge with the "under God" part added in 1954), etc.

Realize that none of this would prevent court systems from working, school children from praying silently in or out of school, Senators, Representative, state delegates and such from praying on their own or forming small group prayer or Bible study on their own time and after their government work hours.

Removal of Christmas/Hanukah and Easter/Passover would also make them what they really are — commercial events to sell stuff parading under the guise of religion. It is something to think about, particularly for us skeptics of anything religious.

GOD'S NONSENSICAL FIREPOT AND TORCH STORY LEADS TO THE DEATH OF THOUSANDS LATER

Among the many nonsensical tales in the Bible is the one about the magical smoking firepot (or furnace) and the torch (or lamp). These are floating in air, not water like the floating iron ax of 2 Kings Chapter 6.

This floating-in-the-air smoking pot and flaming torch are found in Genesis 15:17. "When the sun had set and darkness had fallen, a smoking firepot with a blazing torch appeared and passed between the pieces." The pieces were pieces of a heifer, goat and ram, split lengthwise along the body. Kindda peculiar, if you ask me.

This New International Version differs from the King James Version and refers to a "smoking furnace, and a burning lamp." For this, you have to assume that there are two items, whereas with the NIV the blazing torch might be considered a part of the smoking firepot.

The pieces that this firepot and torch passed between were the pieces of a heifer, goat and ram, each three years old, along with a dove and young pigeon. The wording "divided them in the midst" or "cut them in two" suggests a mid-line cut down the middle of the three animals to make right and left halves. Ok, that is a little strange, but apparently not that uncommon in ancient times. This was a part of an important pact — a covenant between God and Abram.

But we have to assume that the firepot and torch just came floating along on their own, almost like the magical broom when Mickey Mouse tried to control it in the 1940s Disney film, "The Sorcerer's Apprentice." The broom went on about its business of carrying buckets of water while Mickey, still wearing his purloined sorcerer's hat, was sleeping.

Realize that there is no previous immediate reference to the firepot or torch, no reference to anyone holding them and moving them between the two pieces of slaughtered cattle, no way in which the firepot and torch got there. They just floated along, doing their own thing.

There is also no reference as to how this firepot and torch were important to the whole procedure and covenant, other than the fact that it was part of some ritual, some rite, that was a part of the God and Abram deal.

The result was hard on ten peoples — the Kenites, Kenizzites, Kadmonites, Hittites, Perizzites, Rephaim, Amorites, Canaanites, Girgashites, and Jebusites. God gave them and their lands to the

Israelites. They all would lose their lands, with the book of Joshua devoted to the unwarranted and hideously cruel killing of citizens of all 30-plus cities in Canaan.

This is an example of a just God? This is an example of a fair business deal? This is an act of a loving, giving, tolerant God? Even the monsters of recent history were not this bad. And it all started with a torch and a fire pot?

PAGAN RELIGIOUS RITES — WERE THEY STOLEN BY CHRISTIANS TO MAKE THE "NEW" RELIGION SOUND BETTER?

Much of Christianity and Christian dogma revolves around the belief that the only route to heaven, salvation and life eternal after this earthly life is available through the acceptance of a few basic beliefs. Naturally, these have to be Christian beliefs. One of these, in an often quoted or paraphrased statement, includes the rite of communion and the accepting of bread and wine as a substitute for the body and blood of Christ.

The Catholic Church, through Elevation of the Host and wine by the priest, at the altar, and through transubstantiation belief, states that the wine and wafer truly — truly — become the true body and blood of Christ. In Protestant Churches, this act is thought to be symbolic only, not a real change into human or Godly? flesh and blood.

In most churches, this "communion" is accomplished using wine and bread. The Catholic Church uses a cracker, communion wafer, or "host," with this host distributed by a priest in front of the altar to lined-up parishioners. Protestant faiths use a communion wafer or cubed bread.

Protestant churches use wine, sometimes grape juice, as representative of the blood of Christ. Catholic churches often use wine. This is distributed in small cups passed out to pews (mostly Protestant) or from a communal cup or chalice in front of the altar (Catholic or Protestant). It is looked upon as a Christian rite and is certainly not done as a sign of faith by most other religions, including Judaism.

The quotes on this vary only slightly in the four gospels, with the basics as follows: "Take and eat; this is my body," Matthew 26:26, Jesus says of the bread. Also, "This is my blood of the covenant, which is poured out for many for the forgiveness of sins," said by Jesus of the wine (Matthew 26:28).

But you can also read similar exhortations for this rite of communion from other different early translations of the same rite. "He who will not eat of my body and drink of my blood so that he will be made one with me and I with him, the same shall not know salvation."

That quotation? Oh, that's from an early pagan holy communion rite, probably Mithraist, and perhaps existing at least several hundred years prior to the gospels of Jesus.

This just makes one wonder how much of the Bible the Christians stole and plagiarized from other earlier religions to force Christianity into the driver's seat and throw other earlier religions under the bus. That was not nice and brings to question all of Christianity. Isn't this something to think about?

Christian Bumper Stickers To Make You Believe — Or For Non-Believers — To Ignore The Nonsense

The fish is one of the many symbols of the Christian religion. Some years ago, little fish symbols started showing up on car bumpers and trucks to indicate that the owners of the car were Christians.

These were simple — two curved lines, meeting at one end and crossing at the other to make the head and tail of a stylistic fish. These are usually self-stick, molded of plastic or metal, and do stand out on a car.

Then they started to get fancy, the curved fish lines with the word "JESUS" along the body of the fish and between the two curved lines. Fine. It makes the point that the car owners wanted to make. There is no question about the meaning of these stickers, these symbols.

Then secular types created and sold — and are still selling — symbols with the fish to which are added a little front leg and rear leg protruding from the belly to make the point of evolution. In some cases, the name "DARWIN" is imprinted between the lines where the word "JESUS" is on other symbols.

The religionists fought back, producing these same symbols but with the feet pointed upwards to indicate that Darwin was dead, and often with "JESUS" printed right side up on the dead fish (feet in air) of the symbol.

Of course, you also have both religious and anti-religious decals and self-stick slogans about religion. Some of the religious of these are along the lines of "Jesus loves you — but I'm his favorite," "Jesus is the answer," "Got faith?," "Got Jesus?" and "Are you following Jesus this close?"

The American Humanist Association has a nice sticker that says "I Believe In Good." That's not bad, since their motto/slogan is "Good Without A God." They also have a sticker that states "I Trust In Reason." That does sometimes seem to inspire the vindictive hated of the Christians who cannot tolerate any belief other than their own belief in the baby Jesus. Those with the "I Believe In Good" stickers on their vehicles have had occasions in which the sticker has been gouged, defaced, scratched over, written on with felt tip markers, etc.

Of course, there are also bumper stickers for the opposing view along the lines of, "Thou shalt not inflict thy religious crap upon others," "Too stupid for science? Try religion," "Imagine religion," and "Darwin loves you."

The one that I have liked best recently was on a yellow Corvette parked on the street. It stated in nine words and three lines as follows:
"God said it,
I believe it,
That ends it."

Well, that pretty well goes to a careful examination of religion in all its many aspects, doesn't it? (Sarcasm intentional.) How do you talk intelligently to someone who sports a sticker like this?

This kind of goes back to that other anti-religious sticker, "If you could reason with religious people, there would be no religious people."

GOD BLINDING PEOPLE — FIGURATIVELY AND LITERALLY — BOTH JUST SICK IN SO MANY WAYS

The idea of a literal meaning and literal reading of the Bible can often leave one in a quandary. Should we really follow all the dictates of the Bible or is there any wiggle room? Should we really do what the Bible says, especially the dictates of Jesus? Were quotes by Jesus absolutely perfect, without error or flaw and should they be followed exactly?

The usual answers by fundamentalists are respectively yes, you should follow biblical dictates and there is no wiggle room. Yes, you should do what the Bible says and yes, quotes by Jesus are perfect and must be followed.

That being the case, how you are going to get along being blind the rest of your life? Would a guide dog program work for this? Are their Christian guide dog programs? After all, in Matthew 5:28-29, Jesus says, "But I tell you that anyone who looks at a woman lustfully (as past president Jimmy Carter has admitted doing) has already committed adultery with her in his heart. If your right eye causes you to sin, gouge it out and throw it away. It is better for you to lose one part of your body than for your whole body to be thrown into hell."

That is pretty severe, since most of us look at anything with both eyes and both eyes are necessary for perspective, parallax and judging distance. Presumably if the left eye was equally offensive, Jesus would want you to pluck that out also to prevent a one-way direct flight to hell.

Sticking to the Jesus quote, a similar terrible punishment exists for sinning with your hand, according to a following passage in Matthew 5:30. Here, Jesus says, "And if your right hand causes you to sin, cut it off and throw it away. It is better for you to lose one part of your body than for your whole body to go into hell." But then it is our brain that causes us to move our bodily voluntary muscles such as hands, arms, legs and such.

Just how a right hand alone could cause sinning is questionable, unless it is involved with stealing something, unfairly striking or hitting someone, or commits some other act considered sinful. If the hand sins, it should be cut off and thrown away, according to the Bible. But it is really the brain that is controlling the rest of our body. Our hands are innocent.

Quite frankly, many would agree that being blind or half-blind and handless or one-handed is a pretty high payment for believing in Jesus. But realize that in this inerrant Word of God, the Bible. There is no wiggle room. So say the fundamentalists.

If these references are meant as a parable, they are disgusting. However, it is dictated as fact — an edict in the Old Testament and an order from Jesus in the New Testament.

It is to be taken literally. Now that is pretty sick.

GODLY CHILD ABUSE IN TEACHING CHRISTIANITY TO CHILDREN

When we think of the horrors of child abuse, we often think of physical damage, torture, denying children those normal activities, pleasures and needs that are necessary and normal in most households.

But there can also be psychological, mental and emotional child abuse. These include unwarranted anger at the child, excessive or violent arguments between parents, being inconsistent with the child or playing adult "mind games" to upset the child.

But it could also be argued that to authoritatively and definitively teach the child something about which there is a great deal of speculation or error is also child abuse. Some things like this are harmless, such as the early concepts about Santa Claus, the Easter Bunny, the Tooth Fairy and similar tales and messages. We also accept our Teddy bears and girls accept dolls, along with stories like Alice in Wonderland and Winnie-the-Pooh wandering through the Hundred Acre Woods. We accept and encourage all this because (wink, wink) we know that it is not true and as they grow, our children will learn that also.

The abuse comes with teaching toddlers as young as one and two about the Bible and Christianity, and teaching it as absolute truth, even if it is a very simplified watered-down version of Bible tales of right and wrong. But we adults (wink, wink) "know" that it is all true and that our children will continue to be brainwashed with more elaborate, fanciful and detailed versions of this long and twisted tale, all of which might be no truer than tales of Santa Claus, the Easter Bunny, the Tooth Fairy, Alice in Wonderland and the Wizard of Oz.

Part of that difference is that with Christianity, the entire story, truth, or fable (you pick) is treated seriously. It is also laced with the fear of death, and the awful thought that an alternative view would tragically hurt our loving parents. It mars the minds of the young with the vague but promised pleasures of an impossible heaven or the tortures and pain of hell after death. Once the hooks are in the brains of toddlers and their mental capacity warped, no one ever lets go or suggests another alternative story or even a non-story.

That's abuse. A fair and even approach would be to leave kids alone until they are of adult age of 18 or 21, and then allow them to pick and choose their religion if they wish, based on their thoughts, learning, concepts and experiences. Better still would be to forget religion and to face life full on with all the variables of life experiences.

Would children grow up believing in religion, or a particular religion, if they were not conditioned early on by their parents taking them to brainwashing Bible camps and Sunday school classes? Does youthful Christian teaching equal child abuse?

Jesus, Fables, Christianity, Chickens, Horrible Fires And Belief

"There was once a farmyard," the young male Sunday School teacher began, speaking softly in the classroom-like area. "In this farmyard there was a chicken coop — a chicken house (we were little — I was about seven — we might not have known what a "coop" was), where there were lots of chickens and their little baby chicks.

"'Peep, peep, peep!' The little chicks were all saying. They were all happy.

"One day the chicken house caught on fire. It was a terrible, horrible fire and it burned down the chicken house.

"In this terrible fire, all the chickens were engulfed by flames and horribly burned and killed. After the fire was over, there was movement of the burned wings of one dead chicken. Out from under the stiff burned wings of this dead, blackened chicken came all of this chicken's little chicks.

"These little baby chicks were protected by the hen — their Momma — so that they would not burn up. She protected them under her wings, even while she was being horribly burned and killed.

"All those little chicks survived. See boys and girls, that is how Jesus Christ protects us. He died for our sins. He gave up his life and was crucified 2,000 years ago to save us through his gift of salvation. Jesus Christ is just like that chicken in saving her little chicks. Jesus Christ has saved us if we only believe. We have to believe in Jesus Christ and his saving grace to gain Salvation and go to heaven."

I was terribly upset. Even when I was little, I liked animals — barnyard animals, wild animals, pets, dogs and cats, raccoons, birds, fish, lions, ants, butterflies, goats and yes, chickens.

I did not give a hoot about Jesus Christ. I was upset about the burned chicken. And I am still upset about the chicken story, even though it was an obvious fable.

In a very real way my care for the chicken and disinterest in Jesus made sense. It still makes sense in this fictional story. That chicken put its life on the line — to protect its offspring — the baby chicks. In this fable, those baby chicks lived as a result of the direct and immediate action taken by the chicken.

The story about Jesus did not — does not — make any sense. Jesus did not do anything direct and immediate to save me, as the Sunday School teacher suggested. Jesus did not pull me from a burning building, losing his life in the process. He did not throw me out of the middle of the road with an oncoming bus, him being crushed under the wheels. He did not dive into water to give me his life preserver so that I could live, with him drowning in the process.

He presumably did something — maybe — 2,000 years ago which had nothing to do with me. So what? That chicken impressed me with its dedication and love, even if only instinctual; even if fictional. Jesus did not. The chicken was a real hero; Jesus was and is a sham, a fake.

In my early teens, I formally and officially left the church, and I was the first to do so in that church. That was a long time ago. I never looked back

Jesus, Church, Sermons, Lunch, A Price, Proselytizing, And Chicken Salad

I went to church yesterday. I often go since it keeps my wife happy. It also gives me ammunition for my atheistic writing, articles and possibly books. All of this writing is on the problems with religion and specifically Christianity. It is a never ending subject.

Naturally, I can only hit the tip of the iceberg with the many, many problems with religion, Christians and Christianity.

The church visit yesterday was no exception to my past expectations of visits to other churches. The sermon on Christianity and Science was interesting, well done from a logistical view but also a little disappointing and certainly a slick con job. But my wife was happy and I got some ammo.

What I did not know was that my wife had signed us up for a lunch immediately after the service. I knew that there would be "price." I just did not know that it would be three hours of pastor-proselytizing and a 101 introduction to Christianity and that church. It was slow, pedantic and very boring, despite a somewhat charismatic minister.

The arrangement was to have the collected and confused seated at round tables, eight to a table and each table with a "mentor" or church spokesperson to herd us along towards delusional Christianity and that particular church. The pastor gave the sales pitch. It was sort of like one of those free luncheons or dinners that you go to when being sold stocks, bonds, retirement homes, time shares in property, assisted living insurance policies, pork belly futures, etc.

At each table we were to give the others our names and family history, our occupation or interest, what we would do with a free Saturday, how we found this church, our relationship with God, and what we would ask God if we could.

My answers beyond the obvious were my occupation as a writer and photographer, that on a Saturday I would do whatever my wife wanted to do, I came to the church with some slight coercion from my wife and that I have no relationship with a fictional God.

My question for God was simple. "Prove yourself." Nobody said a word. The mentor was silent and the rest at the table did not know what to say. End of tale — perhaps.

Well, I guess with no explanation and with no booming answer or truly miraculous event from God in that room, we all know the answer to that one.

On the other hand, the lunch of a chicken salad wrap and potato salad side was pretty good. It was just came at a high price.

Is God A Mass Murderer?

To believe that the Bible is the literal Word of God as to the events of that time period, you would have to look with horror at the book of Joshua. Joshua is a history of the Israelites conquering of the land of Canaan and all the peoples dwelling there.

In Joshua 1:2, God commands that Joshua and crew should cross the Jordan River into the land (Canaan) that the Lord is "giving" to the Israelites. This is despite the fact that from an earthly standpoint that land already belonged to and was inhabited by the Canaanites.

Clearly, the Israelites planned for war as mentioned in Joshua 4:13 where it states that 40,000 armed advance troops crossed to the plains of Jericho to do battle.

This is followed by the well-known scene of Joshua's soldiers marching around the city once a day for six days and on the seventh day marching around seven times, blowing a trumpet and causing the walls of Jericho to fall down so that the soldiers could enter and destroy the city.

What follows, from any standpoint, is sickening. "They devoted the city to the Lord and destroyed with the sword every living thing in it — men and women, young and old, cattle, sheep and donkeys." (Joshua 6:21)

This was not the end of it however, since the Israelites through God's orders did the same thing with over 30 additional Canaanite cities. In each case they destroyed and killed not only all defending soldiers, but also all innocent men, women, babies, children, teenagers, old men, old women, the crippled, the infirm, the sick, the pregnant, fetuses, and wounded, along with all cattle and other domestic animals.

Joshua 12:9–24 lists the kings of 31 cities and their inhabitants that were destroyed. The rest of Joshua lists the disposition of treasures that were all to go to the Lord and the "Lord's treasury." (Joshua 6:19).

Looked at honestly and realistically, this means that all these thousands — tens of thousands — of peaceful, non-warring, innocent Canaanites were killed — murdered — as per orders from God. This included people of any age and gender, all totally innocent, all killed without any valid reason or justification.

What does this do to the reputation of God as a loving, caring deity? Does this not make God intolerant (at the very least) to promise these lands to the Israelites then kill all others living there? Does this not make God at least highly questionable as to the so-called love and care of God as postulated in the Bible and promulgated by Christians? Was God a mass murderer?

Do We Atheists Have To Prove That God Does Not Exist? Nope!

One of the confused Christian challenges to atheists, agnostics, those of other religions and skeptics when confronted about the reality of God is to insist that the questionable or non-believers "prove" that God does not exist.

We don't have to. You have it wrong, Bunky. A basis of reason and logic is that no one has to prove the lack of something; others (believers in this case) have to prove the existence of something.

I do not believe in the existence of pixies, fairies, trolls, ghosts, leprechauns, dragons, elves (Christmas or otherwise), unicorns, winged horses (Pegasus or Buraq who took Muhammed to heaven to visit Allah), goblins, demons, Cerberus (the three-headed dog of mythology), etc. And I do not have to prove that they do not exist. There is no evidence for the proof of any of them. They do not exist, they are fictional, they are myths, and they were invented by mankind. If you believe in these, then you have to prove that they do exist.

In the same way, there is no proof of God or a god or deity of any religion. If you believe in a God, then you have to provide the proof of his existence. And don't start telling me that the Bible proves it. Don't start telling me that I have to prove that God does not exist.

Who wrote the Bible, according to the Judeo-Christian faiths? God wrote it and God is in the Bible. That's a circular argument. And don't start telling me that some prayer was answered somewhere so that proves that there is a God, because prayer can't be proven and does not work either.

Don't give me all the other lame reasons why there has to be a God. Steven Hawking said recently that the universe does not need and has never needed a God and you have to give Hawking some credence.

Don't point to "miracles" of the New or Old Testaments for proof, since they are not much different than the myth of the birth of Alexander after his mother was impregnated by a snake or the god Minerva being formed from the head of Jupiter, another god. Oblique references, old myths, old miracles and old fables are weak, tired and false. They just will not work.

Things that work well or go right in the world are not proof of God. Good people doing good things are not proof of God, but only that people can do good, regardless of their faith, religion or lack of it.

People saved and rescued in a tornado, hurricane, tsunami or the like are not evidence of a God or God's benevolence, but only that God, if one exists, could have perhaps rearranged the forces of nature to prevent any deaths that so often occur in these destructive events.

Or perhaps that God is as quixotic as a 16-year-old girl planning her first prom date.

Want people to believe in a God — your God? Prove it. Go ahead — prove it.

A 3-In-One Oil Makes Sense — A 3-In-One God Does Not Make Sense

As a youth I went to Sunday School in a Protestant church. My parents insisted, inculcated as they were from their own youthful indoctrination and brainwashing into their particular delusional sect of the Christian religion.

I never did then — and still don't today — understand the concept of a 3-in-one god. I know about "3-IN-ONE" oil (lubricates, stops rust, protects metal) which has been around since 1894, but I don't and didn't know how you could get three people or gods into one, or why you would want to.

As a youth, I remember wondering if Jesus was talking to himself when he was talking to God, when Jesus was hanging on the cross. If Jesus and God are the same, how can Jesus be the bad God of the Old Testament, going around and killing everybody, and then the "good God" of the New Testament, forgiving everybody for anything and everything?

If God was pleased with Jesus, does that mean that he was pleased with himself? How come Christianity is not considered a polytheistic religion, since there are three Gods, or three parts to one God, or three different philosophies or religions in one, or something? I don't get it.

If the Holy Ghost (Holy Spirit, Spirit of God) was in the Old Testament beginning in Genesis 1:2, where was Jesus? Did Jesus have to hold off, waiting in the wings, until the New Testament? Did that make for a dualistic God in the Old Testament and then the three-in-one God of the New Testament?

What does the Holy Ghost or Holy Spirit do? Does he/she/it have a job? I can see that the job of God is to run the world and universe and that Jesus' job is to save mankind (all according to Christian beliefs, of course) but what does the Holy Spirit do? Really?

Does this mean that the Holy Ghost is the sidekick of God, just the way that Little Beaver, Gabby Hayes/Andy Devine and Smiley Burnette played the second banana and doofus/goofus buddies to Red Ryder, Roy Rogers and Gene Autry respectively in the 1940s cowboy movies? On second thought, I don't think that God would want a bumbling sidekick.

But then if God is omnipotent, why would God need an assistant in the Holy Spirit or Holy Ghost arena anyway? It is all very confusing.

It is all very mixed up, not that there will ever be any conclusion or satisfactory answer to all of this casserole of different beliefs and confused thinking that makes up the Bible. But it is something for a serious skeptic to think about.

TEACHING AND LEARNING IN SUNDAY SCHOOL

I am not sure that Sunday School in a Protestant church helped me that much. As I view it now, Sunday School was a waste of time.

In fact, later in life I probably could have done a talk "What I did not learn in Sunday School," along the lines of the "what I did during summer vacation" that we as children often had to recite upon returning to school each fall.

Here goes — what I did not learn in Sunday School:

- I did not learn that there are no longer any originals of the Bible, or originals of the important four gospels. I did not learn that we have only copies of copies of copies of copies — all subject to mistakes and errors in copying.

- I did not learn that the more religious an area, state, country or group is, the greater the likelihood (or higher percentage) of child abuse, domestic abuse, animal abuse, petty crime, rape, childhood pregnancy, illiteracy, high school drop-outs, out of wedlock pregnancy, etc. That is true of US states and also foreign countries.

- I did not learn that as a general rule, the less schooling a person has, the greater the religious fervor.

- I did not learn that there is no anguish by religious folk that the Ten Commandments left out an admonition against slavery. In fact, the idea of slavery and owning another human was endorsed in the Old Testament and basically ignored in the New Testament and by Jesus.

- I did not learn that the ritual of worship and church service is not from the Bible or God, but from man-made ideas that have little to do with religion and worship; more to do with a show and getting that tithe money.

- I did not learn that prayer really does not work, and that no valid scientific studies have ever shown it to work.

- I did not learn that there is little information — almost none — on heaven and hell, despite the heavy religious emphasis on it as a carrot and stick — reward or punishment — in a supposed important but fictional afterlife.

- I did not learn that there are many errors and contradictions in the Bible.

- I did not learn that "original sin" is a man-made confection — if you can call it that — and that the concept of original sin was not codified by theologians until the Second Council of Orange in 529 CE. Original sin is not listed in the Bible.

- I did not learn that the concept of a Trinity — God, Jesus and the Holy Ghost — did not arrive on the scene until it was codified by the Nicene Creed, decided upon in 325 CE.

Perhaps it is no wonder that I did not care about the Bible or Jesus or religion or saints or miracles, or virgin birth or Ten Commandments, etc. The only wonder is that more people do not at some point start to look at the teachings of their youth, ask questions, become skeptical and check the facts of beliefs and Bibles, pastors and priests.

A Crushing Blow From God — Or So God Says

One of the favorites of the fundamentalists is to point to someone — often in their family or a friend — who is not a Christian and thus does not agree with their particular brand of delusion. "God is going to bring you down to your knees," they say, often with a fair amount of hostility and venom and sometimes some finger shaking. And they are going to be really, really glad of it when God crushes that person — perhaps you or me — and brutally teaches you or me about God's importance. Yeah, I've gotten that.

They want that family member or dear friend to be crushed, broken (another favorite word), destroyed, or ruined because that friend/family member is not agreeing with the religious bunkum being offered up and sold as snake oil. What about the love, care, understanding, forgiveness and tolerance of Christianity? I guess that we can forget that with these Christians who obviously through their actions hate their fellow man.

If this were not so serious in the mind of the religionists, it would be funny. It is funny because this punishment by God does not happen, has never happened, and will never happen. It is sad also because in a right and wrong, black and white world, it would be nice if something like that could happen to bad people. But then we would have to worry about who is making the decisions of right/wrong, black/white and if they are looking at it from truly moralistic standpoint or as just cockeyed views of the latest sermon from their pastor.

There would be room to debate this kind of punishment if we were talking about cruel and barbarous humans, but that is not the case. Life often visits crushing blows on the good just as readily as the bad. (As a side note — that ought to also prove that prayer does not work!)

A close-by example is a friend of the family who has some serious spinal problems, even though he is a good person. His father was a pastor, and also presumably a good person. The question then is: what did this good person do to irritate God to the extent that God would curse him with serious spinal problems that for a time even prevented walking? What did he do to piss off God?

When asked of those of the "bring him to his knees" ilk, they somehow stumble, mumble and bumble that this individual is doing OK now, he is better, he just got a new house or some other weak-kneed (pardon the pun) sorry explanation that does not really explain anything.

Let's have these crushing blows of life happen only to the bad guys like murderers, child molesters, robbers, drug dealers, dictators, rapists, wife beaters, and the truly evil. Let's leave the good, caring, kind, benevolent people alone. Were that to happen, it might give people pause and something to think about when it comes to God, religion and worship.

It doesn't. So it is far more likely that God just doesn't care or is not there anyway. Think about it.

THE PROS AND CONS OF ANIMAL SACRIFICES

God surely dislikes the animals that he placed here on earth, all according to Genesis. God always wanted his chosen people, the Israelites, to offer burnt animal offerings or animal sacrifices.

I would hate to have the task of counting up the sacrifices or the numbers and types of animals killed throughout the Bible. But it was a bunch. Almost every chapter of this massive book has animals being killed, slaughtered, sliced, diced, cut, chopped, dismembered, skinned, filleted, disemboweled, beheaded, divided in half lengthwise, cooked, incinerated, burned, grilled, barbequed, etc.

But you have to wonder why. Why would God need this, or why would he require such a sacrifice? Oh sure, I can hear the Christianists now. "It's not for God, silly. It's for us. It's to help us remember God and worship God. God wants us to show that we're willing to give up something for him."

Say again? Say what? And this is supposed to make sense? OK, then why aren't we using animal sacrifice today, other than in a few religions such as the Santeria religion of West Africa and the Caribbean (and in the US) where such sacrifice is still quietly (sometimes illegally) practiced? Did God change his mind for the rest of us? Did he forget to tell us? Did we not get the memo?

And if you can't remember your God any better than with an animal sacrifice, did the Israelites really have a good, Godly belief? Or was it just fake and posturing to please this invisible sky guy? How about living a good life, following the Ten Commandments of Exodus? In the New Testament, how about following the life of Christ and his Golden Rule? Wouldn't that work and be better for the tribe, church, society and fellow humans?

Animal sacrifice? We are talking God here. He — if you believe in this God — does not eat or require food, although he does — for some strange reason — like the smell of burnt flesh. God must have a different olfactory system than the rest of the made-in-his-image people scurrying around earth.

Check Genesis 8:21, Leviticus 1:17 and Leviticus 17:6 for some examples of God enjoying burnt animal odors.

The point is — or should be — why? In that age of nomadic peoples, animals represented security, wealth, value. Would it not be a better use of those animals to charitably give a small flock to the poor so that they could start being contributing members of society?

Would it not be better to cook these animals for the ancient history equivalent of a soup kitchen or homeless shelter meal? Since there is no evidence of God coming to earth to gobble up these burnt offerings, these animal sacrifices were nothing more than a waste.

What did these early nomadic peoples get from such a waste? Even then, they should have had better sense about the use of property other than to burn it up for an invisible god? Was anybody thinking back then? Is anybody thinking today? Shouldn't this make one skeptical?

MATERIAL SACRIFICES FOR AN IMMATERIAL GOD. NOW, THAT DOES NOT MAKE MUCH SENSE!

If there is anything more ridiculous than God wanting animal sacrifices from his people, the Israelites, then it would be God wanting riches such as fine cloth, precious metals, coin of the realm, and such.

And God surely did want this stuff. Just check Joshua 6:17 for this. Joshua, following God's orders and speaking of Jericho, said, "The city and all that is in it are to be devoted to the Lord." Then Joshua said, "All the silver and gold and the articles of bronze and iron are sacred to the Lord and must go into his treasury." Wait — God had a treasury? I didn't know!

Naturally, this happened except for a Babylonian robe, two hundred shekels of silver and a wedge of gold stolen from God's cache by Achan. Achan was caught with the stolen items. He, his sons and daughters and even cattle and donkeys, were killed by stoning for this act of disobedience. That's petty harsh.

Then they were all burned, including the robe. But the gold and silver would have survived — you can't burn up gold and silver by methods available to these nomads. What did God do with it? Nothing, it seems. There is no mention of the use or possible good works of any of this Godly treasure anywhere in the Bible. But I have an idea here. . .

The Levites, one of the twelve tribes of Israel, were the priestly class and involved with all the religious aspects of the Israelites and early Judaism. It would have fallen into their safe keeping, and one can only imagine how safely they kept it.

There are references in many Bibles suggesting that the treasures devoted to God and given to God's treasury were often destroyed as a sacrifice to God. This presumably refers to both material goods farm animals and animal sacrifices, along with people all of whom are killed.

That's a complete waste and a human horror, but apparently common in the Old Testament. Reference is also made (Joshua 8:27) of the Israelites taking plunder for themselves and God, "as the Lord had instructed Joshua."

In another battle, God specifically ordered destruction of property. God said in Joshua 11:6, "You are to hamstring their horses and burn their chariots." Well, that was kindda hard on the innocent horses which had the tendons in their back legs cut so that they could not walk, run, forage or feed. It is sort of a slow death sentence.

The bottom line of all this sacrifice for an invisible spirit-god is totally absurd. God, if God were really real, could have his choice of millions of tons of precious metals such as gold, silver, platinum, etc., from billions of planets and stars. But what would he do with it?

For God to pick on us is like stealing from a beggar. Shame on him.

Newspaper Delivery And Godly Religious Tithing

As have many people in their youth, I served newspapers after school to make extra money. Each day, Monday through Saturday, I served newspapers to 220 households.

These were individual households, not the envied apartment routes of other newsboys. In those, you could enter the main door, pick up your papers and leave a newspaper in front of the subscribing doors by walking up and down each apartment floor. You didn't even have to fold the papers.

You were dry when it was raining, cool when it was hot, warm when it was freezing, and comfortably strolling along when there was two feet of snow outdoors. It was a snap job, quick to do and without the discomforts of being outside.

I was outside through blistering heat, drenching rain, piled up snow, hail, winds that made throwing the paper difficult, if not impossible. I learned many ways to fold a paper, depending upon the number of pages. Wednesday, with the many store ads that bulked up the paper, was the only day that we deigned to use rubber bands, otherwise the mark of a lazy newsboy or a beginner who did not know how to fold papers. We carried our papers with a strap, not a bag, not a bicycle basket and we walked the route.

For this work, approximately 1-1/2 hours per day of rapid walking in all kinds of weather, I was paid $3.00 per week or 0.50 cents per day. Yep, this was a long time ago.

From this, my mother wanted me to tithe (ten percent) to the church. The idea was that I "owed" it to the church, to God, to the Bible edict, to the congregation, to society. I figured it differently.

I figured that it was going to a church about which I cared nothing at all, where there was preaching about a God in which I was extremely doubtful, where they were selling the baby Jesus, because of a Bible that I questioned. The preaching was to a congregation that looked very well-to-do in their Sunday finery. I didn't think that my contribution of 0.30 cents per week or $15.60 annually would make that much difference.

Sometimes, succumbing to my Mom's wishes and completely abandoning any principles, I would contribute a little, but not much, and that on an infrequent basis.

I think that it was the time when I delivered papers through a hurricane, with limbs falling off trees all around me, that I took a stand. I decided that God was not out there in the weather, wind and rain with me, he was not going to deflect a falling tree limb aimed my way and that I deserved to keep all of the 0.30 cents tithe money that I made that week.

With that, along with increasing disbelief, disinterest and even disgust with religion, I left the church. Mom was not pleased; I was delighted. No more guilt and no more paying out hard-earned money to those who did not deserve it. Skepticism had started in my brain some years before when I was 8 or 9. Maybe, just maybe, with the 220 newspapers, the 0.50 cents per day, the rain, the hurricane and no God at least holding an umbrella over my head, some serious atheism took hold then.

SHOULD YOU BLASPHEME ON SEPTEMBER 30? AFTER ALL, IT'S INTERNATIONAL BLASPHEMY RIGHTS DAY!

I don't know when you are reading this, but remember that September 30 is International Blasphemy Rights Day, according to some semi-serious Web sites along with some highly virulent ones. The idea is to project and protect the idea of free speech, perhaps some skepticism about religion, and the ability and right to say what you want when and where you want. Including blasphemy.

Of course, you have to be respectful as to the time, place and event involved in which to use blasphemy and to whom if anyone you want to blaspheme.

And of course you always want (to protect yourself) to check out the laws regarding blasphemy and cursing in your locality, or even nationally, given the efforts of some areas and countries to make blasphemy a crime.

Of course, there are various ways to upset people with free speech. Blasphemy by a dictionary definition is the strongest of several terms and specifically means any remark or statement that would be mocking or contemptuous of God or even a god.

Profanity extends this to remarks regarding a person of thing. Swearing and cursing refer to comments that are profane and not accepted in polite society.

The skeptical will accept this and use this freedom wisely and judiciously and maybe mocking God a little. Of course, the religious will usually look at this like a one-way street, as they do everything else. If you blaspheme against them or their God, they will get a decided twist in their knickers. Otherwise, it is OK. Mock Krishna, Thor, Osiris, Buddha, Shiva, Horus, Ra (or Re), Vishnu or others and it is probably OK.

Being basically intolerant, Christians will not be bothered one whit if they or you blaspheme or make fun of something else or some other god or religion. Thus, I might speak of a nut, or cashews or filberts, or people being "nutty" and no one will be bothered by this.

That's unless of course they still worship ancient Egyptian gods. If memory serves me, Nut was the goddess of the sky and also of cows in early Egyptian religion.

Similarly, people today use the word/non-word "frigg" or "frigging" as a semi-acceptable substitute for a much more crude curse word derived from Old English. It is the word that you see in print and on TV and hear on radio in place of the real original word.

This assumes that no one knows that you are partly blaspheming, since Frigg was the supreme goddess of Norse gods and ruled over the godly city of Asgard. Now, here we are using it both as a semi-sanitized curse in English while at the same time expressing blasphemy for those good ole Norse gods.

Sometimes, it seems, it is possible to get a two-for-one deal in the blasphemy and cursing department. Enjoy the day and stay skeptical.

HOW LONG IS ETERNITY? FOREVER? DOES THAT MAKE SENSE? NAH, I DIDN'T THINK SO EITHER!

Eternity. It is a word thrown about casually in religion and Christianity, just as the term "blue-light special" used to be thrown around in a K-Mart store. Or the term "price roll-back" is used in a Wal-Mart. Or the gleeful term "happy hour" is used daily in many bars.

Ministers and priests use the terms forever, eternal, unchanging, perpetual, timeless, etc., in describing both heaven and hell. Take your pick, they all argue, using the ultimate argument in their religious sales pitch. You are going to heaven or hell. Pick one. One or the other. Forever, eternally. It is the ultimate carrot-and-stick argument, the joys of the heavenly carrot or the punishment of the stick-beating hell.

What these minions of the cloth do not realize is that we humans can't wrap our minds around the idea of something "forever." Oh, maybe Steven Hawking can, with his latest book *The Grand Design*, but the rest of us can't.

Once some visiting missionaries of the Jehovah's Witness or Seventh Day Adventist type wanted to talk to me about heaven and eternity. I told them that I had a question first.

"Describe to me a piece of string with one end," I posed to them. They looked quizzically at each other, not understanding the question.

"Look," I started, "we die. Eternity starts there, just like one end of a piece of string." They agreed. "And it continues on, just as the piece of string continues on." They agreed again.

"If it goes on forever — as in eternity — then there is no end, just as there is no end to a piece of string. Explain that to me."

They looked quizzical again and were never able to answer my question. They left shortly after running out of questions and not at all liking my comments or answers. Everything has to have a beginning and an end.

We think of the earth as being about 4.5 billion years old, life starting about 3.5 billion years ago, the universe about 13.7 billion years old, with all of these figures plus or minus a few million years here and there, depending upon the scientist studying them. We can't even wrap our minds around these figures.

Look under the umbrella of religion and Christianity and you have to believe in the eternal life of salvation through Jesus. But does that make sense? When this does not make sense, can anything else make sense in the Bible, in religion, in Christianity, in Jesus, in the resurrection, in salvation? Is it all suspect as it must be if one of the Domino pieces in this long chain crumbles apart?

Isn't it a lot more comfortable and satisfying to be a skeptic and questioning of all this, rather than buying the pig in a poke that religion ultimately becomes and in fact always has been?

IDOLATRY IS NOT SO GOOD — BUT WHO IS DEFINING THIS ANYWAY?

Idolatry in Christianity and Judaism is specifically forbidden by the First and Second Commandments. Specifically, it says "Thou shalt have no other gods before me" and "Thou shalt not make unto you any graven image." In Islam, idolatry in imagery is also forbidden and even more restrictive than in Christianity and Judaism. Just ask some Danish cartoonists.

In Christianity, Catholicism and Protestant faiths differ a tad on this, but both include as non-idolatry various pictures and images that represent the holy family of Jesus, Mary, Joseph, and various saints and apostles. The Catholic faith is also heavy on images of Mary while Protestants seldom if ever use this imagery. Islam prohibits all images as being idolatrous or sinful.

Exact definitions of all this to suit all purposes are a little difficult, sort of like trying to nail Jell-O to the wall. The dictionary usually has a definition of something like "an image of a god, used as an object or instrument of worship, sometimes said of any heathen deity." Tied in with this is the excessive devotion, admiration and worship of such an image or object.

Idols are usually man-made and thus have no life traits of humans. They can be made of anything — a painting or drawing, or crafted of any material be it silver or stone, platinum, papier-mâché or road tar. Under the right circumstances, the Tar Baby of the 1880 Uncle Remus stories about Br'er Fox and Br'er Rabbit could have been an idol.

In addition, many faiths consider the gods of other faiths as "idols" in contrast to their own symbolic or fashioned god or God, which for that particular faith is the only true God. Thus, any concept of another God is not looked upon tolerantly, but only as an idolatrous belief that deserves scorn and punishment.

Whether or not something is an idol depends upon the use to which it is put by the religious. Is it strictly a reminder to be good and holy, to say prayers at a certain time of the day for a specific purpose? Is it an object of worship, to be bowed to, venerated or the subject of money, material or animal sacrifices? The answers either make it a thing or a god, depending upon the religious person or worshiper.

What makes this interesting is the vagueness of any real definition of an idol, and the difficulty of trying to describe how it is used. If an object becomes or is considered for worship or constant veneration, it is an idol. If not, it is not an idol and fine for that particular faith. But all these nuances of objects tying into a religion make one wonder just how "religious" religion really is anyway. Sometimes you just have to be a skeptic about it all.

GOD'S SCHEDULE, SLIPS, FALLS, WET TILE FLOORS, BROKEN HIPS AND ACCIDENTS

Accidents happen. One happened to a friend of my wife recently when she slipped in a bath house at a swimming beach and ended up with a broken hip. Wet after taking a shower, this friend slipped in a slight puddle on the tile floor. After a stint in a hospital and with some surgery, she ended up mended, but with a severe need of a walker, cane and crutches.

She had all of these from her insurance which covered the accident, but a second set of equipment would allow her to use these aids on the second floor of her home. She is single and lives alone.

My family had all of the above ambulatory devices on hand after some previous injuries in our household, and we kept those items that might prove useful in the future for us or for others. Another friend had recently used these and returned them to us.

We took the items to our friend and were glad to have them to help her. She is a devout Christian woman, one who, like many, has a plethora of small religious plaques and framed religious pictures around her house. These are with the typical blessings and sayings that we all know from being exposed to them throughout our lives in the homes of family, friends, and acquaintances.

While we were at her home, my wife and I tried to do small things at her request to help her, arrange things to aid her during her period of convalescence, and to complete some small chores to make her recovery time easier.

We finally completed what we had come to do and were ready to leave. When we were leaving, this devout Christian woman was thanking us for our help and also thanking God for healing. As I recall, there were no thanks for the doctors, hospital, surgeons and nursing staff that got her mended and on the way to recovery and on the way home where she would rest and heal.

As we left, her final comment on receiving the items that we had brought and on other needs was, "The Lord always provides."

My thinking at the time was that if God really, really, really provided, perhaps a few days earlier he would have noticed the puddle of water in the bathhouse and mopped it up. That way, God could have prevented this accident, bad fall and broken hip. That would have been better — a good thing. But that is just me and my skeptical thinking.

I guess that God was busy elsewhere.

OK GOD — IT IS UP TO YOU AND YOUR FRIENDS, THE RELIGIONISTS — WHERE IS THE BEEF? I'M WAITING. . .

A 1984 TV ad for Wendy's fast food restaurants featured actress Clara Peller asking "Where's the beef?" after being shown a hamburger from a fictional Wendy's competitor. The competitor, known as the "Home of the Big Bun" featured a big fluffy bun topped with a small hamburger.

So I am asking religionists of all types, "Where's the beef?" Where is the beef in your religion? Where is the proof, where are the facts, where is the substance, where is the beef of your claims? What claims do you have anyway?

Where is the proof of a heaven and/or hell that are the carrot and stick of your belief in a God, salvation and hereafter? Sure, you can note that heaven and hell are mentioned in the Bible (over 600 times for heaven, some 50 times for hell, all depending upon your translation), but where is the proof?

And don't give me the Bible for proof. That is a circular argument at best and ridiculous at worst. Nobody ever — EVER — came back from heaven; no crispy critters have shown up from hell.

Where are the miracles that you constantly reference as "proof" of your God, your religion, your belief? "The Miracle at the Mine" (CBS) or "the Miner Miracle" (ABC), with the rescue of the trapped Chilean miners at Copiapo in October 2001, was nothing more than headline-grabbing advertising hype that references the excellent technology and expertise of several countries that resulted in finding a way to accomplish the deed and, fortunately, get all 33 miners out safely.

Despite the claims of miracles, God and faith, it was the hardhats and engineers at the site who accomplished this deed. They should get the credit, not the "miracle" of God. There are no miracles anywhere, any time, and I challenge you to prove — yes, prove scientifically — otherwise.

Some constantly say that there are no errors or contradictions in the Bible. Yet books and substantial parts of other books have been written outlining the failures of those claims, the errors of the Bible, the contradictions in this written "inerrant Word of God," the Bible.

Where is your evidence that prayer works? If prayer — as it seems to be — is so important and vital in your religious life, why do you not insist — yes insist — on tests to prove the efficacy of both personal and intercessory prayer?

Why aren't you out there screaming for a test, an experiment, a gauge, something — of the proof of prayer? You know that you are not doing this — and why you can't. It is because there is no proof, there is no test result that backs up the fable of the prayer that you want to believe. You can't prove what is not true, not provable, and not factual.

There are only proofs that prayer does not work and that any efforts to show otherwise are only a waste of time, a waste of effort and a proof of the failure of faith, the ridiculous of religion.

Go ahead — I'll wait here while you check your Bible, check your studies, check your books and concordances, check with your ministers and priests and rabbis and imams to convince me that I am wrong. I am just afraid that I might have a long wait for the proof of anything on the religious front.

Should I wait?

You Don't Need God And Religion To Do The Right Thing And To Be Ethical And Moral

You don't need God or religion for morals and ethics, despite what the preachers and priests tell you. Morals and ethics have been around long before there was any Judeo-Christian religion. You don't need religion to do the right thing.

I have friends who are atheists, agnostics, humanists, secularists, I-don't-carers, Catholics, retired Catholics, lapsed Catholics, Lutherans, Baptists, Presbyterians, semi-Presbyterians, Episcopalians, Methodists, former Methodists, others. I know that all — religious or not — could have and would have done the same thing in the story that follows.

It was the period of the late 1950s and 1960s during the height of the civil rights conflict: posters and sit-ins, police dogs and fire hoses, marches in Selma and Birmingham, bus boycotts, church bombings, tear gas, Freedom Riders, H. Rap Brown and Stokely Carmichael, Dr. Martin Luther King and the 101st Airborne with fixed bayonets to open schools in the South to blacks.

During this time, I was teaching, south of the Mason-Dixon Line, at a state university medical school and it was the summer — no students. My boss assigned me to monitor state prisoners — all black — who over a period of days were delivering custom prison-made furniture for special laboratory needs.

On the third day of my directing these prisoners and while we were all eating lunch,, one of them asked to speak to me privately. We did. He explained that he had been in prison several months too long and that his paperwork had been lost. He had served his time and wanted to get out and start rebuilding his life. He was regretful for the mistake that he had made.

"Mr. Boyd," he said, using the Southern method of respect of addressing an elder (we were both young) or authority figure. "Could you help me? I've served my time and been in prison months too long."

His state-appointed lawyer could not/would not help. He was from out-of-state and had no local family. His few friends could not/would not help him. No one in prison would listen to him. The guards and warden ignored him. He was lost in a bureaucracy. He seemed sincere.

I got from him all the necessary information — his full name, inmate number, prison, cell number, crime, name of the judge, sentencing court, sentence, time entering prison, time that his sentence should have been served, etc.

After lunch I called the judge. I explained everything, including my relationship with this case — just trying to do the right thing. I gave him all the information that I had. The judge took my name and a phone number and said that he would get back to me.

The call came later that same day, after the inmates had returned to prison. "I checked into it, and your prisoner is right," he began. He was a good judge, obviously interested in people and true justice. He further explained that he had thoroughly checked it out and had already sent orders through the system for the prisoner to be released immediately.

The next morning, the same prisoners were delivering another batch of furniture. The subject of my phone calls was absolutely beaming, joyous, and delirious with happiness. Deferentially, because of our totally separate positions and races, he almost hugged me. He was getting out — the next day.

"Mr. Boyd," he burst out, "I can't thank you enough. You helped me when no one else would even listen to me. I'll come to your house every week and mow your lawn, landscape your property, help you do anything. Just tell me what you want! You saved my life!"

I thanked him but of course refused his offer. You don't help someone for reward or gain. You help because it is the right thing to do. I did ask him to go on the straight and narrow and to never — never again — commit a crime or end up in prison. He promised that he would.

Race relations that day between us — in the middle of civil unrest and riots — could not have been better. I never heard from him again and only hope that his life has been good. Then and now, I wish him well.

Got A "Personal Relationship With Jesus"? Uh-Oh. This Could Be Trouble

You have to have a personal relationship with Jesus, so say the so-called born-again Christians. Jesus loves you, Jesus knows you, and Jesus wants a personal relationship with you. Really. He is watching out for you every minute of every day. Really.

Really? How? How are you going to do that when there is no evidence at all of a Jesus, a living, breathing God or Jesus, a talking, walking Jesus and son of God? I have personal relationships with friends. We talk, visit, correspond, and communicate to cement these relationships. We enjoy mutual interests together, backyard barbeques, mutual friend parties, and conversation.

I have personal relationships with friends who are distant, either a few hundred miles away or a few thousand miles away. I write them, call them, talk to them, email them, sometimes fax them, but am in contact with them as best I can, and they do the same with me. Were I to do all the above while receiving no response from them at all, I would not have a personal relationship with them, nor they with me. And it would be a different scenario if I were to continually try to contact them with no response from them.

In that case, I could be an annoyance at best, or I could even be a stalker. We know about stalkers. Often they follow, contact, communicate with and annoy celebrities, most of whom are not acquainted at all with the stalkers and have never knowingly laid eyes on them or communicated with them in any way.

There are also stalkers who do know or who used to know their victims; these often ex-boyfriends or girlfriends from a relationship that has gone south. The extremes of these cases end tragically. The less extreme cases end with a restraining order, or, rarely, somebody coming to his/her senses.

To strive to have a so-called "personal relationship with Jesus" smacks of delusion, if not outright mental illness. I know of a lot of deceased and living people (but I do not know them personally) — the pope, the president, George Clooney, Andy Rooney of CBS, Brian Williams of NBC TV news, Queen Elizabeth, Billy Graham, Larry King, Nancy Pelosi, Bill Gates, Steven Hawking, etc. I have never contacted any of them. In my role as a US citizen, I have over the years written to various presidents, in their roles as president, to suggest some ideas and concerns, but they would not know me if they fell over me. I do not have a personal relationship with them, nor they with me. I do not expect them to take a personal interest in me and I do not stalk any of them.

To think you have a "personal relationship with Jesus" is to delude yourself as to what or who Jesus is, other than perhaps an idea and a flawed figure from history, if that. Hey, those of you with a "personal relationship with Jesus" — you're stalking the guy! It's a One-Way street! Cut it out! You are making yourself look silly and confusing the rest of us. Fortunately, there is nothing — nobody — there to respond with a restraining order. Lucky for you.

Money For Monuments To God Or Money To Truly Help Children — Which Is Best?

My wife, sincerely religious, started going to a new church recently. I accompany her for ammunition for writing. This large church announced a new fundraising drive in which they want to collect in two years $14,200,000. The money will go to building new churches, salaries for staffing said churches, printing Bibles, and other efforts to sell Jesus. Naturally, they look upon this as working for the good of the world by continuing to promote the pie-in-the-sky Jesus-loves-you salvation folly.

This new $14,200,000 effort is anticipated to come from the regular tithe of at least ten percent they expect from their members and from extra donations on top of that. The commitment card on the back of each pew, in the face of those occupying the row behind, states that clearly.

According to the slick sales pitch, they expect you to fill out a card, committing to an amount for your regular annual tithing for the next two years as well as specifying how much additional money you are pledging to this special $14,200,000 effort.

The result will be more churches, more salaries, more video technology (read sales pitch), and more tax deductible material goods circulating, for which both the faithful and the faithless will be paying indirectly since churches and charities do not pay taxes and the rest of us have to make up public spending shortfalls. They think of themselves as "planting churches" as if they were pansies.

This church — or any church — could have requested money for something that would truly change lives and help children. While there are lots of problems in the world, and lots of notable worthwhile charities, I am thinking right now of Operation Smile and Smile Train. You can find them on the Internet. It is easy to calculate the funding for them. These organizations train local doctors in a region and send volunteer doctors to countries to correct cleft palates and lips of kids whose parents or village cannot in any way pay for these operations. The plastic surgery repair improves the lives of these children immediately and forever, giving them a medical, economic and social chance in life otherwise impossible.

The bare-bones cost of each cleft palate operation is $240–$250. That means that a church with $14,200,000 in donations could forget their edifice complex and pay for operations to truly help 56,800 children who are afflicted with disfiguring and crippling facial deformities through no fault of their own.

In other words, this church can pay $14,200,000 for their egos, material things like monuments to themselves. Or they could use the $14,200,000 to give 56,800 children a chance at a decent life. Interesting choice.

Which one would God want, if there is or was a God? Which one would Jesus want, if there is or was a Jesus?

CHRISTIANS VS. NON-BELIEVERS. WHO IS BEST, THE MOST MORAL, THE MOST ETHICAL?

The religious are wonderful people. They are moral, ethical, good and always concerned for their fellow man. Sure. And I am nine feet tall, wealthier than Bill Gates, and plan to run for president during the next election cycle.

I am sure that many Christians are indeed moral, ethical, good and concerned for their fellow man. Many atheists, agnostics, humanists, secularists, and I-don't-carers are also moral, ethical, good and concerned for their fellow man.

However, checking some figures on prison populations shows that perhaps atheists, agnostics and such are a tad better than the rest of the crew. The Federal Bureau of Prisons figures on the religious beliefs of prison inmates may raise some eyebrows.

Surveys of the general population of the United States show that are about 80 percent consider themselves Christians, with atheists about 16% to 20% (up from about 8% in 1990). Atheists, it seems, are gaining ground out here.

Of inmates in Federal prisons, about 39.164% are Catholic, 35.0008% Protestant and another few percent adhere to the Church of Christ, Pentecostals, Jehovah's Witnesses, Adventists and Mormons. The total of various Christians is about 79.499% of the prison population.

About 16%–20% of the general population declare themselves to be atheists, agnostics and other non-believers, although there are probably more. Many do not want to admit their atheism or religion-denying thoughts, due to the extreme prejudice against them and their thinking, in spite of the so-called but fictional tolerance of Christians.

But the big news is that with the current general population of 16% - 20% atheistic or agnostic and etc., the prison population of these non-believers is — wait for it — drum roll — only 0.209%.

That means that those of a skeptical or atheistic ilk are either better, more moral people, are smarter so that they do not get caught, or are careful to avoid capture and charges. Let's assume for the sake of today's argument that they are better, more moral people.

Let the Christians try to explain that one. Sure, I can hear them now, sputtering and stuttering, mumbling and talking to themselves about this. As they do with the Bible, they will probably play hopscotch with the figures, get a social worker or statistician to explain the error of these figures, explain that Christian morality is better than atheistic morality, or something else. Bet on it.

In the meantime, this is just one more reason to become skeptical or remain skeptical about the false but vaunted goodness and moral superiority of Christianity. Christians certainly do not have the high ground when it comes to morality, social mores or folkways and goodness. At least, not when assessed by the Federal Bureau of Prisons populations.

Stay skeptical.

THE PLEDGE OF ALLEGIANCE AND GOD — SHOULD THEY BE LIVING TOGETHER?

You have to wonder what the Founding Fathers — mostly deists — would think about our current Pledge of Allegiance. You know the one. "I pledge allegiance to the flag of the United States of America and to the republic for which it stands, one nation under God, indivisible, with liberty and justice for all."

And Christians are fighting tooth and nail against anyone who suggests changing this original tenet of loyalty to the United States by taking out the "under God" part. That would be fine, except that the pledge as it is now is not — that's *not* — the original at all. For example, the "under God" part, highly questionable in a nation of supposed religious freedom, was added in 1954, the fourth such change from the original of the pledge.

The original pledge was written by Baptist minister Francis Bellamy in 1892 and first published September 8 in the Youth's Companion, a teenagers' magazine. The original pledge was as follows: "I pledge allegiance to my flag and the republic for which it stands, one nation indivisible, with liberty and justice for all."

Bellamy considered adding "equality" and "fraternity" to the pledge, but he was working with a committee of state school superintendents whom he knew would be opposed to suggesting equality and fraternity where women were concerned, not to mention Negroes (as African-Americans were then called). Obviously, the committee with which Bellamy worked did not want that equality and fraternity thing going too far and becoming too fraternal and equal. There was high prejudice then against Negroes, and women did not get the right to vote for another 28 years.

The original pledge, concocted by a man of the cloth, does not include any reference to God at all. Why would we want or need to include God in a basic secular statement of loyalty to our country?

A salute to the flag was promoted at the same time, to go with the pledge, also initiated in 1892. It consisted of the right arm extended, slightly raised, with the palm turned up at the ending of the pledge. In other words, it bore a striking likeness to the Nazi Third Reich "Heil Hitler" salute that came along in the 1930s and 1940s.

President Roosevelt changed this on December 22, 1942, proposing instead that we hold the hand over the heart, with hats removed and in hand (except for religious head coverings). The "under God" section was only pushed through in 1954, and that's how the pledge remains today.

Seems to this skeptic that if you wanted to change something about the pledge, considering that we boast of the separation of church and state in United States, we might consider going back to the original wording or at the very least take out the words "under God."

I'll bet our deist Founding Fathers would be pleased and proud to see us moving back to the basics. Again, why do we need God in a secular pledge?

ARE BRAIN STUDIES DISPROVING THE IDEA OF RELIGION AND CHRISTIANITY? IS RELIGION A MENTAL DELUSION?

As a former anatomist who taught medical students and third-year physical therapy students, I relish when there is something on TV that covers these fields. I was teaching basic gross anatomy along with histology and neuroanatomy. Today, of course, a lot more is known about these two fields of study.

A TV show on cult leaders recently included information on neurology and neuroanatomy along with current studies on people who have megalomania, a fixation as a god or god-like individual, a religious leader with a fixation on the end times and Armageddon.

It turns out, according to current studies, that overstimulation of the temporal lobe (a lobe on each side of the brain) can cause seizure-like activity in the cerebral cortex which in turn can lead to megalomania and the strong belief that a god (or God) is talking to such an individual, and that they have a direct conduit to god along with supreme powers. It also leads to the strong insistence that others must follow their lead, as per Charlie Manson, Jim Jones, and others. David Koresh, the Heaven's Gate crowd and others were not mentioned, but presumably would be in the same bunch as to their deranged thinking as a god or leader with a God complex.

What this all might do in time — and seems to be beginning now — is to create an explanation as to the source of religion. It might explain those religionists who think that they "hear" God talking to them, and that they must follow God and that God talks to them individually. In short, it might begin to explain the fact that so many agnostics, atheists and skeptics believe that Christianity, in fact all religion, is a product of a delusion, or mental illness.

Think of it. This could explain the mentality of Abraham and his disgustingly evil intention to kill his son Isaac (promoted as love of God by the Christians) as ordered by God. The fact that Abraham did not do this and that God's angel stopped him in the nick of time does not lessen what today would be considered a crime and the possibility of mental illness and/or an evil God.

You can also look at God's so-called instructions to kill 70,000 people after David conducted a census wrong, or Moses on God's orders killing 3,000 who did not immediately accept the Ten Commandments or want to follow them, or God's killing of innocent Egyptians during Passover. There are many such tales in the Bible, but these will make the point of the mental illness of religion.

Could it be that continued neurological and neuroanatomical brain studies will ultimately explain away Christianity and religion so that society no longer needs this crutch?

ARE NEAR DEATH EXPERIENCES REAL? OR ARE THEY A RESULT OF OXYGEN DEPRIVATION?

Near Death Experiences are big things for the Christian crowd. They use these NDE's as absolute facts of good Christian people dying and then visiting heaven, taking the fifty-cent tour, but then not dying and instead coming back to relate all the wonderful things about heaven and how happy we will all be when we get there.

That's assuming of course that we believe in Jesus and accept him as our salvation. It is the carrot part of the carrot (heaven) and stick (hell) deal of Christian belief.

There is evidence that there is a possible rational explanation for these NDE's. You can't slam the door on all this yet, but the rational explanation certainly looks promising. Apparently, this information has been around for a while, but not widely known, or I have somehow just missed it in my reading schedule.

According to some medical studies, people often experience oxygen deprivation during the dying process, whether or not they ultimately die. The lack of oxygen going to the brain can result in pupil dilation. Pupil dilation can range from about one to ten mm, depending normally upon the amount of light or darkness to which we are subjected.

Pupil dilation can also be caused by oxygen deprivation from drug use (prescription and/or illegal). In a normal room or hospital setting, pupil dilation can cause a perception of extreme brightness and a joy in the brightness when compared to normal vision and light level in a typical home or hospital.

In addition to brightness, researchers have discovered that oxygen deprivation can cause tunnel-like vision, as the various external parts of the retina slow or stop working (perhaps temporarily, if death does not occur). It can also cause darkness prior to any bright light, and also cause figures and people to appear slightly fuzzy but also very bright.

This seems to be not an internal or brain-caused manifestation but one in which the patient is seeing, only seeing very brightly as a result of the pupil dilation. Since this dilation, like a camera lens, causes a reduced depth of field in viewing, it is natural that some parts of any vision would be less focused and fuzzier. These visual effects can also be caused by oxygen deprivation by any other cause.

Certainly the research team is still busily exploring the phenomenon of NDEs, but the evidence is mounting that are reasonable, scientific explanations for the visual effects associated with NDE experiences — and perhaps even for the delusion of religious experiences.

THE NAZIS AND THE THIRD REICH — CHRISTIAN OR ATHEISTIC?

Christians are often quick to point out that one reason to hate and discount the disgusting atheists is that they were responsible for Adolf Hitler and thus for the horrible acts of the Third Reich. If that is not a good reason to hate and despise atheists, what is?

The problem is that it is wrong. Hitler was brought up Catholic and was quoted as saying, "I shall remain a Catholic forever. . ." All the leaders under Hitler had Christian beliefs.

In addition, all the belt buckles of German soldiers had the words "Gott mit uns." That's "God (is) with us," certainly a sign that the Germans, from leaders to common soldiers, were not atheistic. They were Christian.

Also, Hitler through his book Mein Kampf, spoke of doing and wanting to do God's work. Wrongly, tragically and terribly, he interpreted this as his mission to destroy the Jews.

He got reinforcement for this from Martin Luther's work On The Jews And Their Lies, a 1543 book which set the stage and reinforced the Nazi acts against Jews 400 years later, including destroying their synagogues, burning their houses, eliminating their books and scrolls, confiscating their property, killing them, etc. For the Nazi leaders and Hitler, Martin's work was the religious and Christian justification for the "final solution" for the Jews in Germany and German occupied lands.

During the war, original copies of Luther's diatribe against Jews were used in Nazi presentation ceremonies and special events of honor and for promotion of Nazi leaders.

An International History channel documentary on the last days of Germany during WWII showed and translated the swearing in of the Home Guard in Berlin. It was during the last days of the war with Hitler hunkered down in his underground bunker and before his suicide. This pitiful Home Guard of course was the "fight to the last man" final defense effort and comprised of the old, elderly, infirm, disabled, youth and children.

The oath was "I swear by God this sacred oath that to the leader of the German state and people, Adolf Hitler, supreme commander of the armed forces, I shall render unconditional obedience and that as a brave soldier I shall at all times be prepared to give my life for this oath."

So the next time a Christian or someone from the religious right erroneously lambastes you for the atheistic Nazi atrocities against the Jews and others, you might remind them of the above. The Christians won't believe you, of course, but a simple check into the history of the period will prove that the above is true. Ask them to check it out through a library or Internet site.

That, of course, is only if the religionists are brave enough to stick a toe into the pool of truth. With Christians, checking on the truth so seldom happens.

If Jesus Was Not Born On December 25, Who Was Born Then?

Every year we celebrate Christmas on December 25th. That's the day established in the Catholic and Protestant Churches for Jesus' birth. Except that December 25th is not the date on which Jesus was born. No one knows when he was born.

Since we know that Jesus was not born on December 25th, the question might be why we are celebrating it on that date? There are several factors to consider.

Late December was the period of the winter solstice and was greeted with celebrations. Past this December period, the days start getting longer again, which has traditionally been taken as a sign of a global rebirth, the coming of spring and summer and warmth and light and food and survival. A great gift to celebrate, after all.

And then, there was the birth date of a competing god. Early Christians hijacked holidays and events from other religions and cultural traditions into their own, just as later on the Catholics did with European holidays and particularly local celebrations in Central and South America.

The god that was born on December 25th was Mithras (Latin), Mithra (Greek) or Mitra, Mithra or Mitras (Persian). The religion was old, had been around for about 2,000 years already, with early primitive stages of 1,500 years and early Zoroastrianism leading to 500 years of popularity from about 100 BCE to perhaps 400 CE.

Interestingly, Mithra, with a birth date of December 25th, was born of a virgin or from a virgin rock. He had twelve disciples, performed miracles, raised people from the dead, had communion rituals, had a last meal, and ultimately died, was buried but then rose from this tomb (rolling back the rock that sealed it) and rose to the heavens three days later riding in a chariot. This sounds a lot like Christianity and a little like Mohammad going to heaven to meet Allah riding on Buraq, his winged horse.

Sound familiar? The fact that Christianity and Mithraism were competitive during that important period of the first through fourth centuries leads one to believe that much of Christianity was stolen from Mithraism or other early pagan religions, of which Christianity was just one more.

Maybe the Jews and early Christians just had a better PR department than the early Mithraists. Maybe if Mithraists had hyped their religion a little more, most religionists in this country today would be Mithraists instead of Christians. It is something to think about.

In any case, as you start to enjoy each winter holiday season, be sure to wish a Merry Mithramas to one and all.

HAPPY BIRTHDAY, MR. DARWIN!

Each fall, there is a seminal date for science, biology and evolution. November 24, 1859 marks the publication date of Charles Darwin's *The Origin of Species*. It was first published in England when Darwin was 50 years old.

This book set the stage for the continued studies in this field in all the various "ologies." Countless research projects and studies continue to validate evolutionary concepts on everything from a micro to a macro level. From cell theory to geology and cosmology, evolution continues to be supported and reinforced. Forget the folly of creationism of the fundamentalists.

This remarkable thinker who set the stage for much of today's biological studies has been celebrated internationally since shortly after Darwin's death on April 19, 1882, at age 73. He is commemorated to this day with celebrations in England, the Royal Society of New Zealand, New York Academy of Sciences, University of Chicago, and the Massachusetts Salem State College. In 2015, Delaware became the first state to mark International Darwin Day on February 12th his birthday. The web site www.darwinday.org has notices about annual events and other information.

Once, I had the opportunity to publicly commemorate the day myself. The letter below was sent to friends who would appreciate it and also to church-affiliated fundamentalist creationists, fundamentalist Christians, evolution-denying evangelicals and other types who would not appreciate it.

Dear Fellow Primate,

I just wanted to be the first to wish you good tidings on this anniversary of the publication of Charles Darwin's *The Origin of Species*, first published on November 24, 1859. This is a great anniversary year, with February 12, 1809, being the birthday of Charles Darwin (along with Abraham Lincoln), and this continued and celebrated anniversary year of Charlie's birth.

I welcome this opportunity to wish good thoughts to my fellow primates and companion-evolving mammals as we hominids have evolved over 7 million years to our present state today. I can't wait to hear what news anchors says on their various TV channels about the importance of this date and this seminal work in biology.

It will also be good to hear about the value of evolutionary concepts, its many related studies and the great accomplishments of Charles Darwin in pushing forward the knowledge of biology and truth while also pushing back the darkness and ignorance of superstition, sometimes called "religion." May we continue, and some day, somehow, reach the Age of Biological Enlightenment.

Best,

Boyd Pfeiffer

PS — Sorry — I could not find a Hallmark card for this important occasion or I would have sent one.

On The Road With The Star Of The East To Find The Birthplace Of Jesus — But There Is A Detour

In the book of Matthew, relating the story about the birth of Christ, the Mithric wise men or Magi (as the Bible likes to call them) followed the star in the East to find the birthplace of Jesus.

But following this star in the East — whatever it was — must have been a chore. First the Magi, "the wise men from the East," must have seen the star in the west — not the east — otherwise they would not follow it from the "east," where they were, to Jerusalem (which is west), to ask about the birth of Christ. Had it been in the east as they viewed it, Jerusalem and Bethlehem would have been behind them and they would have been traveling away from — not towards — these two cities and the birthplace of Jesus.

"Where is the one who has been born king of the Jews? We saw his star in the east and have come to worship him." (Matthew 2:2)

King Herod of Jerusalem was disturbed by this question and found out from his priests and teachers of the law that the king of the Jews — Jesus — was to be born in Bethlehem. " 'In Bethlehem in Judea,' they replied, 'for this is what the prophet has written.'"

Herod reported this to the Magi and sent them to Bethlehem to search for the child that he wanted to kill but claimed that he wanted to worship.

Bethlehem was about six miles almost due south of Jerusalem where Herod was located. According to Matthew 2:9, the Magi followed the star to the house where Jesus was located. This means that the "star in the east" (which had to initially be in the west for the Magi of the east to follow it to Jerusalem in the west) now had to change direction approximately 90 degrees to go almost due south to "lead" the Magi to the birthplace of Jesus. The "star" started out going west and then at Jerusalem had to make a sharp right angle turn to almost due south to get to Bethlehem.

All this is quite a different story from the one that we are taught in Sunday School that leads children to believe that the Magi were following the star towards the east in a direct line from the position of the Magi to the place in Bethlehem where Jesus resided.

To follow the story as literally written, we would have to follow the star from east to west and then make a sharp 90 degree direction change go due south to get to Bethlehem.

That is a defiance of physics and any aspect of cosmology or astronomy. For some, it would sound more like an Alice in Wonderland tale than something that could happen or really did happen. Even comets do not make 90° turns. Could this be a false tale, like much else in the Bible?

Jesus — Was He Born In 4 BCE Or 6 CE? That's A Ten-Year Difference Of Opinion!

The Bible, this inerrant Word of God, tells us in Matthew and Luke of the birth of Jesus. But there is a little problem with all this. For now, let's stick with the problem of dating of these events and when Jesus was really born.

Matthew refers to King Herod in Jerusalem and reports that he wanted the visiting Magi from the east to find Jesus for him. He wanted to kill Jesus, since Jesus, the Messiah, was purported to be a king and Herod could brook no interlopers. There is ample evidence from historical works that Herod died in the year that we now calculate as 4 BCE. Thus, assuming Jesus was born right before the death of Herod, it could have been as late as 4 BCE.

But in Luke, the same (but conflated) story of Jesus's birth, there is no reference to Herod, but only a reference to a census. The census is not mentioned at all in Matthew.

"In those days Caesar Augustus issued a decree that a census should be taken of the entire Roman world. (This was the first census taken after Judea became a Roman province and was conducted by Quirinius, Governor of the province of Syria.) And everyone went to his own town to register." (Luke 2:13)

It follows that Joseph and Mary then went from Nazareth (in Galilee) to Bethlehem (in Judea). But wait a minute — wait a cotton-picking minute! Just as texts outside the Bible confirm the death of Herod in 4 BC (or BCE), so other documents confirm that the census under Quirinius as governor of Syria was not held until 6 CE. And of course, Luke never mentions Herod and Matthew never mentions a census, or Quirinius or Caesar Augustus. What is going on here?

There is a disconnect of ten years here between the two stories of Christ's birth. And that is assuming a best possible scenario between the death of Herod and the census of Caesar. Here in the only two biblical stories about the birth of Jesus, we have separate tales of stars, shepherds, wise men, angels, sheep, a house, a stable with a manger/food trough, guiding lights, Nazareth and Egypt as differing destinations after birth, etc. We also have a big ten-year difference in the birth of Jesus.

Would not this alone make a believer skeptical, if still believing the inerrant Word of God, the Bible? Would not this difference in "facts" alone make one very questioning about all this? Would this be any easier to believe than the Jack and the Beanstalk story? Isn't it time to wake up and reject fairy tales?

JUDGING FACTS AND FICTION OF THE CHRISTMAS STORY. ARE THERE ANY TRUTHS HERE?

Considering how important the birth of Christ is in Christianity, we know surprisingly little about it. In all likelihood, the date of December 25th was stolen from the winter solstice and Mithraism, since it is known as the birth date of the pagan god Mithra. People were going to celebrate that date anyway, so one might as well make the festivities Christian in appearance and thus help convert pagans.

Sadly, the Christmas story as told to wide-eyed and unknowing children and expressed in Nativity scenes each December is a mishmash of Matthew and Luke, and thus a conflation of the two different stories. If you watch the History Channel on TV or read serious books on history, you find notes, quotes and facts that point out the differences of an event as seen or analyzed by different historians. Apparently it's easy enough to mix the two decidedly different stories together and count on the faithful never to read or compare the stories in their Bible — the inerrant words of God.

In Matthew, you find a star in the East to lead Magi to the site of the birth. You have Magi only — no shepherds. This "star" moves until it's right over the site of the birth.

You also have Jesus born in a house, not a stable or manger. "He [Joseph] did what the angel of the Lord commanded him and took Mary home as his wife. But he had no union with her until she gave birth to a son. And he gave him the name Jesus." (Matthew 1:24-25)

Luke has no star in the East, and there was no "house." "And she gave birth to her first born, a son. She wrapped him in cloths and placed him in a manger because there was no room for them in the inn." (Luke 2:7) The manger (animal food trough) and stable are popular props in Christmas stories and nativity scenes, since this creates a more humbling tone than a house. Also, it rounds out the cast nicely in these conflations to have both shepherds and Magi all together, along with sheep and a bunch of cattle, and thus have different classes of people worshiping this Christ child.

With all this semantic word play and idea juggling going on, it makes one wonder how much truth there is in any of these stories from the gospels. . .

JESUS, JOSEPH, MARY, HOLY GHOST, CENSUS, VIRGINS AND THE LINE OF DAVID

In only one out of four New Testament gospels on the life and death of Christ do we find anything about Joseph and Mary having to go from Nazareth to Bethlehem to participate in a census. Their return to Bethlehem was required because Joseph was said to be of the line of David.

According to the Bible, everyone had to return to the city of their biological line and origin. Thus, you can read in Luke 2:4, "So Joseph went up from the town of Nazareth in Galilee to Judea, to Bethlehem the town of David, because he belonged to the house and line of David."

One minor problem with this is that Joseph was not the real father of Jesus, only his step-dad. The real father of Jesus, should we want to believe this fairy tale, was the Holy Ghost, or God, or however you want to phrase it.

But there is even a more major problem with all this. David lived one thousand years prior to Joseph. During any census at any time, would we or should we go back to the city of our ancestors from one thousand years ago? Granted, the migration/immigration rate was different in those days than in the past 500, or 50, years. But even my mongrel lineage would make it hard to go "home." I am mostly German, the rest mixed up with English, French, Scotch and Irish.

Should I, during a census, return to the city of Attila the Hun or whoever else of Germanic lineage was around pillaging Middle Europe at the time? Or should I go to the other countries of my mongrel heritage, to the extent I can trace any of them? I think not. And 2,000 years ago, it is unlikely that most people would have known their lineage of one thousand years prior. I sure don't.

Is it conceivable that this trip from Nazareth to Bethlehem was merely a literary device to make sure that the birth of Christ was in the right town as determined by earlier prophecy? If Christ had been born in any other city or town, would that have prevented him from being the Savior?

If Mary had not made it to Bethlehem before giving birth, would that have taken Jesus off the short list of candidates to be the son of God and the Messiah? If so, would the prophesies of the Old Testament listing Jesus as the Christ child have to be rewritten?

If Mary had not been a virgin but instead been a prostitute, or even a victim of date rape, would that make Jesus any less? Would he or could he not have been the son of God (for those who believe that) as a result of his mother's past?

All this makes one wonder about rewrites, copies, accidental changes, deliberate changes, lies, comparisons with other biblical texts, and translations. Will the truth ever be known or discovered?

THE STAR OVER JESUS' BIRTH HOUSE/MANGER. WOULD IT NOT BURN UP JESUS AND THE WHOLE FAMILY?

Some evening when there are no clouds in the sky and it is very clear, go outside and find the star that resides over your house. It should be bright and visible and definitely over your home and not that of the next door neighbor.

That is the situation found in Matthew on the birth of Christ and the visit by the Magi. It is not mentioned in Luke. Neither Mark nor John has anything to say about the birth of Jesus.

While no one ever comments on this little fiction, it is obvious that if a moving star was to guide the Magi, it would have to have been no higher than a highway street lamp or a low flying helicopter, at least when they were closing in on the target. Nothing else would work.

And yet, buying this fiction is exactly what the Bible suggests in Matthew 2:9–10. "And the star they had seen in the east went ahead of them until it stopped over the place where the child was. When they saw the star, they were overjoyed..."

The Magi were following the instructions from King Herod and the site they were searching for was the birthplace of Jesus.

The important thing to realize is that this "fact" of a moving star ending up over the place of Jesus' birth is clearly impossible. Were this an asteroid burning through the atmosphere, it would not stop over a particular house. Were it a comet, it would continue in orbit around the earth or the sun, leaving nothing but a fiery tail. Were it even a star as described, it would have to be so close that it would appear huge in order to be an effective marker — and it would likely burn up the earth.

In addition, were this to actually happen, it is highly likely that other people in the area would also see this phenomenon and, without even knowing about Jesus, would follow the "star" to discover the meaning or reason for its appearance. Ah, I can hear you saying, the shepherds came, so that kills your argument.

True, the shepherds did come, but not in Matthew. The shepherds were in a different manuscript written at a different time by a different author's hand: Luke. The shepherds did not see any star as a guide. They did see angels who told them about Jesus, but it was only after the angels had left — and with no star or bright light remaining — that the shepherds left their flocks to go and find Jesus. (Luke 2:8-20)

Can we really believe in a magical star that would be impossible in real life? Is it any wonder that some people question the truth and veracity of the entire Bible?

VIOLATING THE TEN COMMANDMENTS ABOUT SABBATH WORK — A LITTLE CRIME BUT A BIG PUNISHMENT

With two acres of property and a lot of trees, I am constantly picking up fallen limbs and branches. I often do this on weekends — Saturday and Sunday. I'm just glad that I live today and not during Old Testament times. Just take for example that poor guy in Numbers 15:32 who was picking up sticks on the Sabbath. That was a big no-no, considering the Ten Commandments and Israeli. Laws of the line.

"While the Israelites were in the desert, a man was found gathering wood on the Sabbath day," says the Bible, beginning in Numbers 15:32. "Those who found him gathering wood brought him to Moses and Aaron and the whole assembly and they kept him in custody, because it was not clear what should be done to him. Then the Lord said to Moses, 'The man must die. The whole assembly must stone him outside the camp.' So the whole assembly took him outside the camp and stoned him to death, as the Lord had commanded Moses."

You would have to assume that he was gathering wood for a fire, for heat or for cooking. Maybe he'd had a bad week and had not been able to gather enough wood earlier in order to provide for himself and his family. No matter, he has to die, so says the merciful Lord.

Certainly there were then and are now crimes for which many Americans would consider the death penalty to be appropriate. And just as certainly, many modern countries have done away with the death penalty in favor of long prison sentences. This is not the time and place to argue the pros and cons of this unending argument. What is certain, in any time and place, is that getting fuel on the wrong day appears to be a less than vital infraction, far short of risking to overturn the social order. Why such a draconian punishment from our loving Lord?

This man was punished for violating the Commandment that forbids doing work on the Sabbath, the day on which one must do nothing but worship the Lord. This suggests an egomaniacal aspect of this God of the Israelites, a god with severe insecurity issues and serious self-esteem problems trying to enforce his "Godness" with the Israelites and surrounding communities.

So when you read today about an Islamic country sentencing a man or woman to death by stoning, just remember that this was also the history — and perhaps current wishes — of the God of the Christians and Jews. After all, all three religions were Abrahamic in origin. This is the kind of God depicted in the Old Testament. Isn't that interesting?

CHRISTIANS HYPOCRITICAL ABOUT TEN COMMANDMENTS FOURTH RULE ON WORKING, ETC. ON THE SABBATH

When it comes to the idea of not working on the Sabbath, hypocrisy abounds. For Christians, it's Sunday, while the Sabbath of the Israelites was Saturday.

Waiters and waitresses working on Saturday (if Jewish) or Sunday (if Christian) are often berated and condemned, especially by Jews and Christians visiting those establishments on Saturday/Sunday. Christian customers may try to "help" the working wait staff by leaving religious tracts instead of tips. That's a big help. But the question for Christians is why would you go to restaurants, or anywhere else, on Sunday when you know people will have to work in violation of this Fourth Commandment which you hold in such high esteem? By going to eat at such establishments on the Sabbath, the religionists — Jewish or Christian — are themselves violating the strict admonitions of their own religion and supposedly beliefs.

Once, with my wife, I attended a Sunday luncheon at a Christian church. It was noted that a church member couple could not attend as a result of their required work schedule. There was much tisking and clucking about this, condemning the workplace and employer that required this church couple to work on Sunday — the Christian Sabbath! How could they?

Ironically, the conversation then moved to those who were attending the luncheon. Some planned to stop to get gas on the way home, buy some groceries, and pick up incidentals needed for the coming week. And of course they had to pay the toll taker — working on Sunday — to cross the bridge to get them home. You probably get where I am going with this.

Some religionists would consider the very fact that they drove to this luncheon as a failure to honor the Sabbath. It would violate Orthodox Jewish traditions of not working on the Sabbath. For Orthodox Jews, even turning on a light switch or an oven is "work" and a violation of the Sabbath rule. Yes, that appears to be why ovens can now be set in advance.

However, the seemingly very devout Christians at this Sunday luncheon had no problem in driving, or in requiring others to work on Sunday at gas stations, convenience stores, grocery stores and other shops. They were perfectly happy to satisfy their needs and wishes while at the same time condemning others for working or condemning those employers for making "good Christians" work on Sunday.

And, if they needed it, I am sure that these same Christians would welcome — if not demand if needed — the Sunday-working police, fire departments, EMTs, doctors, hospitals, Coast Guard, hazmat crews, airport personnel, air traffic controllers, etc. I am sure that they never think of others who must work on Sunday to keep our lives on track. These include those responsible for traffic lights, gas and electric companies, water department, sewage department, etc.

This story speaks for itself about the Ten Commandments and the hypocrisy of Christians. It's far easier to talk the talk than to walk the walk.

THE REAL STORY OF THE RED SEA CROSSING OF MOSES AND THE ISRAELITES MAKES IF ALL PRETTY MUCH IMPOSSIBLE

It has been a while since I read about Moses arguing with the Pharaoh to get the Israelites out of Egypt. Moses ultimately led the Israelites out of Egypt after the final plague killed all first-born Egyptians (Passover). After Moses held up his staff to part the waters of the Red Sea (Reed Sea) to allow the Israelites to pass through to the other side, the Egyptian army followed. The waters, closing in on them, drowned and destroyed them all. We all know this Exodus story.

What they did not tell you in Sunday School was to check Numbers 1:1–4 and Numbers 1:44–49. These verses cast serious doubts on the story. "The Lord spoke to Moses in the Tent of Meeting in the Desert of Sinai on the first day of the second month of the second year after the Israelites came out of Egypt. He said: 'Take a census of the whole

Israelite community by their clans and families, listing every man by name, one by one. You and Aaron [Moses' brother] are to number by their divisions all the men in Israel twenty years old and more who are able to serve in the army.'" Numbers 1:1–3.

The number of able bodied men for each tribe varied from 32,200 (tribe of Manasseh) to 74,600 (Judah). The total number of men for the army (Numbers 1:46) was 603,550. Sure, this was described after the Red Sea crossing, but only by two years later and not enough to seriously change the over-twenty census.

This count includes only able-bodied men. Biblical scholars have calculated from demographics and family sizes of the time that if we count older men, women, and children, too, there would be a population of about two to three million. Add another calculated 600,000 cattle to this mass movement.

Those two million (let's be conservative) Israelites marching ten across would have made a column 200 or more miles long. With hard marching, it would take at least three weeks to four weeks for a 200-mile long column to get through the Red Sea.

The Bible information and the calculations of biblical scholars raise serious doubt about this story. Would the sea waters stay parted for a week? Wouldn't the Egyptian army catch up with the Israelites in a week before they all crossed to the other side? Would the river bed have been dry enough for the 600,000 cattle not to muddy it hock deep and flail around like a house fly in maple syrup?

The Bible (Exodus 14) describes this passing as occurring in one day. This would have been impossible. And would the entire Egyptian army been drowned as described in Exodus 14:28?

Doesn't this fable as described in the Bible and the calculations of biblical scholars make it impossible to believe? Isn't it better to be skeptical and face the truth of the world as we know it from facts and honesty? Isn't it good to be skeptical?

If Jesus Was So Perfect, How Come He Was So Rude And Disrespectful?

We all know the Fifth Commandment — Honor your mother and father. We all know that this is important; otherwise it would not be part and parcel of the Big Ten. Apparently, this skipped Jesus' mind during his short ministry here on earth. Either that, or Jesus was just rude, crude, nasty and impolite to his mother and brothers. You can check this out in Matthew 12:46–50, Mark 3:31–35, or Luke 8:19–21.

The three references are very similar and happen with Jesus preaching to a crowd. "Now Jesus' mother and brothers came to see him, but they were not able to get near him because of the crowd," said Luke 8:19–21. "Someone told him, 'Your mother and brothers are standing outside, wanting to see you.' He replied, 'My mother and brothers are those who hear God's word and put it into practice.'"

Mark says, "Then Jesus' mother and brothers arrived. Standing outside, they sent someone in to call him. A crowd was sitting around him, and they told him, 'Your mother and brothers are outside looking for you.' Then he looked at those seated in a circle around him and said, 'Here are my mother and my brothers! Whoever does God's will is my brother and sister and mother.'" The quote from Matthew is very similar — almost identical — to these.

Well, that's downright nasty, rude, curt, flippant, disrespectful, and dishonoring. Jesus could have excused himself from the crowd to see his Mom and Bros, or he could have passed word along that he would see them just as soon as he finished preaching to the crowd, or he could have asked that his mother and brothers be brought in a join him, sitting at his feet until he could give them some individual attention.

But he didn't. According to biblical references and translations, he did none of these things and openly dismissed them as not worthy of his time. In other words, even though he was an adult and someone who should set an example, he acted like a spoiled brat and certainly did not honor his mother or family.

Did Jesus forget about the Ten Commandments? Did he forget or never learn the social niceties or social mores or folkways of his time? Was he just a nasty clod and a rude lout of a person? Would you not think that Jesus — supposedly a perfect fusion of God and man on earth — would act better than this in front of a crowd and even in private?

Would not this unthinkable act and rudeness by Jesus make one skeptical and seriously question the supposed perfection and divinity of Christ on earth?

"Miracles" Really Aren't "Miracles" Unless They Are True Miracles — And That Does Not Happen!

Today, you can't watch the evening news without hearing about a "miracle" at least once. It might be a miracle of someone walking away from a plane crash, from an automobile accident, from an almost-drowning, from a house fire. It might be surviving tornado, a bear attack or a threatening tornado.

But these are not miracles, only coincidences of nature and circumstance that happen all the time. In the evening news cases, they are events — a little strange — but those that happen with life altering possibilities.

But to check a dictionary definition of a "miracle" you find that said miracle has to be other-worldly, supernatural, caused by a divine happening, a god or God or something other than natural. Any event in which someone walks away from a plane crash, from an automobile accident, an almost drowning or a house fire is just a fortunate coincidence of possibilities.

Often these "miracles" are credited to the event participant's god or God, usually offering praise for something that this god has done or for some person somehow protected. In fact, it could be that the god being credited does not even exist.

In many cases, these miracles credited to God are ones in which some people live and some people die. The hypothetical plane crash and automobile accident are prime examples. Some few — praising God — walk away from a plane crash in which many died. The question is — what about those who died? If God is going to get credit for the "miracle" of saving some lives, is he also going to get the deserved blame for the horrible deaths of those who did not make it? Or is it all just happenstance?

How come no one considers real miracles and what they might entail? How come no one thinks of what God would have to do, if there is a God and whether or not God can do it? How come God does not, with a snap of his fingers, cure all the children with cancers and other childhood diseases? That would seemingly be a miracle.

How come God cannot or does not cause the regrowth of a limb of those amputee Vets returning from wars in Iraq, Afghanistan or elsewhere? That would be a miracle. How come God cannot protect those caught in horrible house fires and burned badly? To do so would be a miracle. There are lots of things that God could do if God wanted to or was able. Or isn't he able?

WHERE DID ALL THE MIRACLES GO?

Think about the quote from Epicurus, the Greek philosopher of 341–270 BCE. "Is God willing to prevent evil but not able? Then he is not omnipotent. Is he able but not willing? Then he is malevolent. Is he both able and willing? Then whence cometh evil? Is he neither able nor willing? Then why call him God?"

The Bible has lots of "miracles", although they don't hold up to the clear light of day or of critical examination. And since none of them are happening today, or have happened in the past 2,000 years, they are highly suspect. Actually, they are not highly suspect — they are impossible. Bible "miracles" are a sham.

Yet they are considered real, even when considered and compared with other things that are obviously fake in spite of being held up as the basis for parts of Christianity. For many Christians, the Bible is true — it has to be true.

Take, for example, Muhammad going to heaven to be with Allah and doing so while riding his white winged horse Buraq. Obviously fake and rubbish, according to Christians. But Jesus going to heaven after resurrection, *sans* horse? Real. Actual. After all, this is Bible business. It is a basis for Christian faith.

The various animals of Winnie-the-Pooh, Alice in Wonderland and Aesop's Fables all talking? Just a little fairy tale for the kiddies, and obviously just made-up nonsense. But the talking snake and the conversing donkey in the Bible? Why that is true, of course! After all, it is in the Bible, the Word of God! Thus, it can't be wrong! But has anyone such as a biblical biologist figured out that the vocal folds of a donkey and snake make talking as we know it impossible? They can't speak English or ancient Aramaic, Hebrew or Greek. They just can't talk.

Jesus walking on water? Of course that's true! It's in the Bible — God's word. But has anyone bothered to look at the physics involved — things such as mass, weight, specific gravity and atomic weights, etc.? Has it ever happened before or after this previous watery Jesus parade and charade? No? Wouldn't that make it suspect at least?

Jesus raising people from the dead? It is in the Bible, thus it has to be true. Restoring a withered hand or curing leprosy? It is in the Bible and has to be true.

All of these things supposedly happened 2,000 years ago, and nothing has happened since. Also, there is no evidence external to the Bible of these miracles. And the Bible is written not by dispassionate journalists of the time, but by enthusiastic supporters of this new Jewish Prophet Jesus and this new religion Christianity. Thus, one might suspect that the truth of anything in the miracle line has been polished a tad, varnished over a bit, gussied-up or created from bald-faced lies and conjecture.

Miracles don't happen and never did happen. It seems that you can't counter the laws of physics, the rules of chemistry or the basics of biology. But Christians don't seem to know this.

As the biblical scribes did, you can write about miracles all you want, even write about what a real miracle might entail. But the facts are that God never did any miracles and sure isn't doing any today to win friends and influence people. Is anybody listening?

A Great Idea For Proving Miracles And Perhaps, Just Perhaps, Proving Christianity!

If you think about it, it would be easy to prove that miracles — as per the Bible miracles — really work, really happened, and can be proven by scientific methods. Or perhaps they don't. One idea from a friend with similar thoughts as mine would be to gather 500 amputees, have a constant 24-hour watch over them by doctors and have God regrow their missing limbs. That would be a miracle.

A second thought would be to have a Godly prophecy of the World Series teams and winning scores for some five years hence. Either of these events should pretty well cinch it for the God team and put those awful atheists and their secular groups out of business.

(If you want to cinch the miracle thing for me alone, just give me the lottery numbers for the next Mega Millions or Power Ball event. But don't tell anyone else — After the drawing, I'll let them know!)

Of those listed above, I like the one about regrowing limbs on 500 amputees. Atheist Sam Harris (*The End of Faith* and *Letter to a Christian Nation*) has suggested the same thing, and all he wanted was a billion Christians praying for the restoration of one limb for one amputee. Of course, theologians have argued for centuries whether or not it makes any difference in prayer effectiveness if the prayer is by one Christian, a few hundred or a million or more.

I don't like the idea of miracle cures of those stricken with cancer, heart disease, glaucoma, diabetes, and similar ailments. I would certainly want all of them cured, but there is too much chance for mistakes, accidents, misdiagnoses, fudging, scams, trickery, etc. to make this valid. There has certainly been enough trickery and conning in these areas by faith healers and other religious charlatans.

But with an amputee, there would be no question about it. Restore the missing limb or part of a limb through a Godly miracle, and the religious faithful win. The missing limb grows, or it doesn't. The atheists, agnostics and skeptics go away, heads down, grumbling to themselves if the missing limb is replaced and a miracle performed.

Were a missing limb to be restored, you could see it grow. You could have doctors and scientists watching every move. You could put it on a video and the Internet and if not growing quite fast enough, do a little time-lapse photography.

The Christians and God would have a big stake in all this. Want to have Christianity take over the whole world, as many ministers and faithful believe and as Jesus supposedly dictated? This limb regrowth event would do it. Put it in a stadium with constant video, hourly updates and daily reports from the news anchors. Think of the sponsors you could get — just like the Super Bowl.

Want to prove that your Christian God can beat all the other gods of Buddhism, Hinduism, Jainism, etc? This limb regrowth event would do it. Want to prove that your God can beat all the other gods in the world today, now, in the future and in the past? This limb regrowth would do it.

We are all waiting. When it is scheduled, be sure to let Richard Dawkins and Sam Harris know. Hey, they would surely want to be in on this.

Fatima 1917 "Miracle" May Be Just Serious Eye Injury And Solar Retinopathy

On May 13, 1917, Lucia Santos and two companions were in a field when Lucia reported seeing an apparition of Mary. They were children from Fatima, Portugal, and this was the first of "Mary" apparitions that continued through October 13, 1917 with three "secrets" that the Mary apparition gave to Lucia.

Subsequent investigation by the Catholic Church ultimately approved of these apparitions, and while not required as an article of faith, were noted to be "worthy of belief." In some of these subsequent viewings by the faithful (not everyone there) looking at or towards the sun, the sun was seen to dance around, rotate, change colors, etc.

While some have accepted these statements as factual, others have pointed out other possible explanations. First, Lucia and her friends lived in Fatima, a town in which the citizens then were reported as accepting without question or evidence a lot of supernatural or divine events. The children in the town were taught to accept these events and to expect the unexplainable as divinely inspired.

Many subsequent investigators have suggested that these sightings of Mary and the dancing sun are all a result of mass hallucinations that occur in both small and large groups of people. Investigations also point out that similar apparitions of a dancing and colorful sun appeared to some of the 10,000 gathered for such an event in Germany in 1949. Other similar experiences have been noted at various times from around the world.

To look at the sun, as these faithful did, is not to court God but to court disaster along with partial or permanent blindness. Staring at the sun, for even the shortest period of time (seconds, not minutes), can cause retinal burn and partial blindness called solar retinopathy. It can later in life contribute to macular degeneration.

This staring at the sun can also cause (sadly noted by those who have done it) the sun to turn blue, later yellow and to be large and colorful — the same visual effects noted by those viewing the sun during this unfortunate apparition.

Thus, this vision and possible damage to the eyes by up to thousands may be simply the visual result of too much exposure to too strong a light with the colors caused by burning and damaging the retinal cells or by the mass hallucinations of many wanting to believe what others are supposedly magically seeing.

It also helps to keep in mind that no unexplained event is a result of God or caused by God. Just because we as a society do not know everything does not mean that the explanation for some unknown event is a God event or God-caused. After all, for the ancients throughout the world, just a simple eclipse was thought to be divinely inspired, a message from God and an event affirming God's control over the earth and mankind.

Hallucination and eye damage sounds like the answer to this Godly "miracle" of Fatima — "worthy of belief" by Catholics or not.

SKEPTICS, LOOKING AT THE SUN, FATIMA AND FAITH

Just for giggles, let's assume that the essay on the mass hallucinations of the Mary apparitions at Fatima, Portugal was all wrong. Let's assume that the dancing sun changing colors really did occur. How would that happen? There are several possibilities, none good. One is that the sun really did change color and really did move in the sky to appear to "dance." Of course, we know cosmologically that this is impossible.

I don't know how many physicists it would take to figure out all the things that would have to occur for the sun to move in place, or the cosmology of our solar system as to other results. This is sort of like Joshua stopping the sun so that he could beat up his enemies, the subject of another essay here. That would and could not work either.

There is no physical reason why the sun should change color. Explaining that would take a bunch of speculating by a lot of smart people. Another possibility is that the earth would move around strangely, so that the sun would seem to move. It would be like wobbling our way down the road on a bicycle with a bent wheel and watching the seeming but non-existent movement of a building or tree on the horizon as it "moved" in front of our eyes. And whatever it would be, it would certainly change our earth's movement in relation to the sun, the length of the day, the tides, and other physical effects including on the atmosphere.

Of course, if the earth were to move or to stop moving, we would have people, plants, buildings, trees and animals spinning off the earth like a wet English sheepdog shaking off bath water. We would know about it for sure, if this happened and if anyone survived.

Another possibility would be that there was some strange meteorological event occurring that would make the sun look different than normal. This could be as a result of dust or vapor in the sky, winds, smoke, or clouds. We can bet that this did not happen either, since astronomers were on hand in 1917 to record any such happenings.

Since we can't ascribe any of these apparitions or dancing sun events to the movement of the sun, the movement of the earth or to meteorological events, we seem to be right back at mass hallucinations as possible explanations.

And as we have said before, that there is no completely satisfactory explanation of all this does not automatically mean "God did it." Such events have happened around the world at different times. This tends to leave us only with the hallucination and eye damage as probable causes. It is better to be a skeptic and never stare at the sun! Never stare at the sun!

COMMUNION OR COMMUNICABLE? A HOST OF PROBLEMS WITH THE CATHOLIC EUCHARIST HOST

Some years ago, Our Lady of Lourdes Church in Massapequa Park, Nassau County, New York, had a little problem with their 10:30 a.m. and noon communion service on Christmas Day, the symbolic day of the birth of Jesus.

It seems that they might have been distributing the communicable disease Hepatitis A along with the wine and Host of communion. Some 1,300 people at the two services could have been affected. The Nassau County Department of Health made vaccines available to all concerned.

While the news reports are a tad incomplete, it seems that at least one of the priests involved did have the disease and somehow it might have been passed along when handling the bread wafer or through the use of a common chalice for the wine.

The irony is that according to Catholic belief, once the wine and the bread wafer have been elevated as the Host by a priest during a service, it becomes the actual, real body and blood of Christ. Could the body and blood of God and the Christian Savior become contaminated with an ancient earth-borne disease? That is funny in the sense of weird, even if it may not be quite amusing.

It certainly raises questions about the validity of all this man-made belief, along with any belief in the powers of Holy Water. Imagine, before the widespread use of hand disinfectants, some priests used Holy Water as a disinfectant prior to the communion service.

After all, Holy Water has special powers, so they say. But apparently a "host" of diseases, including swine flu, were passed along this way and Holy Water is no longer used as a disinfectant.

Instead, bishops and others are suggesting or demanding that priests use hand sanitizers or carefully wash their hands (in tap water, presumably) before any communion service or Eucharist. Some churches, since the 2009 swine flu pandemic, are also suggesting bowing to each other rather than shaking hands as a greeting between parishioners.

One Catholic church in Japan has eliminated Holy Water from their church. At least with the communion wine and wafer, it seems that it is no different from any wafer and wine, and that the power of the church or even of God or Jesus cannot change this.

That's a shame, since it would be wonderful indeed if the power of the blood and body of Jesus could do something helpful in the medical and sanitation field. Too bad it doesn't work that way.

TV Teasers Can Lead To Serious Religious Thinking — And Perhaps Some Religious Rejection

A little teaser I happened upon for the TV show "V" on ABC caught my eye. There was some reference to a giant image of an attractive woman in the sky and her friendly attitude to people. (I think that they turn into really nasty aliens later on. You know, you just can't trust those aliens.)

Jumping from one thing to another, they showed part of a scene where an old priest and young priest in the back recess of a church were discussing what they should tell parishioners about this alien phenomenon. One priest wanted to talk about it from the pulpit but noted that the Bible did not cover such events.

They also both noted that no more than two or three of the neighborhood homeless came to their services anyway. The church was in a down and out, given-up-gotta-get-out neighborhood where most people had left decades ago.

But the priests enter the main part of the church to find — guess what? Yep, the church is filled with parishioners, scared to death and ready to receive the Word of God. It's almost standing room only.

Well, let's admit that the people, parishioners, the cold and hungry just looking for a warm spot, the outsiders, those returning to their religion after twenty years, were all there for one thing: They were afraid. I don't blame them. If this show were real life, I would be afraid too.

But I wouldn't go to church, not to any church of any denomination, for answers — any answers. Churches and religions have not been able to give us any serious, thoughtful, cogent, reasoned answers for anything in life, any time in life, at any point in history. Churches, church attendance and religion are built on fear.

They have the carrot (heaven, golden streets) and the stick (hell, burning flames, lakes of fire) to alternately reward or beat us into shape. And if we don't believe, there is no salve, ointment, or hospital burn treatment center to go to. You just burn and burn and burn, for — well, forever, if you can imagine that. And, if you believe such malarkey (both the burning and the eternity parts), that might scare you.

It scared the extras in this TV show and only showed most dramatically that religion — any religion, all religion — is based on fear. Otherwise, all those extras representing real people would be sitting home, realizing that they could do nothing about the activities of these superior aliens except to try to make the best of their last moments until the last "hoorah."

After all, you just can't trust those aliens. You can't trust religionists either, with their fanciful fairy tales. Do you think that religion or our God or god would have helped in this?

WHEN BAD THING HAPPEN, DO WE NEED GOD? DID I NEED GOD? DO YOU NEED GOD? I DON'T THINK SO

We were driving along a dirt road in a Land Rover, between no place and nowhere in the jungles of Guatemala. We were on our way to explore a new fishing area when several shabbily-dressed men holding Uzis stepped out of the jungle, stopping our car.

They wanted to check our passports, said our interpreter. The Uzi-holders were examining our passports upside down. Neither Spanish nor English literacy was their strong suit. Somehow — to this day I do not know how — we got out of that mess. It could have gone horribly wrong. The hot jungle would have quickly decomposed our bodies without a trace, had we been shot and dumped. The vehicle, if the dim and dazed duo didn't just steal it, would have rusted and corroded in short order.

Later, I was in the lead on a hike in North Carolina when a large, startled black bear ran down the trail towards me, brushing my leg as it went past. I could have easily patted it on the shoulder or rump. He or she could have easily mauled me. It didn't and nothing happened.

On another occasion, we fishermen and our fishing gear were crowded into a small twin-engine Alaskan bush plane when it lost an engine right after lift-off. We were losing altitude rapidly. The pilot barely missed a shack filled with explosives while turning back to slam safely, but hard, onto the runway. If we had hit the shack, authorities would have had to use dental records to identify us.

A fifteen-minute cruise back from the fishing grounds in Delaware Bay turned violent when a bad storm kicked up. It became a two-hour run while soaking us completely despite full foul weather gear. We got back to the dock, unloaded and went home only to learn the next morning that the keel of the aluminum craft had split open from rough water during the run back, the boat sinking at the dock shortly after we left the area.

In a Southern city, after registering at a motel for a fishing tackle show the next day, I was parking my car when two men tried to hold me up with a knife, one squeezing between the car body and door and demanding everything from me. It is a longer story but I ended up fine, my camera and lap top computer were not stolen, the rental car not damaged. Unfortunately, I did not get a chance to run over either of the two bandits.

After a four-hour holding pattern over New York during a flight from Quito, Ecuador, our plane went into steep climb, beverage carts flying and flight attendants falling down. It seems that we were on a collision course with another plane. Then the pilot missed the runway (too high by 100 feet) on his first landing approach. Fortunately, nothing happened and I am here, writing this.

Some of these events — and many others — could have maimed or killed me. But never once — never — during or after any of these events have I felt compelled to hie myself to a church for some solace or re-doubled protection from God, Jesus, religion, a Bible, minister, rabbi or priest. Never once did I think about religion or God, during or after these memorable events.

You have to deal with life as it occurs, rely on yourself and your ability to cope with daily events. That's what life boils down to anyway. Finding a figurative crutch in a church, under a spire or in front of an altar only serves as a futile stop-gap measure anyway. Live life, enjoy each day and deal with it. Stay skeptical. Stay honest. You don't want it any other way, do you?

GOD WOULD NOT LIKE THE FEDERAL DISABILITIES ACT WHICH INSISTS ON FAIRNESS TO THOSE DISEASED OR DISABLED

God would have some issues with the Federal Disabilities Act or any acceptance of or fairness to those disabled. It says so, right in the Bible, the Word of God. In Leviticus, we find all sorts of rules for being holy and clean in God's eyes, from not shaving the sides of your head to not wearing clothes woven of two different materials. Well, there go the trips to the barber shop along with the cotton/polyester shirts! (Leviticus 19:19)

It is perhaps understandable that priests and other clergy should not marry prostitutes, although that rules out some serious opportunities for a second chance or forgiveness for those who have erred but repented. (Leviticus 21:7) And here I thought that God was big on forgiveness. Was I wrong?

Naturally, perhaps, the rules for priests, rabbis, ministers and other clergy should suggest adhering to a strict religious life style as an example to their parishioners. It is questionable when it comes to rules about disease and disability of which no one has any control. For example, a whole bunch of problems are mentioned in Leviticus 21:18 as rules for not allowing a priest with disabilities to serve his people, to make offerings of food or other sacrifices or go anywhere near the holy aspects of the temple and holy places.

This is clear in Leviticus 21:18 where it states that God insisted that "No man who has any defect may come near: no man who is blind or lame, disfigured or deformed; no man with a crippled foot or hand, or who is hunchbacked or dwarfed, or who has any eye defect, or who has festering or running sores or damaged testicles."

I have certainly not been applying for a priestly job, but this section would take me out of the running. I have no running sores, crippled body parts or damaged testicles, but my knee replacement (lame?) and eye operation (eye defect?) would pretty well take me out of the priestly short list.

Perhaps it is a good thing that I turned into a skeptic at a young age and pretty much remained that way throughout life. Had I wanted to be a minister, God would have not wanted me. It says so, right there in the Bible. And we know that the Bible is the inerrant Word of God.

Yet, I bet that there are some ministers, rabbis, and priests who are lame, crippled, or impaired, and I'll bet they are doing quite well. Maybe some of these are soldiers back from Iraq or Afghanistan, making a career change into Judaism, Catholicism or Protestantism clergy. Maybe I would not agree with them and their arguments for God and religion, but they certainly deserve a chance, with or without Leviticus and God.

It is a shame that God throws them out. Skeptics, atheists and agnostics would not do this.

Shouldn't Religious Skepticism Match The Standards Of Secular Skepticism?

Is skepticism good or bad? Sure, when we are little, we like the idea of Santa Claus and only later learn about the impossibility of it all. I feel the same way about religious beliefs and my own skepticism. But let's skip to secular skepticism for a minute. Is it bad or good? Hopefully everyone, or at least most people, would agree that it is good.

That does not mean that we can't accept information from others, but only that we have to be careful about what we accept. For example, I am confident that there is a country called Russia, a Russian people and a past and present Russian culture.

And that is not like being confident that there is a country called Oz through which Dorothy and Toto gamboled and toured. As a basis for my "belief" in Russia, I have books, photographs, newspapers, magazine articles, TV, old Movie Tone News, World War II records, libraries, the Internet, radio, government archives, and personal recollections of those who have been there over the course of hundreds of years.

I do not have that with Oz, or with the countries of Lilliput and Brobdingnag of Jonathan Swift's Gulliver's Travels to the lands of little and big people. Thus, we understand that these countries are entertaining and even educational fictions, fanciful fables, fairy tales.

We have to carefully pick our sources and facts for truthful acceptance of things.

As skeptics, we can — and should — look at medical quackery of the present and past. We have many examples. Laetrile from apricot pits as a cure for cancer was a big thing that the government was supposedly keeping from us 50 years ago — except that it was a fake.

Vaccines were causing autism in kids (just ask that eminent medical researcher "Dr." Jenny McCarthy) until just recently, when it was determined that studies to "prove" the vaccine cause were fudged and manipulated for money. We also know that get-rich-schemes are false — just check out the origin and name of the Ponzi scheme in which those at the bottom of this money pyramid are left with empty dreams and vacant wallets. We are also skeptical of the claims of used car salesmen or anyone else with a vested interest in making us believe something that is too good to be true.

When we receive an email or phone call from the widowed Mrs. Abdulaz Mahumadiz, expressing a fervent desire to transfer to us millions of dollars that she cannot get out of Nigeria any other way except through our bank account, we are — or should be — skeptical. Why not just e-mail her my bank account numbers and information. Sure. Why not? And golly — checking my email — I found out that I just won $2.2 million in the UK-ASIA LOTTERY. Funny thing about that — I never entered that or any other lottery.

We should be skeptical of astrology, sure-fire weight-loss pills, on-line dating services, homeopaths, guaranteed gasoline boosters for my car, Tarot card readers, faith healing scams from TV preachers, any political candidate for office, paranormal "researchers", UFO sightings, herbal remedies, and work-at-home ads. Some of these may be useful in some situations — but real caution is required.

The peculiar thing is that most of us most of the time are skeptical about a wide range of secular things. Why, then, are we not equally skeptical of outlandish religious claims, be they Buddhist, Hindu, Jewish, Catholic, Protestant, Muslim, Mormon, Scientologist, Christian Scientist, Jehovah's Witness or others?

Should not the same standards of our secular skepticism apply to religion? Should we not reject concepts — especially religious concepts — which are too strange for any modicum of common sense?

THE DE FACTO SLAVERY OF WOMEN DEMANDED BY PAUL HAS CHANGED, THANK GOODNESS!

There is an interesting note about women in 1 Timothy, specifically chapter 2:11–12. The writing is from Paul, the man known as a disciple, apostle and herald (his words) of the truth of the Bible. But it does give us a little problem today, were we to strictly follow all this in this short segment about women.

In 1 Timothy 2:11 he states: "A woman should learn in quietness and full submission. I do not permit a woman to teach or to have authority over a man; she must be silent." It goes on with similar nonsense, but you get the idea. Allowing women to own property, be the CEO of a corporation, run charities, patent inventions and many other things was probably a mistake! And gosh, giving women the vote in 1920 in the USA and also around the same time frame in other countries was also probably a big mistake, you think?

I guess that goes along with the old stuff that all women and wives should be kept barefoot in summer and pregnant in winter. And why in the Bible (both Testaments) it is not worthwhile to teach women to read, write, or do anything else above being a scullery maid? This sounds a lot like the worst aspects of Muslims and the Koran.

No point in learning that new-fangled stuff of readin' and writin' when all you are going to do in life is raise babies, wash, clean and cook. Why would you women want to read or write, anyway?

But throughout history we have had some smart, strong women, from Nefertiti of Egypt through Cleopatra to Joan of Arc, Catherine de Medici of Spain, Mary Queen of Scots, Catherine the Great of Russia, Golda Meir of Israel to Margaret Thatcher of England. And a lot more through a couple of thousand years of history.

The problem is that Christians and before them Jews in the Old Testament always wanted women to be near-slaves, property to be owned, sold, traded, married off, given away, with little thought to the wishes of the women involved and less still to the contributions they might have made to society, were they encouraged to develop their potential skills. Paul sure echoes this abhorrent philosophy.

Fortunately we have seen an erosion of this thinking over time, particularly in the last few hundred years. Right now I am waiting for a phone call from my bank manager. This manager is a woman, very learned about banking and always very helpful.

My mother was a teacher — I guess Paul would have scratched her as anyone worthwhile. My wife Brenda is a school nurse and has authority over all the boys and girls in her schools. Paul would not like that.

The third in line for the US presidency before the election of 2010 was a woman — Nancy Pelosi. Major corporations have been and are being run by women. Of course all this is not so good for the religionists, according to Paul.

Disrespect Of Women Common To Bible, Despite The Thoughts Of Others

We got rid of overt skin-color slavery in the US and all developed countries. Riddance of de facto female slavery came later in 1920 to allow them to vote in US national and state elections. The typewriter and later the computer gave women the opportunity to earn a living outside the home to help them escape being "in service" to wealthy estate owners. Equal opportunity laws in this country aided in giving women a valued spot in the work place, the Senate, the House of Representatives, and private and governmental positions throughout society.

Some have questioned the idea of de facto slavery of women in the Bible. Religionists have suggested that women are respected, thought well of and revered throughout the Bible. Yeah, right!

For a few examples, let's start with Genesis, where Adam and Eve were made, Adam first — naturally! — and Eve an afterthought by God. Then we have their kids of Cain, Abel and Seth. Later on they had more sons and daughters, but with none of the daughters named or numbered.

Then Adam and Eve's children had kids, with only the male heirs named, never the women named or numbered. Are we starting to see a trend here? Ultimately we get to Noah with his sons Shem, Ham and Japheth named but no one else in the family named — no daughters or wives named.

By Chapter 11 in Genesis, we get to Abram (later Abraham and his named wife Sarai (later Sarah). But of course Sarah was his half-sister and marriage to her was prohibited by edict from God (check out Leviticus and elsewhere).

And of course on two occasions (with the Pharaoh and Abimelech, king of Gerar) Abraham pimped out his wife by claiming that she was his sister instead of his wife. Nice guy. Nice treatment of women.

The Bible just reeks of disrespect, hatred, lack of loyalty, lack of care, ownership, dominance over, and condemnation of women in all sorts of ways. Women were enslaved, given away, knocked up, traded, sold, burned to death, bartered with, stoned to death, and treated as property right through the entire Bible.

This continues up through Jesus and the New Testament where Jesus dismisses his mother (and brothers) for bothering him during preaching sessions, as described in Matthew 12:46–50, Mark 3:31–35 and Luke 8:19–21. Go ahead — don't believe me — check it out.

Exodus 21:7 describes how a man can sell his daughter as a slave. Sure, modern translations use the word "servant," but servants are hired and paid, not bought and sold. Thus, these are instructions for selling your daughter into slavery, an even stricter type of slavery than that for men.

Even baby females are disrespected. Check out Leviticus 12:2–5. This section points out that a woman giving birth to a male is considered unclean for seven days, then is purified after 33 days. With a female birth, the woman is unclean for 14 days, and then purified only after 66 days. Thus, female babies and perhaps their mothers are looked upon as "dirtier," more unclean or less pure or valuable than baby boys.

Is it any wonder that serious skeptics point out these things and disrespect the Bible because of the disrespect that the Bible shows to half of our fellow humans?

Christians Are Picking Through The Bible To Make It Politically Correct

"What we have here is a failure to communicate," so says the warden to the character Luke Jackson played by Paul Newman in the movie "Cool Hand Luke." We also have a failure to communicate with the waffling that Christians do when trying to wiggle their way into a favorable PC concept of the Bible. For example, I have grown weary of the Christian's response to any comments that point out the many horrors of the Old Testament.

"That makes no difference," they pontificate immediately and very insistently, trying to make you feel as dumb as a worm in a fisherman's bait bucket. "Jesus did away with all that. Read verses in 1 Corinthians 1 (or they will mention other verses in 1 and 2 Corinthians, along with spots from Hebrews, etc.). "When the curtain of the temple was rent in two during Jesus' crucifixion, the Old Testament was eliminated and the New Testament and New Covenant took its place." Sounds like they're trying to segue in a new God to replace the terrible God of the Old Testament.

Of course, what the Christians want to do is to go back to pick and choose those parts of the Old Testament that they want to throw out and those that they want to keep and use to beat you about the head.

They want to throw out all the rape, murder, child killing (check Abraham's plans as directed by God), mass extermination of a people (check the book of Joshua), slavery (check anywhere), theft, multiple wives (check Israelite kings), and their excuses for some of the major players for their violation of the Ten Commandments.

Of course, for the rest of us and even under the New Testament, these same Christians want to keep the Ten Commandments and all the so-called "good stuff." The "good stuff" of course is all those things, sayings, edicts, commands, stories, fables, orders and demands from God that they want to use to threaten you with if you are a skeptic or slightly suspicious of this fairy tale religion.

But wait just a minute. There is a teeny, tiny problem here. Maybe a big problem. It seems that Jesus — yeah, Jesus himself — would not agree with these holier-than-thou Christians about eliminating the Law of the Old Testament. For example, check out Matthew 5:17–18. This is a direct quote from Jesus, so we can't go any higher than that in this argument.

"Do not think that I have come to abolish the Law or the Prophets; I have come not to abolish them but to fulfill them." In this, Jesus, a Jew, is directly stating that he intends to keep and honor all of the Old Testament, all of the laws, all of the Godly demands and commands. "The Law or the Prophets" in this case (capitalized in the Bible translations), refers to the Old Testament and the laws and edicts of Mosaic and Abrahamic eras. One biblical concordance refers to "The Law and the Prophets" as meaning the scriptures — writings — of the Old Testament. No selective picking and choosing here.

"I tell you the truth, until heaven and earth disappear, not the smallest letter, not the least stroke of a pen, will by any means disappear from the Law until everything is accomplished," continues Jesus. No waffling, picking or choosing there either.

Well, with Jesus saying so, I guess that Christians have to pick up their weapons and retreat. They have to believe and continue to include in their beliefs all the rape, pillage, murder, mass killings, stealing, slavery, bondage, multiple marriages, executions (stoning) and the other disreputable acts of early Israelites.

I guess that we skeptics can continue to be skeptical about all this — after all, Jesus says so in Matthew 5:17. Things are looking up for us — but not looking so good for the Christians.

THOUGHTS ON A CHRISTIAN HANGING AND BURNING A PUPPY FOR CHEWING ON A BIBLE

The report about a Spartanburg, SC, woman hanging and burning a female pit bull puppy is old news by now. The woman killed her nephew's dog because, according to news reports, "God told her to do it." If he did that, that is a pretty bad and evil God or god.

The puppy had committed the unpardonable, unforgivable sin of chewing on the woman's Bible that the woman left on the front porch. The woman left it on the front porch! That puppies chew on things is a fact that somehow escaped her. And she was the one leaving it on the front porch as a temptation for the dog. The dog was a "devil dog" according to her and again based on news reports. She had to kill it — had to — since it might be Satanic and harm the neighborhood children.

This story is just one that tends to prove a developing theory of mine. I have long wondered whether extreme religious belief is quite possibly a mental illness. I have also wondered if any or all religious belief is not some form of mental aberration, be it temporary or permanent. Could it not be the cognitive dissonance of psychology?

There can be lots of questions about this and other similar aberrations of individual religious types, but the big question is what people like this would do to the rest of us who do not subscribe to her particular brand of delusion?

We do not know the religious basis or denomination of this woman, except that she is Christian. But if she and others like her had a free hand — legally and religiously — to "correct" those of us who are of different denominations, what would she want done?

Would those who are Jewish, Hindu, Buddhist, Muslim, the "wrong" Protestant denominations, perhaps Catholics, agnostics, atheists and I-don't-carers, suffer in some way? I bet that we would.

And before you say that such thinking by me is patently ridiculous, remember that it has not been that long since the days of the Inquisition, burning at the stake of any named "witches," the Salem witch trials and such.

It was not religious, but we also have the recent McCarthy Era in which innocents were accused of "wrong" political thinking. And their lives were ruined. You could count on Senator McCarthy of 1950 for these reckless, unsubstantiated, demagogic accusations against others.

And remember the words of that great honorable Protestant reformer, Martin Luther. "Witches are the whores of the Devil. That is why they must all be killed." Yeah, try to explain that one for me. Yeah, dress that up for me!

Remember that John Calvin, that great honorable founder of Calvinism and Presbyterianism, accused his theological friend Michael Servetus who was then burned at the stake for Calvin's accusations. And Calvin insisted that he be burned "slowly" to extract the maximum amount of pain for his sin of differing theological views.

I feel sorry for the puppy that had to suffer the hanging and burning for the "crime" of chewing on a Bible. I also feel sorry for the rest of us who are not that far away from similar punishments of the past (and perhaps the future, should religious fundies ever get their way in laws and courts).

How Come God Did Not Give Us A Sense Of Smell As Good As A Polar Bear?

According to the fundamentalist Christians, we are made in God's image, look exactly like God and come with the same equipment. God is the Intelligent Designer who made us just as we are today, they say. No evolution here — we popped out perfect. Well, not exactly. Or perhaps God did not do his best work with us. I can think of a whole bunch of improvements and I make no claims as to what God had in mind when "creating" us.

For one, just take our sense of smell and compare it to that of a polar bear. Among mammals, polar bears have perhaps the best sense of smell in the world, according to biologists. They can smell a ring seal from one mile away — when the seal is under three feet of ice and snow. Shucks, I probably could not smell a ring seal short of sitting on it.

Polar bears so this with one billion olfactory sensors in their noses and a large section of the brain cordoned off for smell. By comparison, our best tracking dogs have about 250 million olfactory sensors and we are a pretty pathetic species with only about 5 million sensors.

Well, you might say, we have no need to smell ring seals and we certainly are not going to track them or dive under the ice to drag one out for a meal. That's all true, but with early man, a better sense of small might have been handy in other ways. (Don't get excited — we are only going back to biblical times — we are not going to touch on evolution and Mr. Darwin here!)

For those shepherds in Luke visiting the baby Jesus, such a sense of smell might have helped them keep track of their flocks. Given that the FDA was not around then, it might also have helped early nomads from eating spoiled food that could sicken or cause death. Maybe by smell, tent makers of the time could have picked out the best linen or other materials for their tent-making.

Personally, I think that a better sense of anything would be an aid to living in this world. With a better sense of smell, we could better detect danger, enjoy life more, be more aware of our surroundings and better bumble our way through life. Of course, with the larger face and nose area required for one billion olfactory sensors, instead of our paltry five million, it would change our facial features.

But if we were grow up with a face like a polar bear (it looking just like Mom and Dad); I am sure that we would love it. And I can't see how it would change the swim suit category in the Miss America Contest.

God should have looked in this olfactory thing more when working on the prototype stage and before whipping out the first assembly line production models with Adam and Eve. God as the Intelligent Designer could have done better. Couldn't he have given us a sense of smell at least as good as say, a polar bear?

IS LEVITICUS IN THE BIBLE TO PERPETUATE A SCAM?

Today we have ministers, priests, rabbis and such all anxious to have you attend their church or synagogue on the Sabbath (the right Sabbath of course) so you can give them money. These characters

— men and women, black and white, old and young, on TV, street corners, in various religious buildings, in retreats and parks, in books and DVDs — are all preaching the Bible as they see it and think that they know it.

And these pikers are all lunging at the leash to pick your pocket, to purloin your pocketbook, eager for your earnings. And it has all been set up that way via that text of untruth, the Bible.

Just take Leviticus as an example. It sets forth the rules of the road, the examples by which mankind is to live, at least if you are Jewish or Christian. In this, it outlines the various offerings to God, not that God could or would use any of it. God is God, so they say — not a wife grinding up grain to bake bread or a husband slaughtering the sheep to cook mutton.

But there are lots of offerings required by God. There are grain offerings, fellowship offerings, guilt offerings, burnt offerings, wave offerings, sin offerings, etc. It goes on and on. You can — and must — sacrifice male and female cattle, male and female sheep, male and female goats, doves, and pigeons, along with grain and oil. Apparently, God needs all that stuff so that the priests can burn it up to make a "pleasing smell and aroma unto the Lord." Sounds like a complete waste to me.

But here comes the hooker. After a portion of all this is made available to the priests to burn up and create that "pleasing aroma" of burned grain, roasted oil and dead slaughtered animals, priests get to keep the rest of it to eat. Look it up — it's in the fine print in the early part of Leviticus. Sounds like a scam to me.

After all, you don't need a church or synagogue to worship, if you really want to worship. People can meet in homes, study a Bible on their own, sing a tad if they like, etc. And with the small groups involved, it would probably be more interesting and worthwhile, assuming that they wanted to follow this dictate of delusion.

The same thing exists today. Give to the priests, rabbis, ministers, and preachers an equivalent of this in money. After all, money is the common exchange medium, since most of us don't have a bullock or ram laying around that we have raised, can slaughter and can give away to ministers and priests who don't deserve it.

But then, perhaps I am just being skeptical of all this built-in Ponzi scheme nonsense.

Ponzi-Schemers Are Pikers Compared To Pompous, Prosperous Preachers Picking Your Pocket

Charles Ponzi did not develop the scheme which goes by his name, but he did perfect it in the 1920s. It was written about earlier by Charles Dickens in his 1857 story, "Little Dorrit."

In principle, a Ponzi scheme is simple, although of course also illegal, immoral, dishonest, unscrupulous, deceptive, unfair, larcenous, and thievery. It involves setting up a fictional or dishonest "investment plan" to pay impossibly high interest rates to gullible investors. Those interest rates are paid for by other subsequently invested money with the whole plan collapsing after creating inordinate wealth for scheme originator. The pyramid gets too big and collapses. One example in living memory is that of Bernard Madoff with monies in excess of $21 billion. He left financial wreckage and ruined lives everywhere.

Churches and religious institutions are just like this, and I am talking about the so-called legitimate ones, not the TV charlatans who want you to "plant a seed" (money) and "invest with God" to make a big killing.

A Ponzi scheme promises something (high interest rates) that it cannot deliver. It takes your money in a lump sum or as a regular scheduled "investment," using that money for enrichment of the scheme operators and to pay out high interest rates to previous investors. It collapses when it runs out of new patsies paying in or when the authorities have slammed the lid on the Ponzi operators.

That's just like any religious group collecting for your "religious welfare." The leaders promise something that they cannot deliver — a ticket to heaven and an eternal afterlife. The religion takes your money, usually with your tithing envelopes when you go to church weekly.

The weekly sermon gives you a message to keep you happy about getting something, sort of like giving a stray alley cat a bowl of warm milk. The money is used to maintain the minister and the church; never mind that the minister may not be making a huge personal investment in the production of a sermon, since such presentations can readily be found in large collections available at Christian book stores, or even online.

These sermon lessons are all laid out for ministers. All they have to do is to add a few personal anecdotes, if they really want to work that hard. It is as if I were to plagiarize from other writers various columns and articles, stick in a detail here and elsewhere, and publish it under my name. Outside of religious circles, this is not considered honest or legal. Were I to do it, I would be fined or jailed or both.

The ultimate promise in all this is not Ponzi high interest rates but something even better, if by better we mean more dishonest and devious. The ministers and priests promise eternal happiness in heaven. Of course the dead never even find out that this is a scam; that the concept of heaven is man-made and based only on the ultimate fear of a loss of life and consciousness.

What a deal for the ministers, priests, preachers, rabbis, TV charlatans and others of this ilk! That's it — promise something that you never had, don't own, can't deliver and never have to prove that it even exists! Ponzi was a piker compared with preachers purloining your pocketbook.

BENDING, MODIFYING, ADDING AND SUBTRACTING THE TRUTH

Experts in ancient languages and literature along with biblical scholars note that peoples of the past were not always accurate and maybe did not even always stick to the truth in their writings. Today, we like to believe we're getting the truth, at least from reliable news sources including mainstream TV, legitimate newspapers and qualified magazines. They weren't quite this extreme in ancient times and their recording of events, and that might explain a few things in and about the Bible.

For example, there were various and different people and numbers of women visiting Jesus' tomb after his crucifixion. There are also various beings there when they got to the tomb — a single man, two men, one angel or two angels — described in the four gospels.

There was also the varied descriptions of Mary anointing Jesus' feet (John 12) or head (Mark 14), take your choice. In Matthew, we have wise men following a star and visiting the baby Jesus, while in Luke, there is no star and only shepherds. In the four gospels, there are varied stories included or excluded so that some parts seem to coincide with others or are completely different.

Religionists often use the ancient literature of others to point out that there are — sometimes — varying degrees of plagiarizing, copying, changing, embellishing, exaggerating and explaining to justify the difference in various stories in both the Old and New Testaments.

For thinking people, this should also lead to other conclusions. Could it be, I ask myself, that these stories are enhanced a little, here and there, by the home team to make their guy look good? Could strong protagonists of the then-developing Christian viewpoint have made up things to counter the other Christian, Mithraic and varying viewpoints and religions of the time? Would some people go to great lengths to make sure that their champion came out better than other champions so that their Christian viewpoint would win?

The answers, of course are yes, yes and yes. Make it up, condemn other viewpoints, destroy documents and manuscripts of the opposition, leaving only one answer for people to consider. That's the way to win wars, battles, and debates and convince people that your story is the true story, in this case, the truth of the Bible. You find it in today's political debates and discussions.

The problem is that there are an awful lot of us who find a huge amount of biblical inconsistencies to think about and to be skeptical of in the Bible. And for skeptics, there is just no way around this. For a lot of us with questions, it seems as if there are no answers — or answers that would make the Christians happy. Are there any real answers?

GOD GAVE US A MUSCLE THAT HELPS IN TREE CLIMBING? WHY?

Creationists and fundamentalists think that the earth began about 10,000 years ago. They also buy into the idea of Bishop Ussher who wrote in 1654 that Adam and Eve popped up about 6,000 years ago (specifically, early on the morning of Sunday, October 23, 4004 BCE).

Naturally, this creationist idea states that Adam and Eve are our ancestors. Our bodies then and now are as God wanted them, perfect, with no extras and no missing parts. But as with other anatomical features such as arrector pili muscles (fight or flight response) and our poor sense of smell (compared to dogs and polar bears), that is not exactly the case. Let me introduce you to the palmaris longus muscle.

You may not know the palmaris longus muscle if you did not attend medical school or have a good college course in comparative anatomy. But we have this muscle, even if it is missing in a few of us, and not always found in both arms.

The palmaris longus muscle is a small slip of a muscle found in the forearm, with one attachment to the humerus and the other attachment (insertion) to a broad tendon-like band covering the palm. Presence or absence of this muscle is easy to check since it is superficial to the carpal tunnel which contains tendons of all other forearm muscles.

Because the palmaris longus is superficial, you can check to see if you have one. With palm up, just touch the tips of your thumb and little finger and bend your palm upward. If you have a palmaris longus, you should see the band of the tendon in your wrist. It is missing in about 14 to 16 percent of the population, with some ethnic variations. Its absence is more frequent in women and it is often absent only in one arm.

The important thing for the creationists to think about is that this muscle is only used in tree climbing and by lower mammals and primates to extend their claws. We have fingernails, not claws, and we can't extend them. We do not do much tree climbing any more. Both uses point to our evolved but now distant evolutionary background.

The absence of this muscle has no effect on grip or hand strength. If you don't have it, you won't miss it. The point for creationists to consider is why have something that we don't need? It only makes sense as a left-over muscle in an evolving body.

That, along with our poor sense of smell and arrector pili muscles (useless goose bumps), is another proof of evolution that the creationists can't explain.

If there is a God, why would he give us something anatomically that we patently do not need and do not use? Why would we need a muscle like the palmaris longus that is totally useless? It is only a remnant of our evolutionary past.

Why can't creationists and fundamentalists finally shed the fiction of the Bible stories when confronted with the truth of science?

What Is So Great About David That He Gets A Pass From God?

If it were not so sad, it would be funny how God plays fast and loose with his dictates and rules when it comes to friends and favored people. At least that how it is portrayed in the Bible, God's inerrant word. It seems that favorites of God get a pass on some big stuff, while the rest of us have to adhere to his Commandments — or pay the penalty. Maybe it is sort of a nepotism example or something.

Take, for example, David, the king of Israel and the leader to whom Jesus was traced back to supposedly (and erroneously) fulfill the messianic prophecy of the Old Testament. Check out 2 Samuel 11 and you find David guilty of adultery and also murder. That's the famous story where David spied Bathsheba bathing, ordered his servants to get her, had sex with her and then had her husband Uriah killed. Great role model.

This is what they say happened. It seems that David had a sleepless night, went up onto his palace roof (flat roofs in that area at that time) and saw a woman in another house bathing. The Bible reports that she was beautiful, that David wanted to know more about her and ultimately sent his servants to get her. She was Bathsheba, the wife of Uriah the Hittite, then fighting the Ammonites with his commander Joab.

"Then David sent messengers to get her," says 2 Samuel 11:4. "She came to him, and he slept with her." Then she went home and later reported to David that she had conceived. She was pregnant.

Naturally, this created a sticky wicket for David. Someone else's wife was pregnant with his child and the husband was still around. David's solution was to "off" the husband, Uriah. David did not do this himself of course, but he created a situation whereby the dirty deed would be accomplished.

David first ordered Uriah out of the field of battle and back to Jerusalem where he stayed for a few days. But Uriah was a decent person. He did not take advantage of the luxury offered to him while his commander Joab and his fellow soldiers were still in the field, fighting for David. He did not sleep with his wife, Bathsheba.

Ultimately, David sent him back to his commander Joab, but with specific orders to Joab. "Put Uriah in the front line where the fighting is the fiercest. Then withdraw from him so that he will be struck down and die," said David in specific instructions to Joab in 2 Samuel 11:15. That's a set-up for a contract murder.

Joab did as ordered, and Uriah the Hittite was killed. Bathsheba mourned, but when the mourning period was over, she was brought by David to the palace, became David's wife and bore him a son.

Today, setting up a hit man or situation for murder is a criminal offense, while adultery is a civil offense. But David gets a pass from God and becomes the king of the Israeli state. Compare that to the unnamed Israelite in Number 15:32 who was stoned to death for merely picking up a few sticks — probably for a cooking fire — on the Sabbath. That's sort of like a school boy given a pat on the wrist for burning down a classroom while his classmate gets expelled for being late for the algebra exam on Tuesday.

King David Gets A Slap On The Wrist — God Would Execute The Rest Of Us

We know that King David of 2 Samuel in the Bible got caught with his pants down and with his hands dirty.

We also know that in our culture today, the murder part would result in a criminal trial with conviction resulting in years in the slammer or perhaps even the death penalty. We also know that the adultery part could have ended up in a civil trial, perhaps divorce, time on the Dr. Phil show, possibly some nasty acrimonious acts or maybe Uriah and Bathsheba reconciling and living happily ever after if everything was stopped before the murder part.

But the biblical punishment of David's acts is pretty clear. All we have to do is to check back in Leviticus for the answer. That's where the wobbly and wonky rules, codes, and laws of the Israelites are listed. Even the Ten Commandments are reiterated here after their initial listing in Exodus.

And Leviticus 20:10 is pretty clear. It says, "If a man commits adultery with another man's wife — with the wife of his neighbor — both the adulterer and adulteress must be put to death."

Interestingly, in the Bible, "neighbor" means virtually anyone. If it means only a neighbor as a person living near you, then this would still apply. After all, King David first saw Bathsheba from the palace rooftop, so she had to be living nearby with her husband Uriah. Either way, this means that David's goose is cooked on the adultery thing. There they go — the two of them off to be stoned to death, separately or together. That's what would have happened or should have happened were the Bible and Godly rules followed.

And there is no wiggle room on the "another man's wife" part, since the Bible clearly states that Bathsheba was married to Uriah. Uriah was then fighting for David under his commander Joab on the front lines, fighting against the Ammonites. In Exodus, the death penalty equally applies to those culpable for the death of another.

There are no exceptions to all this. There are no verses that say "except for kings of Judah" or "except for kings of Israel," or "except for King David who killed Goliath." No exceptions.

Naturally, the death penalty back then was by stoning, where all the guys would get together and clobber the guy or gal (both in this case) to death. That means no jail time, no time off for good behavior.

But David missed all this. Nathan, a prophet in the time of David and Solomon, rebuked David, but that is all. Sure, in 2 Samuel 12:7–13 Nathan points out all that God had done for David and then notes that David will lose his wives (he had lots to pick from), perhaps another sticky wicket.

After David admitted his sin (adultery and murder), the simple answer from Nathan was, "The Lord has taken away your sin. You are not going to die."

That's it? That's the big punishment for David for adultery and murder? That's the slap on the wrist? Big deal! How come David gets a pass from God?

Maybe we should all be a little skeptical about the way God runs his business here on earth. Should we think that in the very least, that this is not fair?

KING DAVID GOOFS — AND GOD KILLS 70,000 INNOCENT ISRAELITES!

More on King David of Israel involves a misunderstanding between David and God. We are speaking of the notations in 2 Samuel 24 and also 1 Chronicles 21. This is the section where God requires or demands that David take a census of the people of Israel and Judah.

This section gives the theological scholars and believers a lot of anguish, as well it should. In 2 Samuel it refers to God ordering the census of the people. In 1 Chronicles, it refers to Satan inciting David to take a census. Who is doing what here and why is God not in control, as the Christians always like to say?

In 2 Samuel 24, there were eight hundred thousand men in Israel; in Judah five hundred thousand — a total of one million, three hundred thousand fighting men. In 1 Chronicles, we have one million one hundred thousand fighting men including four hundred seventy thousand in Judah. That's a slight difference of two hundred thousand men.

What most scholars fail to realize is that God/Satan asked for a census of the people — the total population. David gave him a census of the fighting men, or army. Numbers of fighting men and numbers of the population are always different. Perhaps this goof by David is where God's anger went off the tracks.

Other questioning about this could be because God did not demand and David did not collect the so-called required offering from the people for their pleasure of being counted.

After this, David had a melt down with his "sin" of wrongly taking the census. Perhaps this was for taking it at all even though God/ Satan ordered, or for doing it the wrong way. No one really knows. In both stories, God lashes out — but not against David, who may or may not deserve it — but against the completely innocent Israelites.

God gives David three choices for his people — three years of famine, three months of being vanquished by enemies or three days of plague. David chooses the three days of plague — and 70,000 Israelites die. They die! They are flat-out wrongly killed by God, destroyed because David somehow make a mistake (or not — we don't know) with a bad census. Once again, David gets a pass from God for something that David did wrong, while 70,000 innocents pay with horrible illness and their lives.

Think about this! Innocent Israelites killed by God. Is this another example of God's love, his benevolence, his care for his children, his respect for His Chosen People? I don't think so. Skeptics remain skeptical.

PS — Skeptics would also point out that if God really is God, and if God really is omniscient, God would have all the facts and figures for a census anyway; total population, men, women, children, fighting men, etc. It makes skeptics wonder about all this.

David Killing Goliath — Ballistics, Kinetic Energy And Such — Was It Possible?

We know from 1 Samuel 17 about the conflict of Saul and the Israelites with the Philistines, the 40 days of faux battle plans with posturing and the ultimate trash talking between David and Goliath before David killed Goliath with his sling.

We also know that David used his sling — not a sling shot, as some say. Before engaging in battle, David picked five stones for the ensuing dust-up. In 1 Samuel 17:40 it says, "Then he (David) took his staff in his hand, chose five smooth stones from the stream, put them in the pouch of his shepherd's bag and, with his sling in his hand, approached the Philistine."

The trash talking ensued between the two, and then David approached the giant. In 1 Samuel 17:49 we find, "Reaching into his bag and taking out a stone, he [David] slung it and struck the Philistine on the forehead. The *stone sank into his forehead* [emphasis mine] and he fell face down on the ground."

Not likely; not likely at all. First, the frontal bone in the forehead area is very thick. Since bone can vary depending upon diet, ethnicity, gender and exercise, the forehead frontal bone of huge Goliath may well have been and probably was thicker than that of the rest of us.

Second, there is no fat or muscle in the forehead area for a sling stone to sink into. The stone as described would have had to have crushed the immediate part of the forehead where the stone struck. Admittedly, sling stones varied, according to research done on slings and warfare with slings. The stone — either round or the later styles of football shape — would range from about two ounces to about one pound.

The killing or wounding would come from the kinetic energy, which is a combination of mass and velocity of the stone. Larger stones might kill more effectively with more kinetic energy, but would also be less likely to sink into a forehead, as biblically described.

In any case, the velocity of the stone probably would be less than that of a .22 bullet, which ranges around 1,000 feet per second or a little more for a long rifle casing. And it is known that while a .22 can kill, it often depends upon the angle of the bullet, distance, type of bullet used, and similar factors. It is possible to get a glancing blow and no bone penetration of the forehead from a .22 bullet or certainly no penetration from a slung stone.

It is also possible that the stone to the forehead merely stunned Goliath or knocked him unconscious for the few seconds that it took for David to grab Goliath's sword and cut off his head. (1 Samuel 17:51)

Thus, while there are a lot of variables involved in all this, it is at least questionable that a slung stone would penetrate Goliath's forehead to cause the type of injury or death as described in the Bible.

But even with Goliath merely stunned, that battle still would have ended his life.

God, People Made In God's Image And Sharks. But God Could Have Done A Better Job!

As with everyone else, I have to go to the dentist regularly. My teeth are in good shape, but I still need regular cleaning and the occasional filling. Should we need all this, since God made us in his image? Shouldn't that image and result be pretty good?

Knowing that God made us (if you believe in a God) and that God made us in his image, presumably God made us perfect. But God could have done a better job. This also ties in with countering the fundamentalist concept that "God is God. God can do anything that he wants to!"

With that in mind, God could have given me — and all of us — the tooth basis of sharks. By this, I don't mean the little (or big) pointy things of sharks, but the fact that sharks constantly re-grow teeth their entire lives. Some sharks grow new teeth every two weeks, some over longer periods of time and all of them replace teeth when an existing tooth is lost or damaged.

With a system like this, we would not need dentists, tooth brushes, dentures, denture cream, dental bridges, implants, or to be eating mush by those who have lost all their teeth. Basically, shark teeth consist of endless rows in back of the usable teeth. They are pushed forward as new teeth are needed. Some sharks shed up to 35,000 teeth in a lifetime.

These teeth are in rows, almost like a little cartilaginous conveyer belt to deliver new fresh teeth on demand. They are also imbedded into the gum or skin of the shark, not into the bony jaw as with us. Sharks are all cartilaginous anyway, lacking any bones.

We would not want sharp teeth for tearing flesh, but probably God could modify that. God, since "God can do anything he wants!," could easily modify that to make teeth that are combination choppers and grinders for us omnivores.

Otherwise, we should be in good shape. After all, shark teeth still have a core and enamel covering similar to our current equipment. And there is plenty of power, structural stability and tearing ability in those teeth to tear apart any fish, seal, whale, squid or anything else scooting around in salt water.

Just think — with a system like this, our dental health would be assured. There would be no more cavities, no more ugly fillings, no pain, no trips to the dentist, no dentists, no gaps in our smiles. There would be no more need for toothache cream or whitening formulas to put our best tooth/teeth forward when dating.

We could all relax, and smile. God — if there really is a God — could have done better in making us in his image or with the materials and tools at hand. After all, as the Christians say — God can do anything. It is a shame that he could not/would not make us at least as good as sharks when it comes to dentition.

Therefore, some of us remain skeptical of this whole God thing.

Lots Of Doubts About The Book *Beyond a Reasonable Doubt*

With a book title *Beyond a Reasonable Doubt* and a subtitle of *Evidence for Christianity*, you know what the emphasis of this text will be. Authored by Terry Siciliano and being passed out by churches in my area (which is how I got one) it purportedly answers in 158 pages all the questions one might have about Christianity.

Not quite. It supposedly gives you a solid foundation for Christian thinking, countering Charles Darwin, proving the validity of Christ, outlining original sin, explaining the fall of man, speaking for God with God's Big Plan, etc.

Let's look at one of the points — of many — of poor thinking in all this. In one section, there is a rant about the terrible secular opposition to posting the Ten Commandments in courtrooms, to not allowing official prayer in schools, and the prohibition against teaching creationism or intelligent design along with evolution in the science classrooms.

The emphasis is on the thought that there should be Ten Commandments posted everywhere, that creationism should be taught to all students, and that official prayer should open all schools and presumably anything else secular.

Then there is the follow up plea. "Isn't it wrong to impose one's tastes on others in a free society?" In short, the author in this simple statement argues against herself.

Apparently, Mrs. Siciliano thinks that it is fine and fair for her and her ilk to post in secular buildings and for secular audiences the thinking of HER faith and Fundamentalist Christianity without realizing that she is violating her very statement of the wrongness of imposing her tastes on others in our free society.

According to the author, you can pick A religion, you just can't pick NO religion. You can be, presumably with her blessings, a Catholic, Baptist, Lutheran, Hindu, Buddhist, Jew, Scientologist, Jain, etc. You just can't have the choice of being an agnostic, atheist, secular humanist or I-don't-carer. That is not — or would not be — allowed in her world.

For any critical, careful reader, this short section provides only a glimpse of the convoluted, intolerant and error-filled thinking of the author and of her slight and shallow book.

Post the Ten Commandments on public property and you open the door to the beliefs and mission statements of every other church, religion and belief being posted also. Allow Christian-approved prayer in school and every other religion has an argument for their prayer being announced and publicly recited also. You can pray, just not audibly. What's wrong with that? Besides, it was an 8–1 decision by the Supreme Court, not an act by a lone weirdo or a bunch of atheists.

Her inane and harmful silliness continues, but you get the point. Boy, it really is refreshing to be a skeptic!

THE BIBLE — THE WORD OF GOD — BUT WAIT A MINUTE — THERE ARE LOTS OF MISTAKES!

On the first page of the Preface of my New International Bible, it points out the absolute truth of the Bible. It says, in part, "the translators were united in their commitment to the authority and infallibility of the Bible as God's Word in written form." You can find similar statements of the absolute inerrancy of the Bible in many Christian, Fundamentalist and Protestant Internet sites. They state that the Bible is God's Word and as such is without mistakes — without ANY mistakes.

Well, that's just not true. Let's look at a few examples, leaving lots more for later. First, we are not talking about questions of morality, nor contradictions, nor basic physics. Of those, there are more contradictions, errors and moral questions than a Planter's facility has peanuts. We are talking about flat-out mistakes.

Let's take a look at Leviticus. Right there in Leviticus 11:13–19 you can find a listing of all the birds that are unclean and detestable for food. These unclean possibilities include the eagle, vulture, black vulture, red kite, ravens, horned owl, screech owl, any hawk, gull, little owl, cormorant, great owl, white owl, desert owl, osprey, stork, heron, hoopoe and the bat. Quite a list!

Uh-oh. The bat, the last one listed in these verses, is not a bird — it is a mammal. Mistake. Big, big mistake. A little further down in Leviticus 11:20–23 it states that insects with four legs are detestable for food. Some insects such as locusts, katydids, crickets and grasshoppers are OK for food — the rest are not.

Uh-oh. Insects have six legs, not four. That's true of all of them. Mistake. Big, big mistake. Jump over to 1 Kings 7:23 when Solomon was building his palace. He commissioned work on a large reservoir measuring ten cubits across and 30 cubits around. A cubit is 18 inches.

Uh-oh. That's a mistake also. For something to be ten cubits (or any other form of measurement) across, it would have to be 31.416 cubits around, not the 30 cubits listed. In feet, the above measurements would be a 15 foot diameter and a 47.1240 circumference — not the 45 feet listed in the Bible. The Bible is nowhere near as accurate as measurements by earlier Babylonian and Egyptian civilizations.

Realize that the formula for a circumference is D X pi, or the diameter times the mathematical constant of pi, or 3.1416, etc. You can't change a mathematical constant. God can't make it different from physics and reality.

I can see the arguments against this now. "But they did not know any better in that time period!" "They did the best that they could and did not know about later mathematical calculations or biological taxonomy."

But that misses the point. God — if there is a God — would have known all this, since God is supposed to be omniscient and to know everything — past, present and future. God would have known. And this Bible is supposed to be the inerrant Word of God, without any mistakes. Every Christian says so — including biblical translators.

I can't wait to see the convolutions, calculations, misrepresentations, translations, reinventions, retranslations, reinterpretations, mathematical adjustments, formula changes, and explanations that the Fundies do on this one. Stay tuned — it should be fun for skeptics.

Lines In The Sand For Religion Make It Difficult To Believe In Any Of Them

While attending a fishing tackle show in North Carolina for other writing assignments, I by chance met an Amish gentleman. We were standing side by side in a line to ask questions about the show. He was concerned about getting information from online Internet rod building sites, chat rooms, and forums.

He was allowed by his employer to check these sites when and where he worked, but through his church elders was not allowed to have an email address.

The Amish lack electricity so he had no electric furnace, electric stove, TV, telephone, computer, radio, cell phone or any other electronics. He could not own a car.

His religious faith requires shunning worldly goods and temptations, to abjure members of anything modern. Thus, zippers and Velcro are out. Hook-and-eye fasteners are preferable to more "modern" buttons.

Transportation by horse and buggy (black, please) is fine, and he could travel in, but not own, a car, train or bus. Airplanes are out. That's ironic, since commercial mass transportation by a bus and plane would have been developed in the early part of the 20th century. Neither was any more "modern" than the other.

This gentleman lived in Ohio and the show was in North Carolina; he did not get there by horse and buggy. This also led to my thoughts about hypocrisy, although I did not express this during our too-brief conversation.

If he is supposed to eschew worldly goods, should he not avoid using them in addition to owning them? Would that not also apply to transportation? Would not his viewing and required use of a computer during work — never mind the hobby of making fishing rods — directly conflict with his beliefs? If he could not subscribe to Playboy, could he with good conscience read it (articles only, naturally) at a friend's house?

To me, there are too many lines that have to be drawn for me to be even marginally comfortable with that religion or really any religion. I assume that for the Amish, even the pictures in the Sports Illustrated swim-suit edition and many mainstream publications would be questionable. How do you know where the line is to be drawn? AND WHY?

All religions have lines in the sand — some more or less than others. And these equivocations in all religions lead to the different denominations and the terrible conflicts between them. The Amish are no better or worse than any other religions. Some religions do not allow eating shellfish or ham, or used to prohibit eating meat on

Friday, ban blood transfusions, the use of caffeine, and other strictures that are seemingly pretty petty.

There is no common sense in religion. Isn't that one reason why so many of us are skeptics or become skeptics?

GOD CONFUSES PROTECTION WITH DISRESPECT. THAT'S SAD.

Let's assume that you have something of great monetary or sentimental value in your home. If you are wealthy, it might be a priceless Ming Dynasty vase. Or it could be sentimental — the fragile pottery urn holding the ashes of a loved and revered deceased relative.

Your son has been instructed to never, NEVER touch or go near that vase or urn. He has been told repeatedly the value of such, and that he is absolutely prohibited from even touching these two valuable items. Those are the house rules for any reason, any time, anyway.

Then you get a puppy. During a time when it is galloping around the house, it slides on the hardwood floor into the stand holding the vase/urn. The vase/urn wobbles. It could fall and break. Junior puts his hand on it to steady it and to keep it from possibly falling — and breaking. It breaking — be it a Ming vase or funerary urn — would be a financial or sentimental disaster.

Would you punish Junior? Would you severely reprimand him for touching the vase/urn when he had been specifically told not to touch it - ever? Would you send him to his room or ground him for six months? Would you kill him?

Don't laugh or recoil in horror. Death — that was God's answer for a similar situation involving the Ark of God when moving it under David's rule. You can check 2 Samuel 6:18 for this. For this move, the God's Ark of the Covenant was placed on a new cart with oxen pulling the cart. Uzzah and Ahio, sons of Abinadab, were leading the oxen. The rest of Israel was traveling with it, joyously celebrating this move.

Then disaster happened. "When they came to the threshing floor of Nacon, Uzzah reached out and took hold of the Ark of God, because the oxen stumbled," says 2 Samuel 6:6. "The Lord's anger burned against Uzzah because of his irreverent act; therefore God struck him down and he died there beside the Ark of God," continues 2 Samuel 6:7.

Was God nuts? What irreverent act? Uzzah was trying to protect the Ark! The Ark of God might have fallen and broken or at least been damaged. Uzzah was protecting it and honoring it, not committing an irreverent act.

This is no different than Junior protecting your valuable Ming vase or funerary urn. With Junior you would profusely thank him for his good sense to see the imminent danger to the valued item and to take steps to protect it from falling even though he had been told to never NEVER touch them

God, on the other hand, obviously lacking good thinking or any common sense, kills the guy who perhaps saved the Ark. I am just glad that I never had any Ming vases or urns sitting around with God standing by. No telling what could have happened had God been in charge.

For this skeptic, not having God around to "protect" things means that God won't pull the plug on someone for doing a good deed and protecting something of value.

And with God being God, could he not have instead made the threshing floor of Nacon smooth and even so that the oxen would not stumble? It all makes you wonder. It makes you wonder a lot.

The Supreme Court, The Westboro Baptist Church And Christians

There was and even today continues to be a lot of ire about the Supreme Court 8-1 decision of allowing the Westboro Baptist church of Kansas a continued right to protest funerals of GI's. A suit against the Westboro Baptist Church for picketing the funeral of his deceased son was overturned. But it was not the Westboro Baptist church that won.

What won was the United States Constitution; specifically the First Amendment. Read it sometime. In fact, read the whole Constitution. There is no doubt in my mind and in the minds of so many others that the Westboro Baptist Church is a hateful group who is doing this for no other purpose than to gain publicity and to get its fifteen minutes of fame. Ugly fame, but fame. It, and those who belong to this splinter group, ae hateful, awful people. We all can think what we want to think. But why some would want to deliberately, visually and vocally hurt others is beyond me.

According to this hateful group, God is or was killing American GIs because of the nation's increasing tolerance towards homosexuality. That doesn't make any sense. There is no connection of any sort. We have a basic rule — the First Amendment of the Constitution — that protects free speech by all — even hate groups. Those expressing hate and venom are on an equal par of those expressing love and kindness.

But remember that the group in question is the Westboro BAPTIST Church — emphasis mine. What I find appalling in all of this is that I have never heard, read or seen on TV or in print any conventional religious groups or Baptist churches or denominations condemning the hatred of this offshoot group.

I have never heard from any of the established churches, synagogues, and mosques any response to this disgusting thinking.

As has been asked of Muslims in the cases of extreme Muslim violence, where are the moderate Christians countering such hate by the Westboro Baptist Church? I have never heard or seen from any ministers, pastors, preachers, bishops, priests, imams or rabbis any counter thoughts of Westboro's hateful and harmful message, blatant intolerance and disgusting in-your-face confrontation to those so sadly burying their loved ones.

Westboro calls itself "Baptist." Where are the Baptists on all of this? Where is the largest group, the Southern Baptist Convention, on this intolerance and hate by a group which invokes the Baptist name?

Where are the Catholics, Jews, Episcopalians, Methodists, Lutherans, Presbyterians, Mormons, Quakers, Muslims, etc. on all of this? Why have I and others not heard constantly on TV condemnations by those of God's religions who are supposedly teaching the love, care and benevolence of God? Why don't the supposedly Godly men of the church, cathedral, synagogue or mosque stand up to confront and counter this group?

Why are not congregations of churches out at these funerals to peacefully stand between the haters and those trying to conduct a meaningful funeral of a loved one who died protecting our freedom of speech? Motorcycle groups are doing this — where are the Christians?

Why don't churches and churchmen peacefully confront this hate group to shield those burying their loved ones? Why don't Christians — if they really are loving and Christ-like — put their money where their mouth is? Oh, that's right — they don't have a mouth — just a "tsk, tsk" or two. For shame.

OFFERINGS TO GOD A WASTE WHEN TRYING TO HELP PEOPLE

There must not have been any poor people in Israel or during biblical times. After all, there does not seem to be much concern about feeding them or caring for them, other than with God dropping off the sky-borne manna during their 40 years of travel through the desert when the Israelites were aimless and lost.

The other thing that is convincing of this is all the instances of cattle, oxen, goats, lambs, sheep, birds and grain that are sacrificed to the Lord during these times. Why? You can't read more than a few verses anywhere in the Old Testament without stumbling over a passage where God demands a sacrifice, an Israeli leader or king insists on one, or someone is so contrite that he is gathering up the livestock for slaughter to appease God. I am not sure how this helps God and I am sure that it upsets the livestock.

There are even grain offerings, burnt offerings, fellowship offerings, sin offerings, guilt offerings — all kinds of offerings and sacrifices to keep the God of this people happy and content. While occasionally the priestly clan of Levi were allowed to eat some leftovers, it seems that most of this good meat and grain was burned up for no other purpose than to attempt to please God or stave off some disaster that God is going to inflict for no reason onto "his chosen people."

That all seems a little strange. It seems that the poor and downtrodden are always with us, and it would be a good religious — or humanitarian — thing to help out these people who need a little boost in life. One way of helping out would be — and is today — to provide food and other services to help them get back on their feet.

In my area just recently, some 150 pounds of illegally taken deer was seized by the state Natural Resources Police, with the poaching hunter receiving fines and probation while losing his hunting license, rifle and losing his illegally taken venison. The perfectly good meat seized by the Natural Resources Police was donated to two groups — one a county food bank and the other a service that provides temporary shelter, counseling and rehabilitation services for homeless men down on their luck.

I am sure that the venison will go to make stews and chili for both groups and will be a welcome addition to their diet. And it is obvious that this meat donation is better served helping people than burning up in a bonfire as an offering and sacrifice to some fictional god who even if real would obviously would not need it and could not use it anyway.

The whole concept of burning up perfectly good food of meat and grain just to satisfy an invisible God seems very questionable, to say the least, to a lot of skeptics. But then, doesn't everything in the Bible seem a little far-fetched and ridiculous?

WALKING ON WATER — SCIENCE OR RIDICULOUS SUPERSTITION?

We all know enough physics to know that as a result of mass and weight, certain things float, other things do not. Most woods float, but there are a few woods that do not. We know that most metals do not float, but some do. Certain liquids float (or are lighter than water) while others are heavier than water and sink.

Delve into this far enough and you get into principles of Archimedes, gravity, formulas for buoyancy, etc. Iron (specific gravity of 7.21) sinks in water (specific gravity 1.0), but floats on mercury (specific gravity of 13.56). Ethanol (specific gravity of 0.78) will float on water.

The bottom line is that we know that despite the fact that we can float when horizontal on the water, we sure can't stand up and walk. Unless you are Jesus.

Three of the four New Testament gospels note Jesus walking on the water after serving meals to 5,000 men and assorted women and children. But instead of a firm belief of this as the inerrant Word of God in the Bible, should we not look upon this as a fairy tale of the same scope as other animal and human tales and myths of story tellers of the past?

And of course, all of these stories of walking on water differ in the various Bible books. In Matthew 14, the tale is told of feeding the people, Jesus' disciples going out in their boat, the seas becoming violent and Jesus walking out from land to his boat-bound buddies — the disciples. Peter asked to come to Jesus, walked on water until becoming afraid and then upon sinking was rescued by Jesus.

In Mark 6, Jesus is described similarly walking out from land to the boat occupied by his disciples. The same story, again without Peter mentioned, occurs in John 6, while in Luke Jesus was sleeping in the boat with his disciples and when wakened, "rebuked" the wind to comfort his disciples. No water-walking there.

Thus, in only one story do you have Peter walking on water, in three you have Jesus walking on water, in one story you have Jesus in the boat and calming the winds. In none of the gospels do you have anything that has the remotest acquaintance with logic, truth, facts, physics, specific gravity, density, buoyancy, Archimedes, floating displacement theories, etc.

Could this not be just one more ancient story teller or tale or fable of the likes of myths of Greek and Roman times? Could this instead be like some legend of Poseidon, or a Norse myth, or a tale of talking animals from Aesop's Fables?

Knowing modern physics, even if we do not want to delve into the complex formulas of this subject of buoyancy, can we really believe in a man — a Jesus — walking on water? I didn't think so either.

This Story Is "Sweet" Enough To Make You Vomit!

Here we go again with the Christians and an exercise in ignorance, stupidity, hypocrisy, arrogance, or perhaps a combination of all of these. The story going around parts of the Internet is titled "Saying Grace in a Restaurant — Priceless!" It is a small warm fuzzy tale, worthy of the Oprah OWN channel or a Hallmark card. But it is wrong.

The story is that a six-year-old wants to say grace in a restaurant, says it with permission of his grand-mother, and at the end asks for ice cream if his grandmother will get it for him.

A nearby woman comments that kids don't know how to pray and that asking for ice cream of God takes a lot of gall. A nearby old man talks to the boy, tells him that it was a great prayer and that God liked it and that ice cream is good for the soul.

Naturally, the kid gets his ice cream from grand-mom, and then he promptly gives it to the complaining woman, telling her that ice cream is good for her soul and that his soul is good already.

Sweet, unless you gag and vomit over all the sugar being delivered in the same dump truck. The small things to stumble over are numerous. The old man does not know what God thinks. We don't know if God — if there is a God — likes or does not like ice cream. The adjoining woman does not know if God — if there is a God — likes or does not like kids praying for ice cream. The woman does not know what God would or would not like in a prayer. Etc.

The biggie in all this is the Bible, specifically the New Testament and a quote from Jesus, which apparently Christians hardly ever, ever read. Just take this quote from Jesus out of Matthew 6:5–7.

"And when you pray, do not be like the hypocrites, for they love to pray standing in the synagogues and on street corners to be seen by men. I tell you the truth, they have received their reward in full. But when you pray, go into your room, close the door and pray to your Father, who is unseen. Then your Father, who sees what is done in secret, will reward you. And when you pray, do no keep on babbling like the pagans, for they think that they will be heard because of their many words."

I guess that slams the door on praying in public. We can excuse the little kid, since he is only parroting what his elders tell and show him. But there is no out for the grand-mother, the old man, or the complaining woman at the adjacent table. There is no place for this tale which is the antithesis of Christian thought and being.

Sweet? I don't think so. It is another example of the Christians picking and choosing what they want to believe, or not even reading the "good book" that they claim holds the literal Word of God which we should all follow.

It is Christians wanting to make up a "sweet" story for a warm fuzzy feeling. How about the truth? Or is that too much to ask of religion and Christianity?

More Bad Tall Tales From The Good Book

Among the fables often ignored in the Bible is the one in the short book of Jonah. There we have Jonah swallowed by a "great fish," to quote Jonah 1:17. The Bible follow this up by stating that Jonah lived in the "great fish" for three days and three nights, and ultimately was "vomited" onto dry land.

Remarkable. According to some Christians, this is one more tale that we are supposed to believe, mouth agape, agreeing that this really, really happened. Nonsense. This is the story about Jonah ordered by God to go to Nineveh, but Jonah running away. He got on a ship, storms arose, the crew wanted Jonah to pray to his God to suspend the winds. They tried to row back to land and failed. At Jonah's request, they threw him overboard as a sacrifice. That was supposed to help things and get the ship going straight again.

Jonah was swallowed by a "great fish," got spit out, then went to Nineveh, Nineveh fasted, and the city was not destroyed by God. It all ends happily ever after. Thus, we have the same thing here as in other parts of the Bible. We have an ignorant, primitive post-stone-age people, obviously not knowing any science and thus relying on a fictitious God to make things right through sacrifice, fasting and similar superstitions.

Examples are the storms as a result of Jonah's disobedience to God, the sacrifice of Jonah so God will calm the winds, the fish swallowing Jonah, Jonah living for three days in a fish, being vomited up by the fish, the fasting of Nineveh that saved all 120,000 residents from the destruction planned by God.

It is all pixie dust of course and it is hard to pick the most ridiculous part of this rambling tale. OK — I pick the fish part. We know that the King James and New International versions of the Bible both say "great fish."

If nothing else bothers you about this tale, this should. First we know that a whale shark is the largest fish in the sea, but we also know that it eats only krill — small, shrimp-like creatures.

It could not have been a sturgeon (fresh and brackish water only). Had it been a great white shark, Jonah would have been in the shark, but in pieces, not whole. Then there is that little problem of breathing inside a fish. Breathing is important to all creatures. Jonah could not have lasted for three minutes, much less three days and nights.

What we need here is a story like Pinocchio, who got swallowed by the Terrible Dogfish, a kilometer (3,281 feet) long (not counting the tail), five stories high and with a mouth that could accommodate a whole train. Read the story. Now that is a fish!

That is a tale along the lines of Paul Bunyan and Pecos Bill. Maybe the Bible writers were a little lax when it came to really telling a tall tale. But a person in a fish for three days is perhaps enough of a tall tale for one Bible book. Forget the fish swallowing Jonah — try swallowing the tales of the Bible.

Do We Need A Tailbone To Have Been Made In The Image Of God?

God must have a coccyx. After all, we are made in his image, and we all have a coccyx — or tail bone — so God must have one. After all, we were made in God's image, so the Bible says. If God did not have a tailbone or coccyx, how would we get one?

I do not know why God would have a coccyx, but I think I have an idea as to why we have one. It's called Evolution.

In the same way that we have other features that have evolved from animals, we have a coccyx, or a remnant of a tail. It is the end of the spine, consisting of three to five jointed or fused vertebrae. It is not useless. It is important for connection of various lower pelvic muscles. It even serves as an attachment point for a little bit of the gluteus maximus, the large "derriere" muscle important for bipedal walking. It is found in the great apes, or tailless apes, those same apes that have a common ancestor to us.

No, we are NOT, as so many religionists like to accuse us, thinking that we evolved from a chimp or an ambiguous "monkey". We just have common ancestors with apes including chimps, bonobos, orangutans and gorillas.

Without the coccyx, we might get along fine. Thus, perhaps we did not need one if God were making us from scratch, as is biblically suggested. Certainly, if coccyx removal is medically suggested (it is sometimes done) , the surgeon does have to check to make sure that its removal will not impede other functions such as attachment for support of the pelvic floor, walking and even sitting in an upright position.

The important thing is that the coccyx is one more anatomical feature that helps to prove the facts of evolution and our ancient hominoid, mammalian and primate history.

The fact remains that as an upright biped, we no longer need the long tail that was perhaps a part of our ancestry long before our ancestral primatehood. In many creatures, that tail is necessary. For some creatures like the big cats, it is important as a rudder and for balance as they make sharp turns in chasing down a lunch that does not want to be a lunch. For others such as opossums, monkeys and similar climbing creatures, a prehensile tail is important as a safety catch, or for balance in a tree, or as a balance stabilizer.

One would think that anything made in the image of something else would have to be the same on the inside as well as on the outside. Following that religious theme, one would think that our insides have to be God approved, almost like a UL sticker on an electrical device or a purple USDA stamp on a side of beef.

The interesting thing with all of this is that a coccyx does not point to God. It only points to evolution and the further proof that Charlie Darwin was — and continues to be — right.

ARE WE MADE IN GOD'S SPIRIT OR PHYSICAL IMAGE? INQUIRING MINDS WANT TO KNOW

The Bible is the Word of God, right? And that Word of God is certainly inerrant, right? Christians — or at least a lot of them — believe that. And right there in Genesis 1:26, it quotes God as saying, "Let us make man in our image, in our likeness. . ."

Check your Webster's dictionary for a definition if "image" and "likeness" and you will find it stating definitions such as a painting, sculpture, representation, close in appearance, etc. It would seem that if this Bible really is the true Word of God, and if God had meant that man was in spirit like God, he would have said so.

Thus, you could have had Genesis 1:26 read "Let us make man of our same spirit, of our same ideas, of our same disposition. . ." But Genesis does not say that. But for the sake of a friendly discussion, let's say that is what God meant and let God's writers and translators off the hook.

So then we have to consider the nature of mankind. We have to consider that God could have added or substituted a gene or specific internal quality in all of us all the time for goodness, honesty, fairness, helpfulness, tolerance, etc. Sure, we have that in many people and in many events in history. But God could have — we would hope — been able to insert a "good" gene or "Godly" gene or character in all of us.

But we know that throughout recorded history and before, mankind has been warring, intolerant, biased, bigoted, murderous, thieving, dishonest, lying, etc. We certainly could have used an inerrant part of the Ten Commandments — specifically numbers 6 through 9. These, in order, are the ones dealing with a prohibition against adultery, murder, stealing and false witness (lying). In this case, are we to blame all of this on God, since he might have meant that we are made in his spirit and not his physical image? Does this mean that God is and has been warring, dishonest, murderous, intolerant thieving, etc. and that we are just a cloned copy of his evil morals and ethics?

But the fact remains that the Bible — this inerrant Word of God — does not say "spirit." It says "image." So we are left with three choices in this definition and selection:

1. The Bible is not the inerrant Word of God and Genesis 1:26 really means "spirit" or something else, or nothing.

2. If the above is true, it means that God is really the originating spirit as mankind, and thus blatantly both good and evil as mankind has proven to be over the centuries.

3. If a physical appearance as "image" is true, then with many evolving anatomical and physiological aspects, mankind is really evolved from lower primates.

Maybe we have all three of these going on at once. After all, for evil, just check out Joshua, Passover, David's census, Moses, Abraham and Isaac, Achan's children, Job's children, Lot and his family, Jesus' rudeness to his family, and so much more in the Bible.

It is all there — meanness, dishonesty, murder, lying, intolerance, unfairness, evil, bigotry, bias, etc. And a whole lot more — with God playing a major part of the middle of all this and causing most of this evil.

No wonder skeptics keep right on being skeptical. Stay skeptical — it will keep you sane, mentally alert and critically thinking.

PROSELYTIZING, WITNESSING OR IN-YOUR-FACE CONFRONTATION?

My brief acquaintance with an Amish gentleman during a North Carolina trip and fishing tackle show was not without a minor glitch and disappointment. I suspect that it would have occurred with any member of any of the established Christian religions. Our conversation took a turn toward him asking about my faith — my religion. I explained very briefly my highly skeptical views of all religion, God, Jesus, resurrection, miracles, prayer, heaven, hell, etc. I was and am, I explained, an atheist.

His answer disappointed me. "At some point," he admonished demonstrably, "you are going to have to consider God. You are going to have to face God, the idea of God," he said, his voice and his rapidity of speech rising a little. "I know this. I hope that you make the right decision. You are older and I know that you will have to deal with this and I know that you have to decide this soon. I know that you are going to have to consider God, to listen to God."

He had noted that I, as an older person, am much, much closer to the end of life than the beginning of life. Unsaid was the common Christian overtone of the looming specter of death with a choice — to be made now — of heaven or hell. The carrot or the stick?

I found this so disappointing. How dare he tell me what he thinks I will face, what I must think, how I must face the future? Who gives him the right to lecture me? Of course, Christians call this "witnessing" and thus excuse the fact that such confrontations are patently in-your-face-proselytizing of their particular brand of delusion. It is their ugly way of "being right," by telling you what you MUST believe, telling you HOW you must live and WHAT you must think.

Suppose instead, the conversation from me to him had been along these lines: "At some point, my Amish friend, you are going to face the nothingness of death. You are going to have to face the fact that there are no proofs of your God, of your Jesus or of his resurrection. There are no proofs of the efficacy of your prayers, of your so-called miracles, of your heaven or hell. There are no proofs of your particular brand of religion or any other brand of religion or Christianity.

"You are going to face the foolishness of your beliefs — in fact the foolishness of all beliefs of Christians, Jews, Muslims, and those of other religions and far eastern beliefs. You are going to have to deal with the fact that all religion is man-made, that it is all pointless and pixie dust and that we are literally nothing but star dust on this small planet and here for only a short period of time." But of course I did not say this. I am nicer than that. I am nicer than most Christians.

We were parting at this point and I did not follow up his minor tirade. I have been considering religion, Christianity and other beliefs since I was about seven years old. I never felt a kinship with Jesus. I never felt sorry for him in life or hanging on the cross. I did feel sorry for the animals slaughtered in all those horrible sacrifices in the ridiculous belief that some god or God would approve.

All my life, I have been thinking about the very thing — God — that the Amish man argued for. The answer after all these years and decades is still the same. There are no proofs of anything about religion or God or gods and I remain — with very good reason, I might add — highly skeptical of it all. I am an atheist.

The Truth Will Set You Free!

Stay Skeptical!

Bibliography

In addition to the works listed here, and perhaps far easier to find, are references to these subjects on the Internet, with the most comprehensive being Wikipedia. While care must be used in sourcing anything in writing or on the Internet, good sources are easily available that enable readers to check on the statements made in this book, and to continue the process of uncovering the problems, flaws and errors of religions.

Aronson, Ronald. *Living Without God, New Directions for Atheists, Agnostics, Secularists, and the Undecided*, CA, Berkley, Counterpoint Press, 2008

Baggini, Julian. *Atheism, A Brief Insight*, Oxford, NY, Oxford University Press, 2003

Baigent, Michael. *Racing Toward Armageddon*, NY, HarperOne, 2009

Barker, Dan. *The Good Atheist, Living a Purpose-Filled Life Without God*, CA, Berkley, 2011

_____. *Godless*, CA, Berkeley, CA, Ulysses Press, 2008

Bivins, Jason C. *Religion of Fear*. NY, Oxford University Press, 2008

Brogaard, Betty. *The Homemade Atheist, A Former Evangelical Woman's Freethought Journey to Happiness*, CA, Berkley, Ulysses Press, 2010

Bock, Darrell. *The Missing Gospels*, TN, Nashville, Thomas Nelson Publishers, 2006

Cresswell, Peter. *The Invention of Jesus*, London, Watkins Publishing, 2013

Charles, R. H. *The Book of Enoch*, Dover Publications, 2007

Crisswell, Jonathan C. compiler, *The Wit and Blasphemy of Atheists*, Berkley, CA, Ulysses Press, 2011

D'Antonio, Michael. *Mortal Sins: Sex, Crime, and the Era of Catholic Scandal*, New York, Thomas Dunne Books, St. Martin's Press, 2013

De Waal, Frans. *Primates and Philosophers, How Morality Evolved*, NJ, Princeton, Princeton University Press, 2006

Dawkins, Richard. *The God Delusion*, New York, Houghton Mifflin Company, 2006

Douthat, Ross. *Bad Religion*, NY, Free Press, 2012

Durschmied, Erik. *Whores Of The Devil*, Sutton Publishing, 2005

Ehrman, Bart D. *Forged*, NY, HarperOne, 2011

_____. *Misquoting Jesus*, NY, HarperOne, 2005

_____. *The Lost Gospel of Judas Iscariot*, NY, Oxford, 2006

_____. *Peter, Paul and Mary Magdalene, the Followers of Jesus in History and Legend*, NY, Oxford, 2006

_____. *God's Problem*, NY, HarperOne, 2008

_____. *Jesus, Interrupted*, NY, HarperOne, 2009

_____. *Lost Scriptures, Books that Did Not Make It into the New Testament*, NY, Oxford, 2003

_____. *Did Jesus Exist?*, NY, HarperOne, 2012

_____. *How Jesus Became God*, NY, HarperOne, 2014

Fetzer, James H. *Render Unto Darwin*, Il, Peru, Open Court Publishing Co., 2007

Cambridge University Press, 2010

Friedman, Richard Elliot. *Who Wrote The Bible?* NY, HarperOne, 1987

Freke, Timothy and Gandy, Peter. *The Jesus Mysteries — Was the "Original Jesus" a Pagan God?* NY, Three Rivers Press, 1999

Galambush, Julie. *The Reluctant Parting*, CA, San Francisco, 2005

Granados, Luis. *Damned Good Company*, Washington, DC, Humanist Press, 2012

Greenberg, Gary. *101 Myths of the Bible*, Naperville, IL, SourceBooks, 2000

Harding, Nick. *How to be a Good Atheist*, Oldcastle Books, 2007

Harrison, Guy P. *50 Reasons People Give for Believing in a God*, NY, Amherst, 2008

Harris, Sam. *The End of Faith, Religion, Terror and the Future of Reason*, NY, W. W. Norton & Company, 2004

_____. *Letter to a Christian Nation*, NY, Vintage Books, 2008

Henze, Matthias. Editor, *Biblical Interpretation at Qumran*, MI, Rapids William B. Erdmans Publishing Co. 2005 Bibliography 225

Hitchens, Christopher. *God is Not Great*, New York, Twelve, Hachette Brook Group, USA, 2007

_____. *The Missionary Position*, NY, Verso, 1995

_____. *The Portable Atheist, Essential Readings for the Nonbeliever*, Philadelphia, PA, Da Capo Press, 2007

Huberman, Jack. *The Quotable Atheist*, NY, Nation Books, 2007

Hudnut-Beumler, James. *In Pursuit Of The Almighty's Dollar, A History Of Money And American Protestantism*, Chapel Hill, NC, University Of North Carolina Press, 2007

Johnson, Marshall D. *The Evolution of Christianity — Twelve Crises That Shaped the Church*, NY, Continuum International Publishing, 2005

Jordan, Michael. *In The Name of God — Violence and Destruction in the World's Religions*, Sutton Publishing, 2006

Joshi, S. T. *The Original Atheists, First Thoughts on Nonbelief*, Amherst, NY, Prometheus Books, 2014

Kasser, Rodolphe, Meyer, Marvin and Wurst, Gregor. *The Gospel of Judas*, Washington, DC, National Geographic Society, 2006

Konner, Joan. Compiler, *The Atheist's Bible*, NY, HarperCollins, 2007

Largo, Michael. *God's Lunatic's*, NY, Harper, 2010

_____. *The Unbelievers*, Amherst, Prometheus Books, 2011

Lewis, C. S. *Mere Christianity*, NY, Harper Collins Paperback, 2001

Lewis, James R. *Violence and New Religious Movements*, Oxford University Press, 2011

Loftus, John W. *Why I Became an Atheist*, Amherst, NJ, Prometheus, 2008

Maisel, Eric. *The Atheist's Way, Living Well Without Gods*, Novato, CA, 2009

Marshall, David. *The Truth Behind The New Atheism*, Oregon, Eugene, Harvest House Publishers, 2007

Meyer, Marvin. *The Gnostic Discoveries*, NY, HarperSanFrancisco, 2005

_____. *Judas*, HarperOne, 2007

Miles, Jack. *God: A Biography*, NY, Alfred A. Knopf, 1995

Mikul, Chris. *The Cult Files*, Pier 9, ?

Mills, David. *Atheist Universe, The Thinking Person's Answer to Christian Fundamentalism*, Berkley, CA 2006

Moorey, P. R. S. *A Century of Biblical Archaeology*, KY, Louisville, Westminster/John Knox Press, 1991

Moss, Candida. *The Myth of Persecution*, NY, HarperOne, 2013

Myers, PZ. *The Happy Atheist*, NY, Vintage Books, 2014

Nabarz, Payam. *The Mysteries of Mithras*, VT, Rochester, Inner Traditions, 2005

Navabi, Armin. *Why There Is No God*, Atheist Republic

Needleman, Jacob. *What Is God?*, NY, Penguin Books, 2009

O'Reilly, Bill and Dugard, Martin. *Killing Jesus*, NY, Henry Holt and Company 2013

Pagels, Elaine. *Revelations*, NY, Penguin Books, 2012

_____. *Beyond Belief*, NY, Vintage Books, 2004

_____. *The Origin of Satan*, NY, Vintage Books, 1996

_____. *Adam, Eve and the Serpent*, NY, Vintage Books, 1988

Paine, Thomas. *Common Sense*, NY, Fall River Press, 1995

Park, Robert L. *Superstition: Belief in the Age of Science*, Princeton, NJ, 2008

Pfeiffer, C. Boyd, *No Proof At All: A Cure for Christianity*, NY, Algora Publishing, 2015.

Phillips, Kevin. *American Theocracy*, NY, Viking Press, 2006

Picknett, Lynn. *Mary Magdalene*, NY, Carroll & Graf Publishers, 2004

Randi, James. *The Faith Healers*, Buffalo, NY, Prometheus, 1989

Rosenberg, Alex. *The Atheist's Guide to Reality, Enjoying Life without Illusions*, NY, W. W. Norton & Company, 2011

Rodwan, John G. Jr. *Holidays & Other Disasters*, Washington, DC, Humanist Press, 2013

Rowland, Wade. *Galileo's Mistake*, NY, Arcade Publishing, 2001

Russell, D. S. *The Old Testament Pseudepigrapha*, Philadelphia, PA, Fortress Press, 1987

S, Acharya. *The Christ Conspiracy*, Kempton, IL Adventures Unlimited, 1999

Sachar, Abram Leon. *A History of the Jews*, 5th Edition, NY, Alfred A. Knopf, 1964

Sagan, Carl. *The Demon-Haunted World*, NY, Ballantine Books, 1996

Schroeder, Robert. *Cults, Secret Sects and Radical Religions*, Carlton Books, 2007

Schweizer, Bernard. *Hating God, The Untold Story of Misotheism*, Oxford University Press, 2011

Shermer, Michael. *Why People Believe Weird Things*, NY, MJF Books, 1997

_____. *Why Darwin Matters*, NY, Henry Holt and Company, 2006

Smith, George H. *Atheism, The Case Against God*, Amherst, NY, Prometheus, 1989

Stenger, Victor J. *God, The Failed Hypothesis*, Amherst, NJ, Prometheus Books, 2007

Stewart-Williams, Steve. *Darwin, God and The Meaning of Life, How Evolutionary Theory Undermines Everything You Thought You Knew*, NY, Cambridge University Press, 2010

Twain, Mark. *The War Prayer*, NY, Harper and Row, St. Crispin Press Book, 1951

Vermes, Geza. *The Resurrection*, NY, Doubleday, 2001

Wade, Nicholas. *The Faith Instinct*, NY, The Penguin Press, 2009

Walter, Philippe. *Christianity: The Origins of a Pagan Religion*, VT, Rochester, Inner Traditions, 2003

White, Mel. *Religion Gone Bad*, NY, Penguin, 2006

White, L. Michael. *Scripting Jesus*, NY, HarperOne, 2010

Wicker, Christine. *The Fall of the Evangelical Church, The Surprising Crisis Inside the Church*, NY, HarperOne, 2008

Zichterman, Jocelyn. *I Fired God*, NY, St. Martin's Press, 2013

Zondervan. *Zondervan's Compact Bible Dictionary*, MI, Grand Rapids, 1993

Printed in the United States
By Bookmasters